FOLENS GCSE P.E.

For AQA

Julie Walmsley

Acknowledgements

The publishers would like to thank the following for permission to reproduce photographs:

Actionplus on pp. 9b, 10b, 12, 45b, 52c, 52e, 53, 72, 98b, 118, 128, 153a, 153b, 160a, 160b, 161, 165, 169, 173b, 175, 183, 184, 188, 192, 217a, 217b, 221; Associated Press/Joe Cavaretta on p. 163; Associated Press/Charles Rex Arbogast on p. 131; Associated Press/Seiko Timing on p.133; BBC on pp. 176, 180, 193a; Consignia on p. 7b; Duomo/Corbis on p. 38; De Vere Group/Greens Health and Fitness on pp. 96, 97a, 97b, 104; Digital Vision on pp. 10a, 11b, 15, 45g, 45h, 67, 80, 88b, 111, 112b, 166a, 166c, 208, 216; EMPICS on pp. 9a, 11a, 13b, 13c, 14, 19, 30, 31, 40, 45d, 45f, 52a, 52b, 52d, 54a, 60a, 60b, 62a, 78, 79a, 88a, 89a, 89b, 101, 108, 109, 112a, 113a, 113b, 115, 117b, 117c, 117d, 121, 123, 126b, 129a, 137a, 137b, 137c, 138, 144, 145, 149, 150, 151a, 151b, 151d, 154a, 158, 162, 170, 171, 173a, 179, 189a, 189b, 190, 191, 193b, 196, 215; Eyewire on pp. 7a, 213; Laurence Griffiths/Getty Images on p. 147b; Shaun Botterill/Getty Images on p. 147a; Mirrorpix on pp. 85a, 154b; Michael Crabtree/PA Photos on p. 34; Owen Humphreys/PA Photos on p. 168; PhotoDisc on pp. 8, 10c, 13a, 16, 17, 18a, 23, 24, 29, 45a, 45e, 46, 49, 54b, 55, 58, 59, 79b, 84, 89c, 98a, 106, 117a, 124, 126c, 137b, 147c, 147d, 151c, 156b, 156c, 166b, 167, 168, 199, 200; Paul Doyle/Photofusion on p. 159; Don Gray/Photofusion on p. 21; Popperfoto on p. 129b; Reuters/Phillippe Wojazer on p. 126a; Reuters/Mike Blake on p. 187; Rex Features on pp. 7c, 105, 156a; Andrew Syred/Science Photo Library on p. 69; Jerry Wachter/Science Photo Library on p. 36; NIBSC/Science Photo Library on p. 70; Phil Jude/Science Photo Library on p. 74; Stockbyte on p. 68; Topham/EMPICS on p. 130; Topham/PA on p. 129c; FootTopham/PA on p. 185; UPPA.co.uk on p. 197

Cover image: Corbis

United Kingdom: Folens Publishers, Apex Business Centre, Boscombe Road, Dunstable, LU5 4RL.

Email: folens@folens.com

Ireland: Folens Publishers, Greenhills Road, Tallaght, Dublin 24.

Email: info@folens.ie

Poland: JUKA, ul. Renesansowa 38, Warsaw 01-905.

Editor: Melody Ismail

Illustrations by Roger Goode, Colin Brown and Maggie Rammage – Beehive Illustration and Mark Stacey.

Cover design: Duncan McTeer

Index compiled by Indexing Specialists (UK) Ltd

Layout by Hardlines Ltd, Charlbury, Oxford

First published 2003 by Folens Limited.

Every effort has been made to trace the copyright holders of material used in this publication. If any copyright holder has been overlooked, we should be pleased to make any necessary arrangements.

British Library Cataloguing in Publication Data. A catalogue record for this publication is available from the British Library.

ISBN 1-84303-237-6

Contents

Introduction

The contents of this book cover the theory content for AQA Paper 1 *Factors Affecting Performance and Participation in Physical Activity* and *Analysis of Performance* from the coursework part of the course. The course content for Paper 1 is set out in four sections.

Section A – Health, Fitness and the Factors Affecting Performance: looks at how health and fitness are related, the reasons for undertaking exercise, the importance of a balanced diet and anatomy and physiology and how the body systems interrelate to allow for different types of physical activity.

Section B – Principles of Training: covers how to apply the training principles, the effects on the body of different training methods, sport and drugs, how sports injuries are caused and treated and what could be done to prevent them.

Section C – Factors Affecting Individual Performance and Participation: this section looks at how school, society, social groupings, leisure time and availability of facilities are all important in promoting physical education and how these factors interrelate with health and fitness.

Section D – Social and Cultural Factors Affecting Participation: the factors studied are sponsorship, media, social and cultural aspects and the influences of local and national providers.

Knowledge and understanding of the topics covered in this book can be useful in jobs needing a level of physical fitness, like working in the police force or fire service. The elements of first aid that are covered may bring about an interest that could lead to a pursuit of a job or hobby involving first aid. In general, the whole course is useful to those hoping to pursue a career in the sports leisure industry, as a coach or as a participant at any level.

The book layout

The book is set out so that it matches the AQA specification. The headings of each of the sections and the order in which topics are covered relate directly to the specification. This means that if you carefully work your way through this book you will cover everything that the exam board requires of you. To help you further, the material is presented in small, easy-to-digest chunks that are broken down using frequent sub-headings.

There are many photographs, illustrations and diagrams used to give you a visual way of remembering the work. Each photograph has a caption bringing your attention to the main point so the link with the information is unmistakable. There are also numerous learning features built into this book:

What you will learn in this section

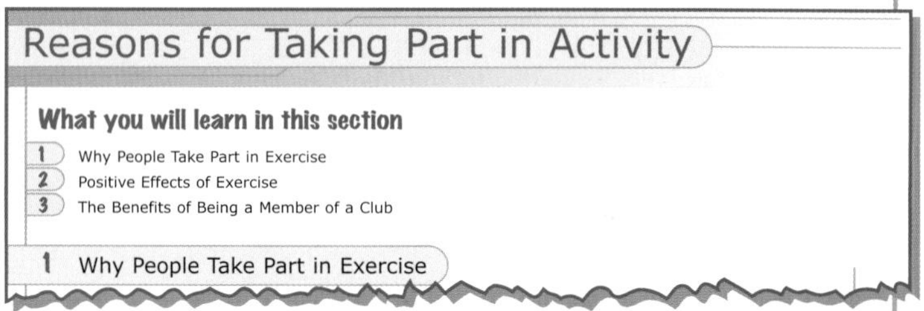
Reasons for Taking Part in Activity

What you will learn in this section

1 Why People Take Part in Exercise
2 Positive Effects of Exercise
3 The Benefits of Being a Member of a Club

1 Why People Take Part in Exercise

At the beginning of each section, you will find a list of all the topics you will learn about in that section. Each topic is numbered, which is especially useful when you are revising, as it will be quicker to find relevant information and to check you know all the points you are supposed to.

Tasks

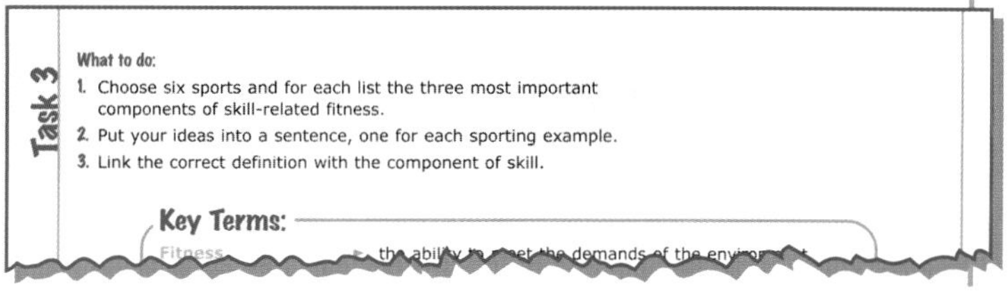
Task 3

What to do:

1. Choose six sports and for each list the three most important components of skill-related fitness.
2. Put your ideas into a sentence, one for each sporting example.
3. Link the correct definition with the component of skill.

Key Terms:

Each section of work involves completing a series of numbered tasks. Completing tasks involves referring to the work just read or discussed in class. Tasks need to be recorded in your own book or file.

By keeping your book up-to-date and tasks complete, the work recorded will build up into your personal revision document. It is important that when you are working, information you write down can be read easily when you refer back to it. Take enough time to make your words legible.

Active Challenge

These are thought-provoking tasks, which often involve working with a partner. Completing these tasks will open your mind to the section being worked on and give you the chance to add verbally to the topic.

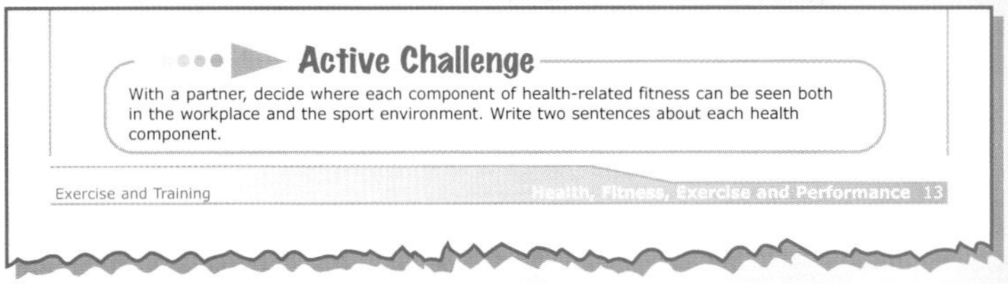

Using a spidergram

Spidergrams are quick and easy to complete. They are an excellent way of recording and remembering the main points of a section.

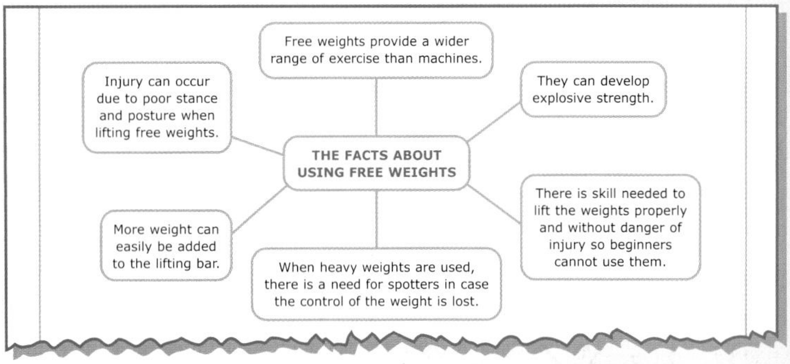

Key Terms

Wherever there are words in **bold** in the book they will be found in the key terms section. This indicates important words for you to remember together with their definitions.

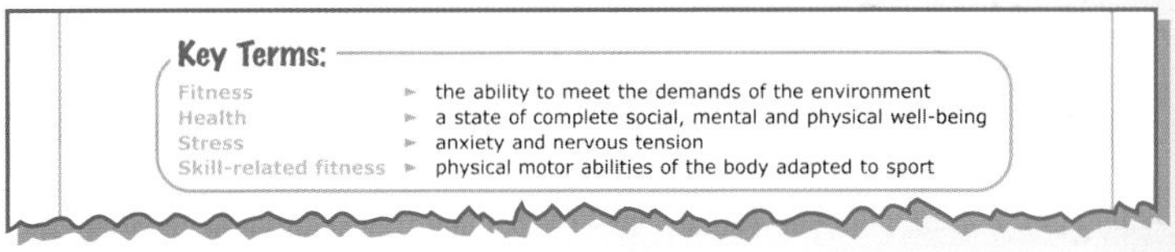

Summary

At the end of each section there is a summary that rounds up the essential information that you need to remember from the topics covered. It acts as a short collection of the ideas that are the most important to the section. When revising, the summaries can be used as a starting point to remind you of the main ideas. You can then add to them with more detailed information from memory or by re-reading the text.

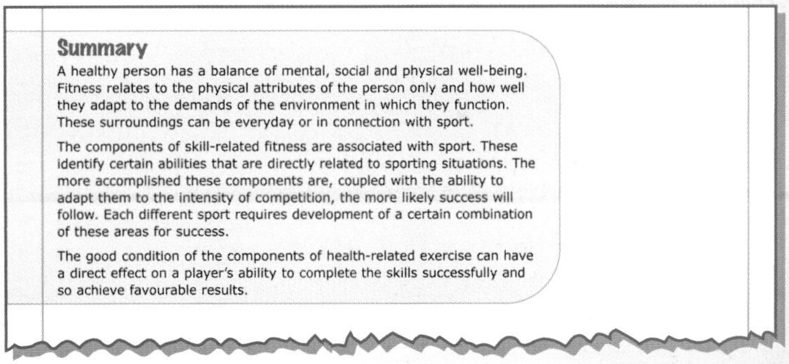

Glossary

Many words that you come across in the text are explained in the glossary. When you come across a word for which you are unsure of its meaning – look it up in the glossary.

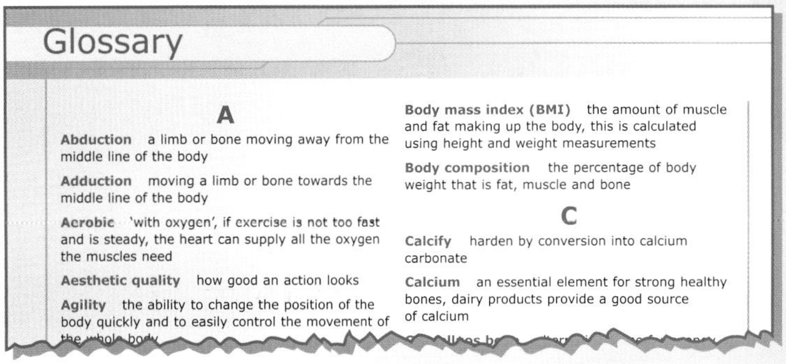

You and the exam

You could view the exam as a competition – a competition to get a better grade than pupils nationwide who have chosen to take this exam. So give yourself the best chance. If you are absent it is up to you to copy up any work missed. Gaps in work are gaps in knowledge. Pupils who have completed all of the work give themselves the best chance of success.

Health and Fitness

What you will learn about in this section

1. The Definition and Components of Health
2. Exercise Needs for General Health
3. Different Exercises for Specific Activities
4. The Definition and Components of Fitness
5. About Performance
6. Physical Activity for the Performer
7. Mental Fitness for Sport
8. Different Levels of Fitness: Club and International Performer

1 The Definition and Components of Health

The World Health Organization (WHO) give a complete definition of what it considers **health** to be:

'a state of complete mental, physical and social well-being, not simply the absence of disease or infirmity'.

Mental health can be regarded as the ability to concentrate on a subject for a long period of time, control emotions and think logically through a problem. This could be achieved by regularly meeting people that you take part in activities with. In a sports context this could be as a member of a club, gym or society.

To achieve physical well-being, a performer would concentrate on five areas of health-related exercise (HRE), possibly following a programme of exercise conforming to the minimum level of **fitness** required, which would improve the condition of the cardiovascular system.

COMPONENTS OF HRE

Cardiovascular fitness relies on a healthy heart, blood and blood vessels. How active a lifestyle a person can lead depends on the condition of these.

Muscular endurance is the ability of the muscles to move weight over a long period without tiring and losing effectiveness.

Flexibility is movement at a joint to its fullest range. With regular practice the joints can get nearer to their maximum range of movement.

Muscular strength can be seen in a person who can lift heavy weights. Strength is defined as the ability to lift a maximum weight in one attempt.

Body composition is how the body is made up in terms of bone, muscle and fat. Bone structure gives us our build. The percentage of fat and muscle can be changed according to diet and exercise.

2 Exercise Needs for General Health

Maintaining the condition of the components of health, at a level at which people can carry out their everyday working lives without excessive fatigue, is essential. The effort required to get these components into a good condition will vary according to the individual. Each person has their own natural fitness level and so everyone has different requirements to maintain their minimum level of fitness.

Each type of work demands a certain level and type of fitness. Sedentary jobs – those where little physical effort is exerted, like working in an office, need a lower fitness level than manual jobs, like working for a removals firm. Yet, each active job differs as the type of fitness required by a removal person is different from that needed by a postal worker, for example.

Sedentary work only requires low fitness levels.

High intensity effort requires muscular strength.

Working moderately over long periods needs endurance qualities.

3 Different Exercises for Specific Activities

Just as each job has a different demand on fitness levels, so too do the various sporting activities. Some activities depend on the development of only a few health components, others need a combination of all of them.

To exercise effectively for any length of time, without tiring or becoming less efficient, requires the training of the cardiorespiratory system. The better the heart and lungs work, the greater is the efficiency of the body getting oxygen to the working muscles and removal of waste products from the body.

The development of muscular endurance requires light to moderate exercise over long periods, whereas developing muscular strength needs short bursts of maximal effort. To execute actions with the correct technique and least likelihood of injury relies on the joints having good flexibility and muscles that can control the movement of the joints safely.

Body composition plays an important part in the effectiveness of the performer. There is an ideal body shape for each activity (somatotype is explained in detail on page 118). Athletes can improve their shape:

- by controlling their diet and choosing the correct combinations of food
- by eating the right amounts of food
- by the amount of exercise completed.

Active Challenge

With a partner, decide where each component of health-related fitness can be seen both in the workplace and in the sport environment. Write two sentences about each health component.

4 The Definition and Components of Fitness

Fitness is different from health. A definition of fitness is:

'the ability to meet the demands of the environment'.

Having the minimum level of fitness will allow a person to go about their everyday life and meet its demands without tiring. Fitness, therefore, is concerned with the physical condition of a person. Walking to the bus stop and completing tasks at work are both actions that should be completed without exhaustion. Each person has a different set of physical demands in their day, so each person's minimum level of fitness differs. If a person does not exercise and does not keep each of the components of HRE in good condition then daily tasks will become more difficult to complete.

The idea of various levels of fitness applies to different sports too. To take part in any sport requires a combination of fitness and performance. Exercise is a series of physical activities that improve health and physical fitness. A person may be fit to play badminton, but not fit in the necessary way for tennis. Each activity has its own set of requirements that the player must meet in order to succeed. The exercises, therefore, for each activity's training session will be different in order to fit with the requirements of the sport. The performance will improve by choosing and working on the most appropriate exercises.

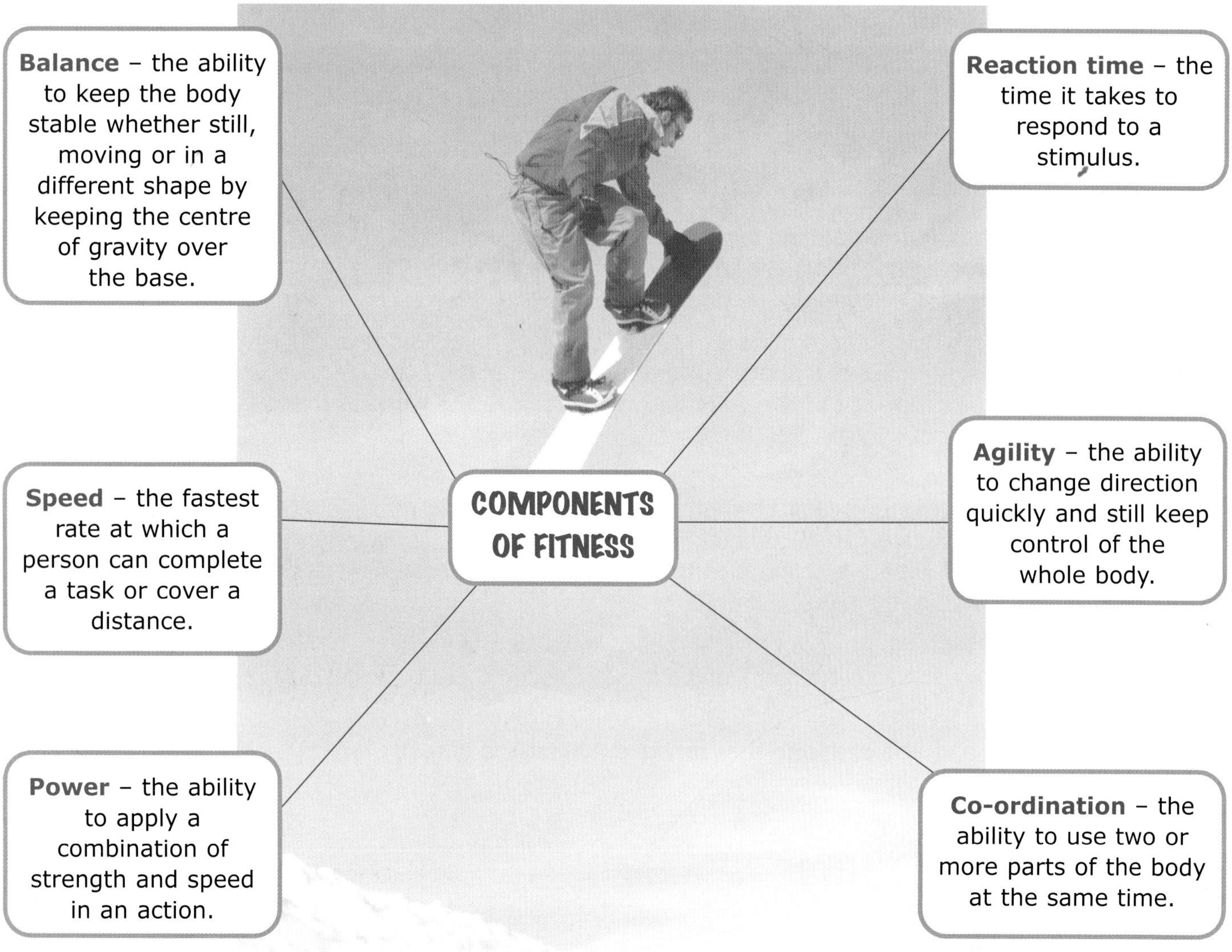

Most sports have a combination of all the components of fitness. Each sport has its own special mix of **skill-related fitness** components to master in order for a player to be successful. These are the specific requirements unique to successful performance or participation of that sport. Some sports need more power and strength, like throwing events in athletics, whereas others, like badminton, need agility and co-ordination.

5 About Performance

Performance is 'how well a task is completed'. This may be judged on whether the skills are performed with correct technique or whether the action, irrespective of technique, resulted in success. Often players who have good technical ability are successful. Top-class sportspeople spend much time perfecting their technique in order to compete successfully at the highest level.

The correct technique is how accurately the body matches the acceptable way of performing a skill. Although each performer will have a slightly different action depending on their height and build, good technique involves:

- good body shape at preparation, moment of contact and follow-through phases
- balance of the body
- speed of execution.

Identify the differences in hurdling technique between Colin Jackson and the school pupil.

Task 1

What to do:

1. Look at the pictures above and spot the points of good technique. Write a sentence on each of them.

Example: Colin Jackson's body is square to the lane, maintaining the running action as much as possible.

The condition of the five components of health has a great effect on the amount and quality of exercise, training and performance a person can achieve.

Cardiovascular fitness

Ice skaters need good cardiovascular fitness.

The good condition of the cardiovascular system allows for efficient transportation of blood to the necessary parts of the body in order that the body can meet the extra demands of exercise.

In training, if the cardiovascular system is not fit then the ability to keep working is reduced and so the required skill level is less likely to be reached. In competition, fatigue and breathlessness would prevent a person playing to the required standard or even continuing the activity in some instances.

Muscular strength

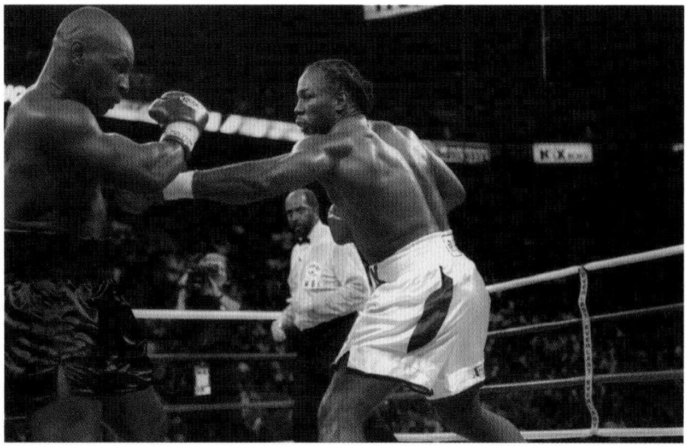

Lennox Lewis uses his muscular strength to overpower Mike Tyson.

Muscular strength, in itself, can be used to overpower an opponent. A player who can combine strength with speed can create power, which is especially useful when playing a forehand drive down the line in tennis, in order to pass an opponent at the net, for instance.

Having poor strength may prevent a player shooting with the required amount of power to beat a goalkeeper. In contact sports, like judo, a weak player gives little resistance to an opponent with muscular strength.

Muscular endurance

Good muscular endurance prevents the body tiring quickly.

Muscular endurance is essential for long-distance events such as 10 000m racing. The body is able to keep working for a long time without tiring and so the performer has more chance of winning.

Flexibility

Controlled use of the full range of movement available at a joint can allow for the execution of the correct technique, improving performance and lessening the risk of injury. Where resistance to a force is necessary, the muscles must be strong enough to prevent over-extension beyond the fullest range. For example, players in a rugby scrum must have muscles strong enough to prevent over-extension of their shoulders.

Romanian Dana Carteleanu demonstrates her flexibility.

Body composition

Success in sport can depend on choosing the most appropriate sport for your build. The amounts of fat, muscle and bone in the body will change the shape of a person, making them more or less suitable for a particular activity. A particular-sized skeletal frame may lend itself to a certain sport or position in the team. The longer the bones making the frame, the taller a person is; this would be advantageous to a basketball player or goal shooter in netball. Shorter skeletal bones make for a smaller frame, suiting the needs of a jockey, for example.

Most jockeys have a small skeletal frame and a minimal fat component.

A person's frame size is an important part of their body composition. To determine your frame size, measure the circumference of the smallest part of your wrist. Use the table below to determine your frame size.

Determining frame size based on average height using wrist circumference

Frame	Men	Women
small	less than 165mm	less than 152mm
medium	165–191mm	152–159mm
large	more than 191mm	more than 159mm

Body fat

Retired sumo wrestling champion, Konishiki, weighed over 275kg.

Extra weight is good for some sports. A member of a tug-of-war team or a prop forward in rugby usually has a high level of fat proportion, but this is usually combined with strength in order to make the person efficient in the activity.

Having extra weight can make a person slow and unable to keep working at a moderate to hard level for long periods. This is because the extra oxygen needed to keep the muscles working cannot be supplied at the pace needed by the cardiorespiratory systems (heart and lungs). As a result, fatigue sets in, injury is more likely and so the activity has to stop.

Task 2

What to do:

1. Describe the positive effects in sport of having well-developed HRE components.
2. Describe the negative effects in sport of not having well-developed HRE components.

Write your answers in sentences and give an answer for each of the components of HRE.

Use the examples previously given as guides, but try to think of your own.

The examples below show three different sports each requiring different components of fitness.

Track cycling requires aerobic fitness.

Hockey uses both aerobic and anaerobic fitness, as shown by Australia's Alison Peek.

The javelin event, performed here by Denise Lewis, uses anaerobic fitness.

Task 3

What to do:

1. Choose six sports and, for each, list the three most important components of fitness.
2. Put your ideas into sentences, one for each sporting example.
3. Link the correct definition with the component of skill.

7 Mental Fitness for Sport

Not only do competitors have to be physically fit, but they also have to have a mental strength too. Sport brings different pressures on the performer and the way these are handled can have a big influence on the outcome of the game or event. By using the following mental preparation techniques the performer can have a better chance of completing the task successfully.

Relaxation – in an attempt to keep relaxed the player will use different strategies; some deep breathe, clearing mental tensions and anger of any previous play and shake tension from arms to relax the muscles so that they can perform the skills properly.

Mental rehearsal – the performer will go through a routine in their head before and on the day of the event giving them a familiar order to their day. The performer, during the competition, will **visualise** the successful action or shot to be completed. This method is used to great effect in athletics and golf. Players taking a penalty kick in rugby create the shot they want to perform in their head before taking the actual kick so they 'see the shot' before playing it.

Focusing – here, an attempt is made to clear the mind of other thoughts so they do not interfere with the successful outcome of the action. The crowd may be chanting, other players making comments or personal doubts may be in the performer's head – focusing attempts to shut all interferences out. The aim is to think only of the job in hand and to concentrate on the technique to be used.

Before an event British athlete Natasha Danvers visualises her successful outcome.

8 Different Levels of Fitness: Club and International Performer

The difference between a top-class sportsperson and an average club player may be obvious when looking at their skills, but this is not the only factor making the elite athletes reach the highest levels of success.

Although club members are competitive, they are also participating for fun, not financial reward or the prestige of a gold medal or cup final victory. Often the time devoted to the sport is limited as they usually have the commitment of having a full time job. Some club players use sport as a release of tension and aggression from the daily routine and to socialise with others. Access to top coaching and facilities are often not available to them and many do not have the physical or mental requirements to develop their involvement to this level.

The top-class sportsperson has a different reason to participate. They have physical skills and talents in their chosen area and see it as a way of making a living and gaining prestige. Professional footballers and rugby players, for example, are paid for playing, and with recent lottery money many other athletes receive a grant to train full-time. This enables them to compete at the highest level worldwide.

People who make it to the top are very often driven to be the best and win. Often, their background provided the encouragement and accessibility to acquire skills at an early age. Some top athletes had the support of their parents when they were younger, who gave their time and financed their travel expenses, coaching and provided equipment.

Key Terms:

- **Fitness** ► the ability to meet the demands of the environment/lifestyle
- **Health** ► a state of complete social, mental and physical well-being
- **Skill-related fitness** ► physical abilities of the body adapted to specific sports
- **Visualise** ► to create a positive mental picture of a desired outcome

What makes a champion

Category	Club player	Top-class player
Personal	• enjoys competing • participates for fun • uses sport for social reasons	• very ambitious • desire to be the best • highly motivated to train and compete • ability to cope with anxiety, tension and stress • determined to do well and gain success • dedicated to training and competing • willingness to make sacrifices to be the best
Physical	• some ability and development of some skills • fair to good level of health and fitness • skills often lost under pressure	• high levels of skills and natural ability • good fitness and health • ideal shape and size for the sport • skills remain under pressure
Background	• family who may have played the same sport • encouraged by school	• encouraged by family tradition • family support, who accept level of commitment • school tradition in the sport • school provided opportunities
Facilities	• some facilities available in local area	• near to best facilities • top coaches available • influenced by highly trained people • in training full time • member of strong, often influential, club • attracts sponsorship
Lucky breaks		• talent recognised by scouts • played well in trials

Summary

A healthy person has a good balance of mental, social and physical well-being. Fitness relates to the physical attributes of the person and how well they adapt to the demands of the environment in which they function. These surroundings can be their everyday environment or in connection with sport.

The components of skill-related fitness are associated with sport. These identify certain abilities that are directly related to sporting situations. The more accomplished a person is at these components, coupled with their ability to adapt them to the intensity of competition, the more likely it is that success will follow. Each different sport requires the development of a certain combination of these areas for success.

The development of the components of health-related exercise have a direct effect on a player's ability to complete the skills successfully and so achieve favourable results.

Reasons for Physical Activity

What you will learn about in this section

1. Why People Take Part in Exercise
2. Positive Effects of Exercise
3. The Benefits of Being a Member of a Club
4. Posture and Good Health
5. Seasonal Training
6. Three Parts to an Exercise Session

1 Why People Take Part in Exercise

There are many reasons for taking part in sport. A person will choose a type of activity according to the benefits they want from physical exercise and which suits their personality. A person may choose exercise because they enjoy the activity, but other positive changes may result as well. General health (both physical and mental) and social behaviour (how people mix with others) may improve, whether planned for or not. In some cases people can gain employment in an area linked with their sporting interests. Owing to the wide range of rewards from exercise, most people can benefit whether the activity is strenuous or not. It is the health and fitness rewards that make exercising special in comparison with other leisure pursuits.

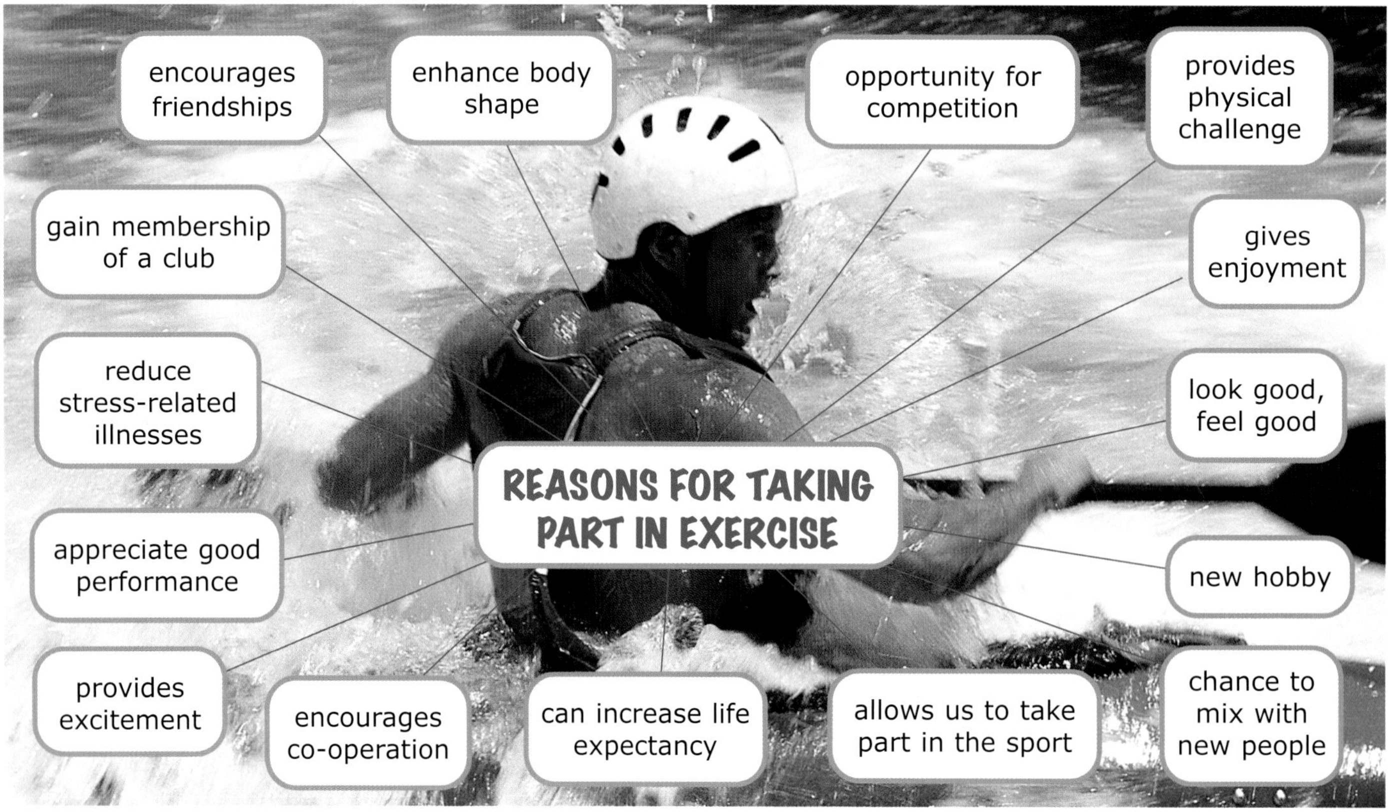

Active Challenge

Choose five reasons why you participate in sport and discuss them with a partner.

2 Positive Effects of Exercise

Health

The general health of a person, both physically and mentally, may improve as a result of regular exercise. Not only may the heart and lungs become more efficient but success in sport can improve self-confidence which can influence other parts of life. Failure in sport can lead to disappointment or depression.

Physical effects of exercising

Fitness

Generally, the more you exercise, the more your body is able to meet demands of exercise. Toning muscles can help posture. Exercising can increase strength, stamina, mobility and flexibility.

Enhance and change body shape

With regular exercise the muscles become toned: this is a tightening of the muscles in a state of readiness to work. Depending on the type of training programme, the shape and size of the muscles will begin to develop. Many people want greater **muscle definition**. Exercise at the correct level burns calories and, as long as the dietary intake remains the same, a person may lose weight with the extra activity.

Increase life expectancy

Regular exercise increases the efficiency of the heart, circulatory system and lungs. This also leads to an improvement in a person's general health. A person who has good general health can suffer less from minor ailments and may recover from serious illness more quickly due to the condition of their body.

Research carried out by the Department of Medicine at the University of Dundee came to the following conclusions: 'Older people with better health habits live healthier for longer' and 'Regular physical activity in old age can rejuvenate physical capacity by 10–15 years'.

More energy

When exercise is carried out regularly the body begins to respond to the activity. The body may become stronger, more enduring and more flexible. As a result, the body can work harder without becoming tired and breathless.

Reduce stress-related illnesses

When involved in physical activity the **stress** a person may feel is often forgotten for a time. This can have a positive effect on the functioning of the heart and so **stress-related illnesses** may be reduced.

Offers physical challenges

Whether taking part in a team sport or an individual training programme there will be targets to meet. Following a plan will help the performer to meet targets of physical self-improvement in skills, techniques, speed and strength.

Mental effects of exercising

Look good, feel good

The improvement to general body shape and posture can result in people feeling more positive about themselves and also feel they have more energy to do more things in life.

Feeling of well-being

An improvement in the efficiency of the body systems and body shape brought about by regular physical activity can give a person a sense of well-being.

Sets physical challenges

A person may take up physical activity later in life for the first time since school or be a regular exerciser. Whatever the circumstances, targets for development can be set so progress can be made. The satisfaction of reaching a higher standard through hard work, determination and effort can be the feeling that keeps a person continuing with exercise.

Personal development

Certain physical activities can present a person with challenging situations. By seeing problems through, whether individually or as a member of a team, and reaching the set goal, a person can develop courage and confidence.

Gives enjoyment

There are various reasons why a person enjoys an activity: it can be the physical challenge, the tactical battle to outwit the opponent or the fun of playing as a team to achieve success. There is a sport suitable for everyone and those who seek exercise can usually find a pursuit to satisfy them.

Interest/hobby

Starting a new interest can extend the knowledge of the individual. New tactics, skills, strategies and safety factors may have to be learned. As the skills develop, personal pride in the new achievement is felt and so pleasure and satisfaction result.

Reduces stress

Some activities are extremely competitive. These activities can act as a release valve for aggressive behaviour so that a person's general life is calmer. Having a hobby is something to look forward to and when taking part in a sport or activity a person deals with a new set of challenges; this can take their mind off problems from daily life.

Excitement through the activity

Some activities are attractive because they are exciting to perform. Skiing, climbing, skate-boarding and BMX track racing are all examples of sports that attract people because of the thrill and adrenalin rush they provide.

Opportunity to appreciate the activity

From taking part in an activity, a person will realise how difficult the skills are to perform. Using their knowledge of good technique, people can learn to appreciate others' skills and recognise good quality performance and the **aesthetic quality** of a move. A gymnast understands the degree of difficulty in a movement; a rugby player, seeing a player avoid several tackles in order to score, may appreciate the skills needed for this action more than a non-player.

Here the crowd are appreciating the performance of Julian Knowle at Wimbledon. However, only those that have played a game can truly appreciate the skills involved.

Task 1

What to do:

1. Link each sentence below to a heading.
2. Make up your own sentence for each heading.

Think about the positive effects of exercise. Perhaps link your ideas to sports and activities you are good at.

Headings

More energy Increase in fitness Feeling good Life expectancy will increase
Appreciating the finer points of the activity Excitement through the activity
Learning new skills Meeting the challenges

Sentences

"Having played the game, I can see how good top-class sportspeople are."

"My pulse rate per minute is reducing; this means my heart is becoming more efficient."

"The rush of skiing my maximum speed downhill is what I really enjoy."

"Despite my training sessions getting harder, I seem to be able to keep working for longer without tiring."

"I enjoy starting a new sport and learning and using the new skills involved."

"Through exercising regularly I have lost weight; this makes me feel positive about myself."

"I am becoming more confident about my ability to meet the challenges of the sport and realise how important it is to keep to my plan."

"I exercise for general fitness so I can keep my heart and lungs working in good order for longer."

3 The Benefits of Being a Member of a Club

A person attracted to sport may join a club so that they can participate in their chosen activity. They will not only improve physically but personal and social benefits may follow as well. As they improve their skills and abilities, a person's confidence may rise and so they feel ready to enter club competitions and compete against other clubs.

Encourages co-operation

In any club there are many jobs to complete for its overall success. The obvious one is to be a member of a team, but there are duties necessary for the general running of the club too. For example, fixtures need to be arranged, finances have to be looked after and the facilities have to be maintained. By working together for the good of the club, a person can be a player and an organiser or helper, co-operating with fellow members for maximum success.

Opportunity for competition

Many clubs arrange matches against other teams. This gives an opportunity for members to pit their skills against others in an effort to outplay and beat the opposition. The competitive approach needed in some sports can link qualities needed in everyday life. In the relatively safe environment of sport, a competitive characteristic can develop that may help effectiveness at work.

Mixing socially with new people

Training with club mates and performing against other teams gives a person the opportunity to meet a large number of people. This can expand the variety of acquaintances a person has. Through these experiences a person can become more outgoing and confident in the company of others.

Some sports provide time during the game for socialising.

Encourages friendships

By being a member of a club, a person meets others with the same interests. After a club event there is usually a social drink and, by regularly attending such social events, friendships can form.

Allows us to take part in a particular sport

In some instances the only way to participate or compete in a sport is to be a member of a club. Clubs make taking part in an activity viable, as the equipment and coaching may be too costly otherwise.

Task 2

What to do:

1. Write out what you would say to a friend to encourage and persuade them to join a sports club. Include at least four different reasons.

4 Posture and Good Health

Posture not only makes a person look good but also plays a part in keeping a person healthy. In order to have good posture the muscles supporting the body need to have good tone and be trained to keep the body in the correct position. The muscles of the back (latissimus dorsi) help to pull the shoulders back and prevent round shoulders. Poor tone in these muscles can, in extreme conditions, lead to a curved back and permanent damage to the spine.

A person who does adopt a bad posture can damage the skeleton, strain the muscles and cramp the internal organs of the body. This could have the effect of making breathing difficult or prevent efficient digestion. In everyday living good posture should be adopted when sitting, standing or lying down. This is called 'static posture' and applies when the body is still. When the body is more active, 'dynamic posture' comes into play and concerns the body in movement. Dynamic posture can directly relate to the athlete in action and the correct technique to use.

5 Seasonal Training

The training programme for the year needs detailed planning. The plan will change according to the sport, the individual and the facilities available. The coach should make the team or individual familiar with the plan and, although it may have to change due to injury or postponed fixtures, the general outline should create goals to achieve and keep the performers motivated. The training differs greatly between the pre-season, peak season and out of season (closed season).

The performer will need to consider the following:

- What is the overall aim of the training?
- When does the training year start?
- What results am I working on – personal best or qualifying performance?
- When is the competition I am training for?

Planning for an individual event

If an athlete is training for a competition taking place in August, then the training starts in the previous October and is divided into six phases each with their own goal.

The timetable sets out with specific plans to develop each of the following areas: condition of the body, strength, technique, mobility, endurance and speed. Each of the activities are building blocks worked on to ensure there is no injury. The goals or objectives of each phase are as follows :

Phase 1 – starts October for 16 weeks. General development of strength, mobility, endurance and basic technique.

Phase 2 – starts February for 8 weeks. Development of specific fitness and advanced technical skills to do with the event.

Phase 3 – starts April for 8 weeks. Competition experience: achievement of indoor objectives helping to bring an edge to performance.

Phase 4 – starts June for 8 weeks. Adjusting technique for the event and preparation for the main competition.

Phase 5 – starts July for 8 weeks. Competition experience and achievement of outdoor objectives.

Phase 6 – starts September for 4 weeks. Active recovery from the season's efforts changing the amount and type of training. Planning preparation for the next season.

Planning for team games

A team game with a seasonal playing time may have the following three phases to the year.

Pre-season

Working on fitness, strength, mobility, power, speed, skills and strategies.

Peak season

Emphasis on speed, work at competitive pace, experience of game situations and improve fitness.

Out of season

Rest from the efforts of the season, keep a level of fitness, keep working on strength, flexibility, aerobic fitness and skills.

6 Three Parts to an Exercise Session

An exercise session consists of a **warm-up**, a **main activity** and a **cool-down**.

Warm-up

There are three phases to a warm-up: aerobic phase; stretch and flexibility phase; skills and intensive exercise phase.

The time immediately before the main activity is crucial. This is the period when the body can prepare for rigorous physical activity. There is no set time for a warm-up. It should be adapted to the demands of the sport and the age of the performer.

By warming up, the body systems, muscles and joints gradually become used to working harder. This gradual increase of stress on the body reduces the risk of injury. The pulse and body temperature are raised to nearer the working rate.

Concentrating on the warm-up activities will concentrate the mind. By focusing in this way an advantage may be gained over the opposition by having a better start to a match.

In the warm-up phase of team sports there needs to be an opportunity to practise the basic skills of the game and start to think collectively as a team. The warm-up creates a link between rest and the main activity. The timing between the two is important. If there is too long a gap the effects of the warm-up will be lost. If actions stressing the muscles and joints, like sprinting, are used in the event then these should be included at the end of the warm-up session.

Types of movement to include in a warm-up

Light aerobic work

This type of activity, such as marching on the spot, starts a session in order to get the heart and lungs working harder.

Stretches

Stretches and flexibility exercises are next. Stretches ease the muscles and joints used in the activity into action.

There are different types of stretches and those performed in the warm-up should, for safety, be performed in the following order:

- static
- assisted
- dynamic.

Athletes using static stretches ease the muscle gradually into the stretched position and hold it there for 10 seconds.

Assisted stretching is when the action is helped by pushing against another person or a wall. A specialised way of stretching is often used in gymnastics. Here, the coach helps the performer by pushing the limb and so stretching the joint further. These are called 'proprioceptive neuromuscular facilitation (PNF) techniques'. These should only be undertaken by an expert and with great care.

Dynamic stretches are the most complex to perform. Care needs to be taken as injury can occur if these are misused. The athlete moves into the stretch position and 'bounces' the muscle. This starts at half pace for two to three repetitions. These gradually increase to full speed. These movements are used when the event or activity needs rapid, explosive movement.

After the aerobic phase, static stretches should follow in a warm-up.

Flexibility exercises

These exercises increase the mobility of the joints of the body – rotating shoulders and hips, for example. Each joint should be given some time, although certain sports may need some joints warmed more than others.

Skills and intensive exercises

Basic skills related to the sport can help co-ordination in a game. The exercises gradually increase in intensity. If the sport includes times when bursts of pace are necessary then, at the end of the session, some short sprints can be included. By warming up, a person will increase their awareness and reaction time ready for the game. Preparing the body will increase the level of work the person is capable of producing in the event. Note that professional football teams have set warm-ups, which they perform on the pitch before a match.

Main activity

The warm-up leads to the main activity. This can be a training session, skills session or a competition, match or performance. Once the body systems are trained they become fit enough to complete the skills practised. When the body is pushed to the limit in competition, the skills can be put to the test without breaking down because of inadequate fitness levels.

Cool down

There are two phases to the cool down: gentle aerobic and stretching.

After the main activity, the body is given the chance of gradually returning to its resting state; the cool down helps to do this. The heart and muscles of the body take advantage of this. By completing a cool down the heartbeat reaches its resting rate sooner; this is called the 'recovery time'. The heart, therefore, does not have to work too hard for longer than it needs to. The speed of the recovery rate is influenced by several factors:

- The older a person is, the slower the recovery rate will be.
- If the exercise is new, then the new stresses will be harder to recover from.
- How 'in shape' the performer is: the fitter a person is, the quicker the recovery.
- Women tend to recover more slowly than men.

Like the warm-up, there is no set time for a cool down; keeping the blood circulating prevents it from having the chance to 'pool' or collect in areas of the circulatory system; this prevents light-headedness.

Gentle stretching stops the build-up of lactic acid in the muscles and so prevents immediate cramp and aching and soreness the following day. Stretches in a cool down should be held for about 30 seconds and should concentrate on the muscles used in the event. Freestyle swimmers will concentrate on cooling down their arms; runners will stretch their legs. A controlled, restful cool down can have a calming effect on a person after the excitement of a competitive match.

Task 3

What to do:

1. Give three reasons why a warm-up helps a performer.
2. List three types of exercise that would be included in a warm-up.
3. Draw a spidergram of the main points and reasons for a cool down.

Key Terms:

Aesthetic quality	► how good an action looks
Muscle definition	► muscle shape
Posture	► a position the body can assume; the way in which a person carries themselves
Stress	► anxiety and nervous tension
Stress-related illnesses	► illnesses such as heart attack, ulcer, high blood pressure

Summary

There are many advantages to taking part in physical activity. A person in the habit of regular exercise could benefit from their healthy lifestyle. Physically, the body and its systems can increase in fitness, and be able to meet the demands of their environment and the added demands of the activity. A stronger body may increase life expectancy.

Personal development can come about through the challenges of exercise. A person may develop determination, courage and a positive attitude as a result of taking exercise; in turn this may spill over into general life and positively affect a person's confidence. Co-operation, teamwork and friendships may develop from being a member of a group, club or team.

Diet

What you will learn in this section

1. Seven Parts of a Balanced Diet
2. How Energy is Calculated
3. Individual Energy Requirements
4. Factors Affecting Energy Requirements
5. Special Diets for Sport
6. The Effects of Over and Under Eating

1 Seven Parts of a Balanced Diet

The food we eat fuels our body just like petrol fuels a car. As the human body is more complex than a car engine, there are different types of food to keep the various parts of the body functioning properly. Food does the following:

- provides energy
- helps our bodies grow
- repairs injured tissue
- contributes to good general health.

It is important to have a balance of all of the seven types of food. Eating the correct quantities and combinations of food will keep the body systems functioning properly, keep hair and skin in good condition and reduce the chances of obesity.

In general, a **balanced diet** is important, but, by changing the amounts of each nutrient eaten, a diet can be adapted to have a specific result for a sportsperson training for a particular event.

FOOD TYPES	ABOUT THE FOOD	AID TO THE SPORTSPERSON
Carbohydrates (sugars and starch) 	Fruit, cakes, beer, sweets, granulated sugar and bread, pasta, rice and potatoes. Stored in the liver and muscles as glycogen. Converts to glucose and used as energy for muscles of the body, brain and other organs. Excess converted and stored as fat. Should provide over 47% of daily energy requirements and if a person is training hard this should rise to 65–70%.	Provides a ready source of energy when the muscles require it. Carbohydrates in the highly processed form of sugars provide us with energy but no other nutrients so it is better to eat more starches. Athletes training hard use carbohydrates quickly, so diets should be high in this food type.
Proteins 	Meat, fish, pulses (chick peas, lentils and beans), nuts, eggs and poultry. Builds body muscle, repairs tissue, enzymes and hormones. Proteins are broken down in the body as amino acids; 21 types are needed for our bodies to work properly. Our body can produce 13 types (non-essential amino acids) but the other 8 (essential amino acids) come from protein foods. Excess is converted and stored as fat.	Builds muscle and repairs tissue within the body. Essential after an injury to heal quickly. Sportspeople who need large muscle size need extra proteins.

FOOD TYPES	ABOUT THE FOOD	AID TO THE SPORTSPERSON
Fats 	Milk, cheese, butter, oils, chocolate, fatty meats, soya beans and corn. Provider of energy – recommended daily intake 30% of a combination of saturated, polyunsaturated and monounsaturated fatty acids. Can be stored in the body.	Increase size and weight of body. Important for performers who benefit from having extra bulk, shot putters for instance. Unnecessary weight can inhibit performance and lead to high cholesterol levels. Fats are a form of stored energy, released slowly when there is a lack of carbohydrates.
Vitamins 	Fruit (vitamin C), liver and carrots (vitamin A), whole grains and nuts (vitamin B1) and vegetable oil (vitamin E). Help with the general health of vision, skin condition, forming of red blood cells and blood clotting, and the good condition of bones and teeth.	The general health of athletes is important if they are to perform well. When training hard, vitamins from the B group are used more and so need to be replenished. This can be done by eating more of that food type or using supplements.
Minerals 	Milk and saltwater fish (iodine), red meat, liver and green vegetables (iron), milk, cheese and cereals (calcium). Calcium helps growth of bones, iron helps the making of red blood cells and the way oxygen is carried in the body by the haemoglobin. The more a person exercises the greater the intake needed, provided by a varied diet or supplements. Excessive amounts of the mineral salt can lead to high blood pressure.	Increase efficiency of carrying oxygen to the working muscles of the body. Iodine aids normal growth, essential for the athlete to help energy production. Iron helps produce red blood cells and so carry more oxygen round the body helping to prevent **fatigue**. Calcium helps blood to clot, aiding recovery from injury, and strengthens bones and muscles.
Fibre 	Leaves, seed cases, cereals and whole grains. Fibre, or roughage, helps digestion but contains no nutrients. There are two types: insoluble – this adds bulk to our food, helping it to keep moving through the digestive system and so preventing constipation, and soluble – helps to reduce cholesterol, keeping the heart healthy.	Less cholesterol in the body makes the heart more efficient. By keeping the digestive system functioning regularly the body retains less waste.
Water 	Fluids and food. Two-thirds of the body is made up of water. We need regular intakes to replenish what is lost in urine, sweat and condensation as we breathe.	Water allows the blood to flow more easily around the body. This is extremely important when exercising, as the body demands more oxygen, nutrients, heat control and waste removal. In endurance events, or when exercising in hot weather, water is lost quickly; this can lead to dehydration and heatstroke if not replenished.

Task 1

What to do:

1. What is the major role in human diet of
   a. carbohydrates? b. proteins? c. fats? d. vitamins?
2. Give three examples of foods that are good sources of
   a. vitamins b. carbohydrates c. proteins.
3. What two types of carbohydrates are there and in what form are they stored in the body?
4. How does the sportsperson use the following:
   a. carbohydrates? b. proteins? c. water? d. fats?

2 How Energy is Calculated

The body needs energy all the time, even when sleeping. This is because the body is still functioning – the heart is beating, blood is circulating, the body is breathing. This lowest form of energy requirement is called the **basal metabolic rate** (BMR).

Each food type has an energy value which can be calculated in two ways:

- Joules are calculated by a moving force = energy needed when 1 kilogram is moved by 1 metre by a force of 1 **newton**.
- Calories are calculated by a rise in temperature = amount of energy needed to raise temperature of 1 gram of water by 1°C.

The main ways we understand the above calculations are as kilojoules (kj) and kilocalories (kcal). This is because diets and nutritional information on food packaging deal in large quantities and so the equation is multiplied by 1000 to make the figures more manageable. A food with a low kilojoule or kilocalorie value will have to be eaten in a larger quantity than one with a high value to do the same job.

3 Individual Energy Requirements

There are many factors that change the energy requirements of people. At different stages of life greater or lesser levels of energy are needed. Teenagers need more than adults. Women, on average, need less energy than men as they have a smaller build. As people get older their pace of life slows down and their energy requirements reduce. Even same age, same gender people rarely have the same energy needs owing to variations in their lifestyles and build. These factors are out of our control but what does dramatically change our energy requirements and is in our control is the amount of activity we undertake.

Below is an approximate calculation of the daily intake requirements for people of different ages.

Boys 15 years old	11 500kj (2700kcal approx.)
Girls 15 years old	8800kj (2100kcal approx.)
Adult men	10 500kj (2500kcal approx.)
Adult women	8400kj (2000kcal approx.)
Older men	8800kj (2100kcal approx.)
Older women	8000kj (1900kcal approx.)

Active Challenge

Discuss with a partner the reasons why people have different energy requirements. Think of four different reasons.

4 Factors Affecting Energy Requirements

- Each sport has a different energy requirement.
- Length of activity.
- Intensity of activity.
- Level of opponent – easy game/lower level opponent.

Energy per hour needed for different activities

Activity	Approx. energy (kj)
Sleeping	252
Studying	420
Housework	798
Walking	840
Golf	1080
Gardening	1260
Cycling	1280
Swimming	1300
Volleyball	1440
Tennis	1740
Disco dancing	2100
Marathon running	4158

5 Special Diets for Sport

An increase in demands on the body from exercise means an increase in energy requirements. This should result in a change of diet to compensate for the new demand. The general diet for an athlete is high in carbohydrates, low in fat, with a high fluid intake, including **energy drinks** and/or water. This provides energy and keeps the fluid levels balanced.

Diets can be organised around an exercise programme. This will involve timing when meals are taken, the content of the meal depending on the activity and the quantity of food to be eaten. A top-class athlete acquires knowledge of how to use the different types of food to their best advantage. Each sportsperson's diet will vary due to individual differences of build, demands of the sport, position played in the team and any injury incurred.

Diet plays an important part in an athlete's performance. It is seen to be so important that many sportspeople are guided by specialist dieticians and follow strict eating habits. The dietician will play their part in the performer's success just as the coach does. There are crucial times when a sportsperson can adapt their diet to help performance.

By adapting their diet over the following periods the athlete can get the best results:

- the week before the event
- the day of the event
- during the event
- after the event.

Carbohydrate loading

Traditionally, **carbohydrate loading** is linked with long-distance events but other competitors can benefit too. Swimmers can use this diet effectively for their event. Carbohydrates are important to an athlete, as they are easy to digest and provide an instant source of energy. By eating more carbohydrates, a store of glycogen is built up in the body. In competition this store will reduce levels of fatigue and so help to maintain a standard of performance.

Diet for a long-distance athlete

Pre-event

The week before an event a runner's training routine and diet change. Due to the excesses of previous training, carbohydrates are low in the body while proteins are high. This combination is not appropriate for a long-distance athlete. So, four or five days before the race, many more carbohydrates are eaten in order to build up these energy stores for the event.

The training programme is now tapered so fewer miles are covered, allowing energy levels to build up and the speed of the shorter runs increases, preparing for a burst of speed during the race. By taking in extra carbohydrates and fewer fats, together with reducing the intensity of the training programme, the body is able to store these nutrients, as glycogen, for use in the race.

The usefulness of carbohydrates is so widely recognised by the long-distance athlete that 'pasta parties' are organised for the athletes two days before the London Marathon. Eating foods such as noodles, rice, potatoes and even beans on toast will have a similar effect.

Day of event

On the day of the event athletes will choose, from preference and experience, either a large meal three to four hours before the race, or a lighter one up to two hours before the race. This is the final chance, before the competition, to make sure that carbohydrates are stocked up and fluid levels are high.

During event

The prolonged, moderate to hard intensity of a long-distance race reduces the amount of water in the body. Low water levels reduce performance and prevent correct circulation and temperature control. Regular water intake is essential to the athlete to prevent dehydration (see page 143). Energy drinks help the body to work hard for longer by using the carbohydrates in them.

After event

An athlete must continue to drink fluids and energy drinks to replace the fluids and carbohydrates lost. High energy food can be eaten immediately after the race. Depending on the training programme following the event, a sensible meal including various carbohydrates is usual.

Taking fluids during an endurance event is essential.

Task 2

What to do:

1. Make a ten-point list about carbohydrate loading and the procedure for food and fluid intake for a long-distance event.

Include ideas on the week before, day of race, during race and after race.

High protein diet

This diet requires the intake of a large amount of protein. Weightlifters and athletes, needing a loss of weight over a fairly short period of weeks, can adopt this diet. High protein diets can also be used in a rehabilitation programme after injury for the repair of damaged tissue.

A bodybuilder or a rugby player will use this type of diet to burn fat and increase muscle size. Taking creatine (a form of protein) supplements increases the effect. A rugby league player can eat as many as six meals a day taking in mainly proteins, some carbohydrates, but little or no fat. Throughout the day, they are encouraged to drink plenty of fluids and eat fruit as well as the prescribed meals. The protein will build up the muscle; carbohydrate will provide energy and fluids will keep the body hydrated.

Eating a high protein diet has the effect of reducing the storage of fat in the body. Some performers, who need to lose weight quite quickly, can use this type of diet. However, there is now evidence of long-term problems with this type of diet.

Problems with the diet

There are long-term effects of using high protein diets. When a bodybuilder takes in a high level of animal proteins this raises the cholesterol levels in the body, leading to a possibility of heart disease, diabetes, stroke and cancer. The performer using a high protein diet to control their weight can develop kidney damage in the long term.

6 The Effects of Over and Under Eating

How to lose weight – more exercise, less calorie intake.
How to gain weight – make calorie intake exceed energy expended.
How to maintain weight – balance calorie intake with energy used.

Changing their diet to make a weight or to keep slim can have major consequences on a sportsperson.

(Normal-sized person)
The amount of food eaten matches the amount of energy used, so maintains weight.

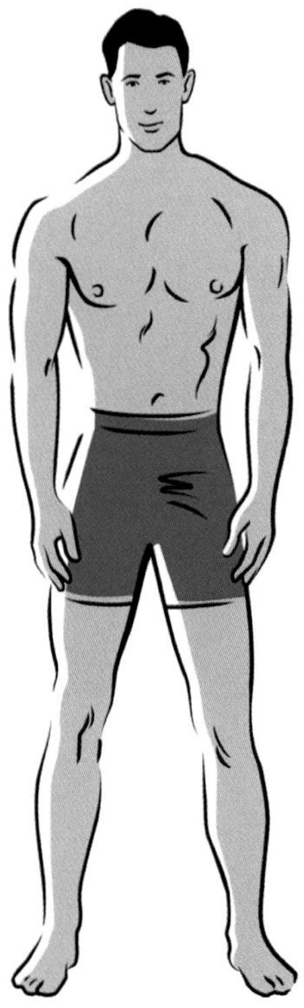

(Underweight person)
The amount of food eaten is not enough for the energy used, so weight is lost.

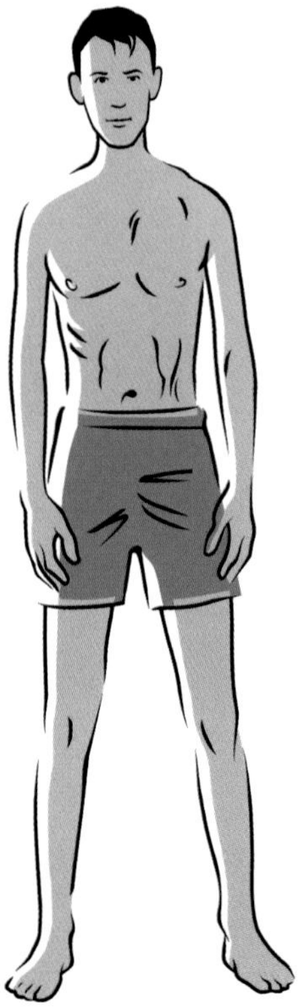

(Overweight person)
The amount of food eaten is too much for the energy used, so weight is put on.

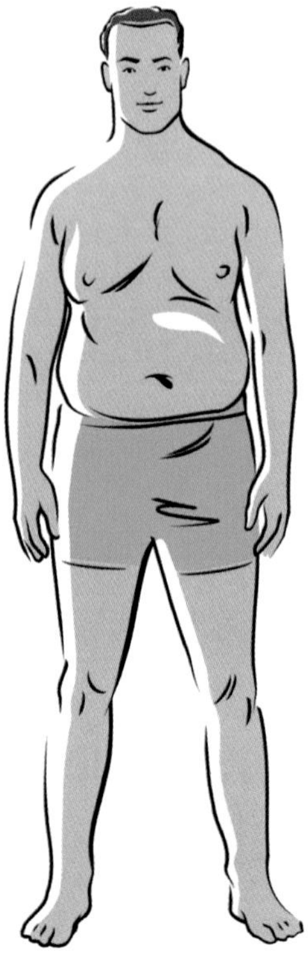

Weight problems affecting performance

Each athlete has an **optimum weight** at which they perform at their best. This depends on the correct balance of height, gender, bone structure and muscle girth (measurement around the flexed muscle). Some athletes can keep to their optimum weight easily, whilst others constantly have to check what they eat. Some sports, like boxing and horse racing, demand a certain weight restriction; so for the boxer and the jockey, diets and quick weight loss are sometimes vital for them to compete. It is the fluids in the body that are lost when an athlete needs to make the weight category in a short period of time. The consequences of losing weight quickly can be that the body becomes dehydrated and the level of performance is reduced, making the competitor less effective. Some athletes will appear to be overweight; their large muscle girth will give a reading that is misleading. If a sportsperson is overweight it can have a bad effect on their performance as well as a poor effect on their health.

The demands of some sports for an athlete to be the optimum weight are essential for the greatest success. The effect of having too much fat can restrict the flexibility of the joints and so the athlete cannot move appropriately to execute the correct technique. Carrying too much weight will decrease the speed of movement, slowing a player down in a game. A performer will tire quickly because of the extra effort needed to carry more weight. In some sports, like archery and bowls, where speed is not a necessity, then being overweight is not a problem. It may even make the person more stable and so help accuracy.

Height to weight chart for adult men and women

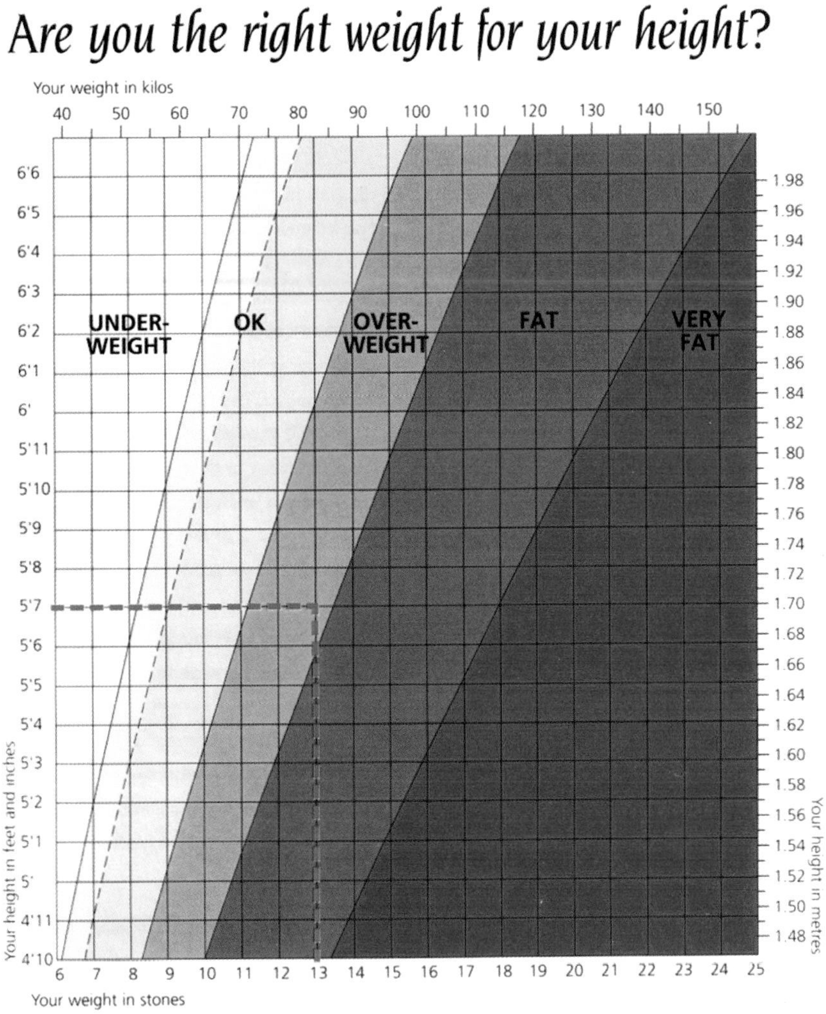

This chart is issued by the Food Standards Agency in the UK. The chart provides a guideline to adults showing what the correct weight of a person should be dependent on their height.

Degrees of being overweight

An **overweight** person can be said to be heavier than the average person of that gender, height and build. (See height to weight chart on the previous page.) The extra weight, however, is not necessarily a threat to the person's health (sometimes a lot of it is muscle).

Being **overfat** can have a direct effect on a person's health. In this category a person will have a high level of fat in comparison with their total body composition. Having this amount of fat can lead to obesity related disease: problems may include high blood pressure, strokes, cancer and heart attacks.

When a person reaches the stage of being **obese**, they are abnormally fat (more than 20% over the standard weight for their height). At this stage the health risks become more dangerous and can include diabetes, high blood pressure, heart disease, osteoarthritis and early mortality.

Being overweight is a problem of the twenty-first century. Many nations now record more than 20% of their population as clinically obese and well over half the population as overweight. This trend has increased throughout the world as fast food chains reach various areas. In the USA 60% of the population is overweight giving America the nickname 'the fat capital of the world'.

Possible dietary problems

In an effort to look like role models seen in the media, people put pressure on themselves about their weight, which can sometimes lead to eating disorders. Athletes may also do the same in an attempt to reach and maintain a low body weight ideal for their sport, but unnatural for themselves.

There are two main eating disorders:

Anorexia – a person does not eat, they see themselves as fat; the problem is the obsessive state of mind. This condition leads to excessive weight loss.

Bulimia – a person eats a lot and then forces themselves to vomit. This has the effect of weight loss.

Both eating disorders lead to bouts of depression and many severe medical problems, including kidney and liver damage, and even death.

Many people feel under pressure to become thin to look like their role models; this can lead to eating disorders.

Task 3

What to do:

1. Choose five different types of sportsperson.
2. Write a sentence on what they may say about their diet and how it affects them.

Include ideas on:
energy needs of the activity, weight problems and how training changes natural food preferences.

Key Terms:

Balanced diet	daily intake of food containing right amounts and types of nutrients
Basal metabolic rate	the level at which energy is used without exercise
Carbohydrate loading	building up carbohydrates in the body to use in endurance events
Energy drinks	fluids containing carbohydrates
Fatigue	the body's inability to complete a task
Newton	a unit of force
Obese	a person who is extremely overweight (more than 20% over the standard weight for their height); this condition can lead to many health problems
Optimum weight	ideal weight for a person, giving them the best chance of success in an activity
Overfat	a person having more body fat than is recommended for their gender and height
Overweight	a person carrying more weight than is recommended for their gender and height

Summary

For general health, a balance of all seven nutrients in the daily diet is important.

Different types of food provide these nutrients helping the body to function properly. It is important to eat a variety of foods within a day so that all the body systems can function properly. In general, there needs to be a balance of all seven nutrients for everyday healthy living.

Each food has a different energy value. A person who strikes the correct balance between food intake and energy output according to activity levels will maintain a constant weight. The performer pursuing high-energy activities will have to increase the amount of food eaten to cope with the energy demand. When athletes understand the different qualities of food, they can use food to their best advantage. Once the requirements of the sport have been identified, the sportsperson can choose a special diet containing foods to help their performance. For example, a weightlifter needs to increase muscle size and strength so a high protein diet is appropriate. Whereas a long distance athlete needs a slow release of energy lasting the whole of the race, therefore a high carbohydrate loading diet suits them.

Combining training with eating certain foods in definite quantities can help an athlete to become more effective in their event. The following changes may then occur:

- change their natural shape (changing the fat ratio and muscle size)
- improve their energy levels
- reduce their recovery periods.

Certain shapes of performer are suited to particular activities. This can be a natural body shape or a person can use diet to achieve the shape they want. Whether a heavier or lighter weight is pursued, both can result in health problems. In sports where weight is required heart disease, high blood pressure and diabetes can result; in sports where lighter weight is more suitable, eating disorders can result.

The Performer in Action

For any performer to function to the best of their ability all the body systems need to interact with each other. The systems working together are the skeletal, circulatory, respiratory and muscular systems. Each system is reliant on the others to work together and adapt to the changing demands of exercise. The efficiency of each system depends on the individual and can be improved by training but can also deteriorate with age. The good condition of the systems make long life expectancy more likely.

Some of the main links you will learn include, how:

- the muscles are attached to the skeleton to aid movement
- the muscles are reliant on the circulatory system to provide oxygen and take away waste products
- the circulatory system transports oxygen, carrying red blood cells, which are produced in the long bones of the skeleton
- extra oxygen needed for energy release in prolonged exercise is taken in by the respiratory system and is absorbed into the circulatory system via the lungs and transported to the working body parts
- how the nervous system has overall control of changes which omit all the other points above.

Regular and specialised training of the body allow skills to be performed.

The Skeletal System

What you will learn about in this section

1. The Function of the Skeleton
2. The Names of Bones
3. The Different Shapes of Bones
4. How Bones Are Grouped Together
5. What is the Function of Certain Bones?
6. How Bones Help the Sportsperson
7. Bones Linked With Sporting Actions

1 The Function of the Skeleton

We take for granted having a **skeleton** but have you ever thought what we would be like without one? A mass of muscle and tissue on the floor is not a pretty sight. The bones of the skeleton have five important jobs to do. Some of these jobs are more obvious than others.

The skeleton gives us our general **shape** and determines whether we are tall or short, broad or narrow.

The bones of the skeleton **support** the rest of the body.

The skeleton helps the body to **move** by providing a framework to which muscles attach.

Some bones help to **protect** the internal organs of the body.

What is not that obvious is that **production** of red and white blood cells takes place in some bones of the body.

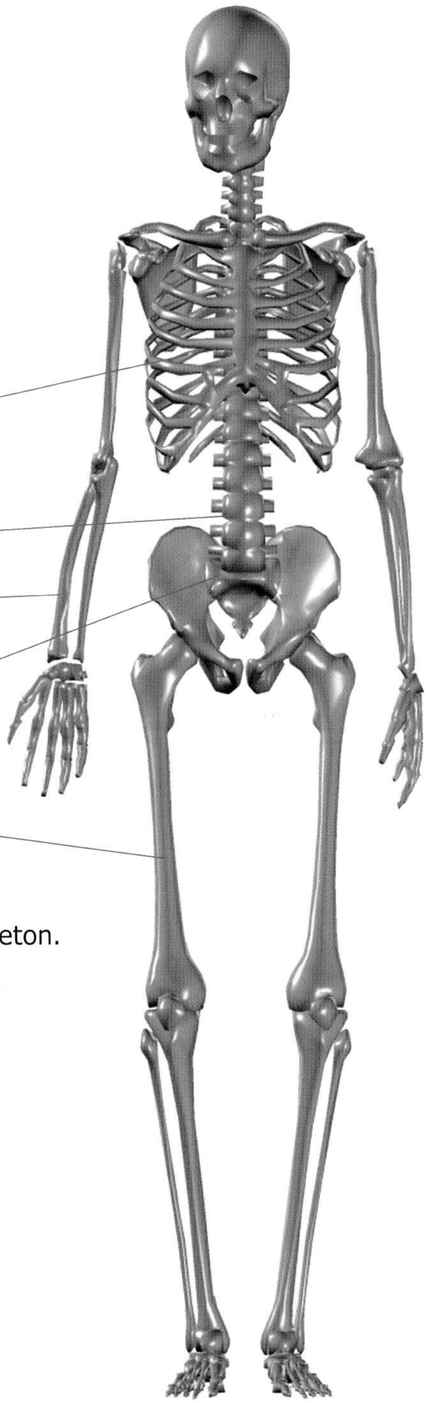

Task 1

What to do:

1. Using the above section, pick out the five different functions of the skeleton.
2. When you have found them, copy the spidergram below.
3. Put one function at the end of each line.

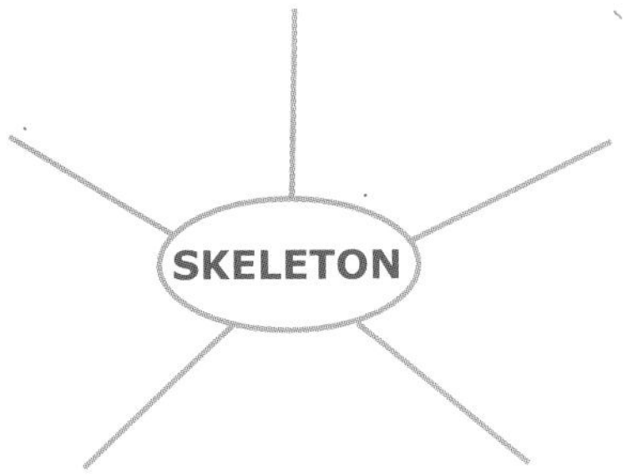

2 The Names of Bones

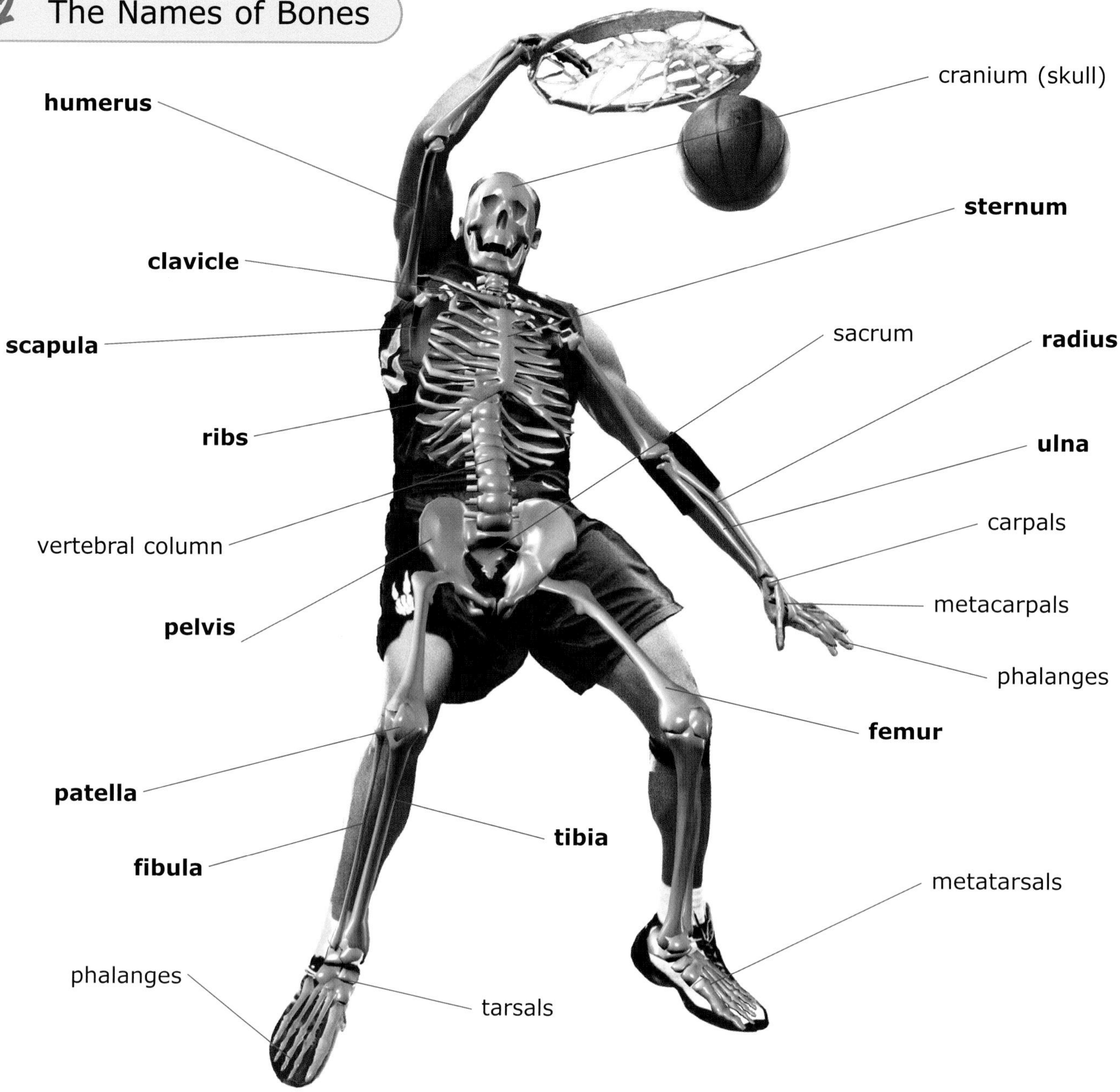

What to do:

1. Learn the names of the bones in the body. The bone names in **bold** are the ones you need to remember.
2. Start by trying to memorise the bones of the upper body.
3. When you feel confident go on to the bones of the lower body.

Remember **u**lna is **u**nderneath the radius and the **t**ibia is on **t**op of the fibula.

The phalanges are both fingers and toes!

Task 2

Active Challenge

Take turns in testing your partner. Point to a bone in your body and see if your partner can tell you its name. Use the picture above only when you need to.

Functions of the bones

Shape

The way bones are arranged gives us our general framework and shape. When someone is said to be of a large build it is partly because of the size of their skeleton. Certain builds are more suited to particular sports. When you look at different sportspeople you will be able to work out their general shape and size of skeleton. Jockeys have a skeleton that is likely to be small and thin; a basketball player's skeleton is often long and thin; a sprinter's skeleton is medium to long but sturdy.

Support

As bones are firm and rigid they can support the rest of the body and keep us upright. Part of the body is made up of muscle, which is held in place by being attached to the skeleton. The bones act as an anchor or framework upon which the rest of the body tissues, like muscles, hang.

Help with movement

When the bones work with the muscles of the body they allow the body to move. The skeleton provides a series of 'anchor points' to which the muscles attach. When bones are made to work by muscles they work as levers and so allow a variety of movements in everyday life and when we play sports. When a sportsperson swings a racket to hit a tennis ball, for instance, the **long bones** of the arm help create the leverage necessary to apply force to the shot.

Protection

Some bones help to protect the internal organs of the body. These are the bones and arrangements of bone that enclose other parts of the body. They act a little like a box. This is especially important to the sportsperson playing contact sports or team games. A volleyball player dives to make a dig, a footballer heads a ball and a rugby player takes a tackle. The vital organs of the body would not last long if they did not have certain bones to protect them. Examples of these protecting bones are: **skull**, **pelvis**, **rib cage** and **vertebrae**.

Task 3

What to do:

1. Use skull, pelvis, rib cage and vertebrae as headings.
2. List underneath each of these headings the part of the body they protect.
3. Use the word bank below to help you.
4. Each word links with only one set of the protecting bones.

Word bank

brain **spinal cord** **heart** **lungs** **spleen** **stomach** **bladder** **liver**

Task 4

Production of blood cells

In the **long bones** of the body, the production of red and white blood cells takes place. As blood cells keep wearing out it is important that new supplies are made. The job of white blood cells is to go to any source of infection to fight germs and bacteria. Cells need to be regenerating constantly so the body can be guarded from disease. Red blood cells transport oxygen from the lungs to the rest of the body.

What to do:

1. Copy and complete the sentences below about each function of the skeleton.
   - a. Some people choose a particular sport because of their ______ owing to their skeleton size.
   - b. Red blood cells are constantly being __________ in the long bones of the skeleton.
   - c. We need our skeleton to work with the muscles to allow different _________.
   - d. The skeleton provides the _________ upon which muscles can hang.
   - e. When a player heads a ball their brain is __________ by part of their skeleton.

Key Terms:

- **Long bones** ► those bones that are the longest in the body, which make up the arms and legs
- **Move** ► a motion, could be an action like running or swinging a racket at a ball
- **Production** ► making something
- **Protect** ► guard against threat of injury
- **Shape** ► form or outline
- **Skeleton** ► the arrangement of the 206 bones of the human body
- **Support** ► helping to take the weight

To perform well in ladies' gymnastics it is vital to develop and maintain good flexibility. Russia's Yulia Barsukova won a gold medal for her performance at the 2000 Olympics.

3 The Different Shapes of Bones

There are four different **classifications** of bones. We have already read and learned about long bones. The other types are **short**, **flat** and **irregular** bones. The way differently shaped bones are arranged in the body allows them to perform certain jobs. It would be hard to imagine an irregular bone, like the pelvis, at the point between the elbow and the shoulder and being as efficient there as the long bone of the humerus. The role that the bone has to perform determines the shape, size and density (compactness) that it is.

Long bones

humerus
radius — arm
ulna

femur
tibia — leg
fibula

metacarpals
phalanges — hands and feet
metatarsals

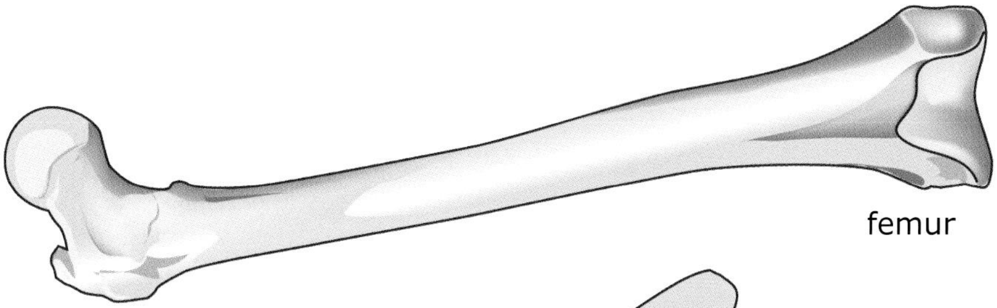

femur

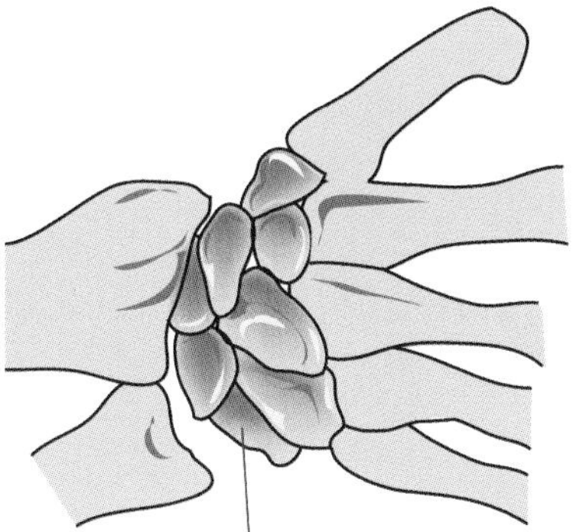

carpals

Short bones

carpals — hands

tarsals — feet

Irregular bones

vertebrae
patella
jawbone
cheekbone

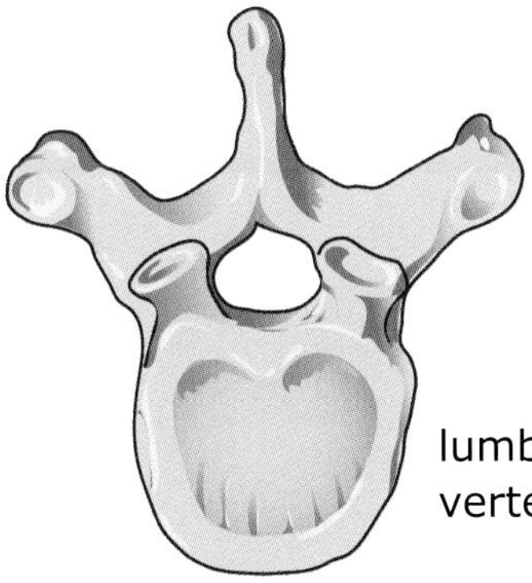

lumbar vertebra

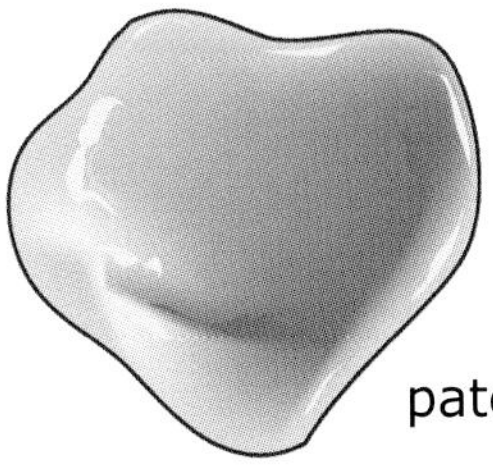

patella

Flat (plate) bones

cranium
clavicle
scapula
sternum
ribs
pelvis

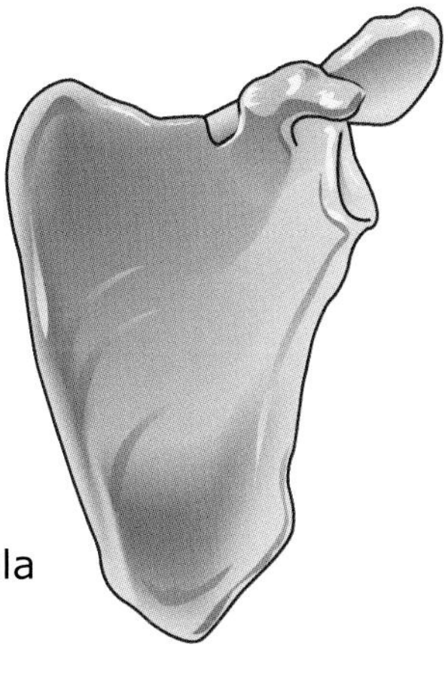

scapula

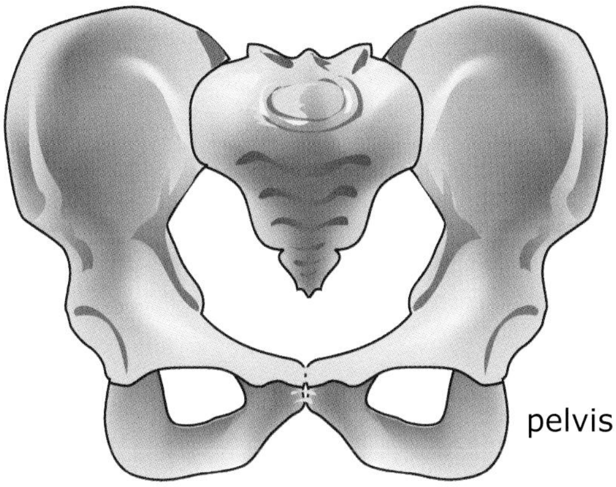

pelvis

4 How Bones Are Grouped Together

Task 5

What to do:

1. Make a list of all the bones in the following groups:
   a. irregular
   b. flat
   c. long
   d. short.

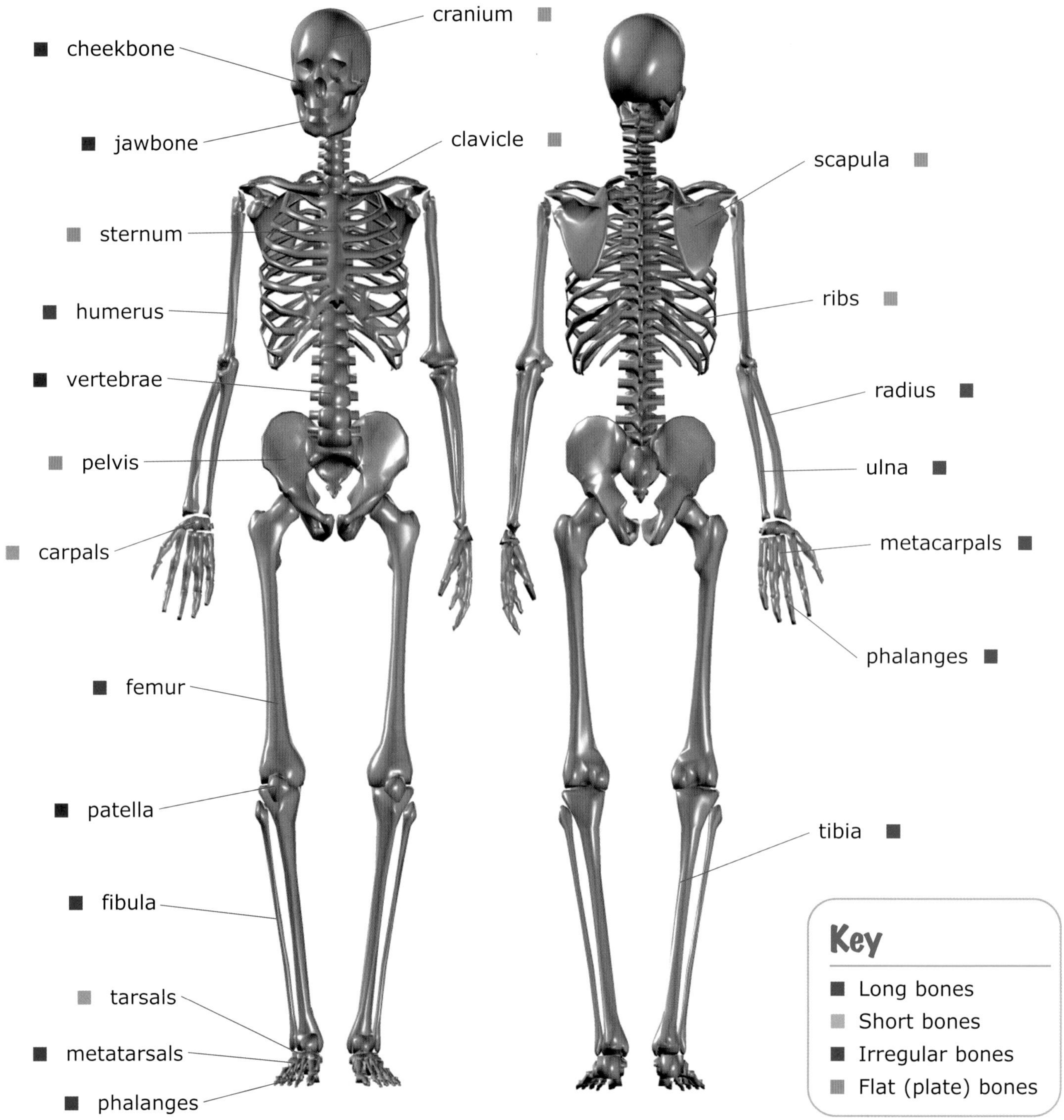

5 What is the Function of Certain Bones?

The vertebrae

The **vertebrae** are irregular bones. There are 33 of these bones making the vertebral column. They are placed in five groups according to where they are along the vertebral column.

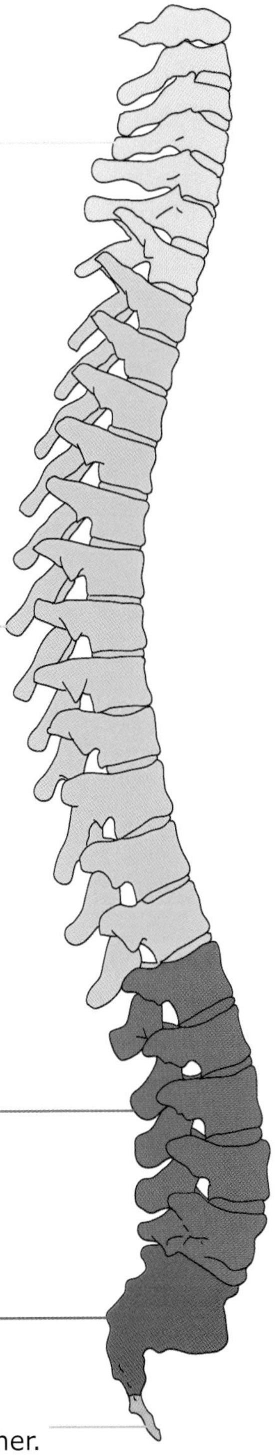

- **Cervical** vertebrae allow different movements at the top of the spine; there are seven of them. The top two vertebrae are called the atlas and axis; they allow you to nod and move your head.
- The **thoracic** region has 12 vertebrae. Ten of these are attached to the ribs and help movement when breathing.
- The five **lumbar** vertebrae are the most robust as they take a lot of weight. They are also large because they are in the area that allows the most movement.
- The **sacrum** has five vertebrae, which become fused together in adulthood. They make up part of the pelvic girdle.
- At the end of the spine is the **coccyx**. There are four vertebrae here, all fused together.

All the vertebrae fit together neatly to protect the spinal cord. This is an important job as any damage to the cord can be paralysing. In between the vertebrae there are cartilage discs. These help stop damage, wear and tear and grinding down of the vertebrae through constant movement.

6 How Bones Help the Sportsperson

Long bones, due to their length, create **leverage** when playing sport. Whether you are hitting a shuttlecock or bowling a ball, long bones play an important role in the performance of the player, helping to generate speed, force and power.

Flat bones are tough and can withstand hard impact. The cranium takes a hard blow when heading a ball. When a rugby player is in a tackle his pelvis and rib cage can protect his internal organs owing to their strength.

Short bones are specialists for fine movements, especially those of the hand. Short bones are responsible for putting spin on a ball in cricket and rounders and for helping a ball accurately hit a target. As these bones can make small adjustments they help keep the body balanced – important for the gymnast and golfer.

Bones have different uses depending on where they are in the body. Some, like the vertebrae, work together and act as a shock absorber. When players land on their feet from a jump it is the vertebrae that help reduce the shock on their backs.

7 Bones Linked with Sporting Actions

Whenever a sportsperson is in action, they are relying on their skeleton to play a supporting role in their performance; bones are also designed to help the action. Whatever a sportsperson does, bones are there, helping them to move efficiently.

- When a bowler spins a cricket ball they are relying on the bones of their hand to help apply the spin, so the carpals, metacarpals and phalanges are important.
- Swinging a racket to play a forehand drive in tennis involves the bones of the arm. Therefore the scapula, humerus, radius and ulna help the swing action of the stroke.
- Landing on their feet after playing a spike or smash, volleyball players require their legs to cushion the landing. Here the pelvis at the hip, the femur, patella, tibia and fibula in the legs, plus the tarsals, metatarsals and phalanges in the feet, are in play to make the landing safe and the body balanced and ready for the next movement.

Active Challenge

Work with a partner. Point to different bones and ask your partner to say what class of bone they are. Take turns to link a sporting movement with the class of bone indicated.

Task 6

There are two levels to this task. Choose **one** of them to complete.

What to do:

Level 1 Give one example of each bone type and link it with a sporting action.
Level 2 Give two examples of each bone type and link them with a sporting action.
Use common names and proper names when describing areas of the body. For example, irregular bone, in the lower back – lumbar vertebrae – bending to field a ball in rounders.

Choose a bone type and say where it is located in the body. Give the name of the bone and explain the sporting action that uses it. Put them together and that is your answer.

Task 7

What to do:

1. Look carefully at the pictures on the next page of people playing different sports.
2. Work out the action that they are performing and name the bones involved.
3. Write a heading for each action that you see and give the names of the bones that are involved in the specific action.

Sporting actions use various bones for movement.

Key Terms:

- **Cervical** ► bones of the vertebrae forming the neck
- **Classification** ► a way of sorting or organising groups
- **Coccyx** ► bones of the vertebrae, fused at the extreme lower end of the vertebral column
- **Flat bone** ► can be called plate bone, mainly linked with protection
- **Irregular bones** ► bones that have no uniform shape
- **Leverage** ► the use of force or effort (muscle power) to overcome resistance
- **Lumbar** ► bones of the vertebrae in the lower back region
- **Sacrum** ► bones of the vertebrae, fused in adults, making part of the pelvic girdle
- **Short bone** ► smaller version of a long bone, found in the hands and feet
- **Thoracic** ► bones of the vertebrae in the chest area
- **Vertebrae** ► irregular bones that run the length of the body from head to rear

Summary

Bones perform seen and unseen functions. A person may choose a sport because their body shape suits that particular activity and so they can be successful. The sportsperson relies on the strength of bones to withstand pressure and knocks in contact sports and so bones protect vital organs of the body. A shot to beat a keeper or a passing shot in tennis needs the length of the long bones to bring leverage to the action. The long bones help movements to be powerful and forceful.

Athletes need their small bones to aid in small movements, such as in balance and agility, important when dodging around the opposition or changing direction in a gymnastic movement. The skeleton supports the muscles. It is this anchoring that enables the muscles to work and bring about movement. Production of red and white blood cells occurs in some bones of the body. This is essential so that the body can function, as the cells transport oxygen and nutrients, and fight infection.

Physical Movements – Joints

What you will learn about in this section

1. The Definition of a Joint
2. Different Joint Locations in the Body
3. The Three Types of Joint in the Body
4. The Significance of Synovial Joints
5. In-depth Understanding of Synovial Joints
6. Functions of Different Parts of a Joint
7. The Importance of Cartilage, Tendons and Ligaments in Sport
8. Different Types of Synovial Joint
9. The Range of Movement at Joints
10. Movement and Levers
11. Effects of Age on Flexibility of the Joints
12. How Joints Help the Sportsperson

1 The Definition of a Joint

A **joint** is the place where two or more bones meet.

There does not have to be movement there.

The **fused** bones of the cranium are as much a joint as the meeting of the humerus and ulna at the elbow. The joints where there are movement are more significant to the actions of the sportsperson.

Some joints allow a large range of movements, such as the hip joint. Other joints, like the joint at the wrist, give much smaller and more restricted movement. This is owing to the size and arrangement of the bones. Although there are elements common to all joints, each type is formed in a different way and it is this arrangement that leads to the different ways we can move.

Task 1

What to do:

1. Write out a definition of the word 'joint'.

Skiing involves a range of movements at different joints.

2 Different Joint Locations in the Body

The following are all **synovial** joints. These joints allow the greatest movement. You only need to remember those in bold.

What to do:

1. Make a table of the body's joints.
2. State where the joints are in the body. Use neck, knee, hip, elbow and shoulder as headings.
3. State the type of joint each is and the bones involved.

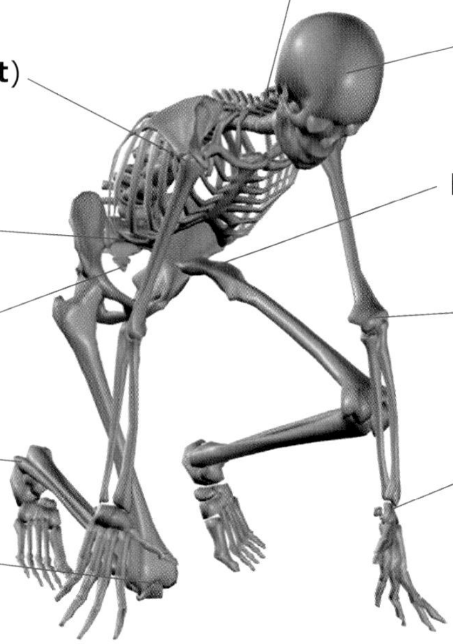

3 The Three Types of Joint in the Body

In the body there are three types of joint. These are immovable, slightly movable and freely movable. They all differ according to how much movement they allow.

Immovable joints are fixed: here there is no movement at the joint. Any place where the bones are fused together is an immovable joint. These occur in the crown of the cranium and the coccyx, which lies at the base of the spine. Slightly movable joints have gaps between the bones, which allow a small amount of movement. These gaps are usually filled with cartilage. The bones of the vertebral column and the joint of the ribs and the sternum are examples of this type. Freely movable joints are the most complex of the three types. They are designed for movement and have the most obvious relevance to physical activity.

4 The Significance of Synovial Joints

Freely movable joints are common in the human body. The components of this type of joint have built-in safety factors to help guard against injury. These joints are designed to reduce wear and tear, absorb shock and reduce friction. These factors are especially important when performing skills at pace and with power.

5 In-depth Understanding of Synovial Joints

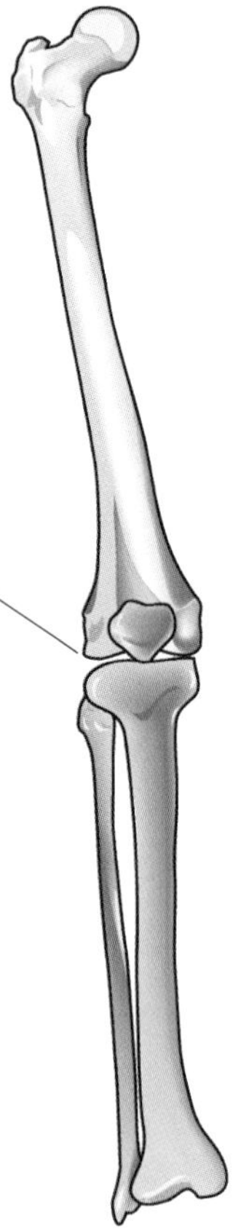

Knee joint

There are many parts to the knee joint. Its position demands that it can withstand hard pressure. This makes it a robust joint. The ligaments that hold the bones in place are called the 'cruciates'. When footballers have serious knee injuries it is these ligaments that are often damaged. Between the femur (thigh bone) and the tibia (shin bone) is the semi-lunar **cartilage** that helps lubricate the joint. This is also the damaged or torn tissue in knee-twisting injuries and cartilage problems.

Task 3

What to do:

1. Copy the diagram of a knee joint.
2. Refer to work already studied on the skeleton and then label your diagram.

6 Functions of Different Parts of a Joint

Cartilage covers the ends of the bones where they meet and stops the bones touching each other. This is called 'hyaline cartilage'. The cartilage acts as a cushion and creates a barrier, reducing the amount of **friction** that occurs when the bones are moving against each other. This stops the bones wearing each other away.

Synovial fluid lubricates the joint. Like oiling the chain of a bike or putting oil in the car, synovial fluid allows all the parts to move against each other smoothly. It also keeps the joint free from infection.

Synovial membrane lies inside the capsule. It is here where the synovial fluid is produced.

Synovial capsule is a tough fibre that surrounds the joint holding the fluid in place.

Ligaments surround the sides of the joint. Ligaments are made of tough elastic fibres. It is the ligaments that hold the bones in place, so keeping the joint together. The stability of the joint relies on the strength of the ligaments and on the muscles supporting the joint.

Tendons are not strictly part of the joint, although they play an important part in the joints movement. Their job is to attach muscle to bone. Without tendons muscle would float around the bone and movement would be impossible. It is this attachment that creates an anchor for muscles to shorten and bring about different actions. Tendons are very strong because great exertion is required for some actions. As the muscle needs to be held firm, the tendons act as a non-elastic anchor.

Task 4

What to do:

1. Link the matching words. Each word can be used only once.

elastic **hyaline** **lubricate**

barrier between the bones **synovial fluid**

reduces friction **tough fibre** **ligaments**

stabilise **tough** **acts as a cushion**

attach bone to bone **helps move freely**

synovial capsule **cartilage**

surrounds the joint

Key Terms:

Cartilage	► tough, flexible tissue; can be found at the end of bones
Friction	► action of two surfaces rubbing together creating heat
Fused	► two or more bones knitted together so no movement occurs
Joint	► the point where two or more bones meet
Ligament	► tough, rounded, elastic fibre attaching bone to bone at a joint
Synovial capsule	► tough fibre surrounding the synovial joint
Synovial fluid	► fluid; found in synovial joint
Synovial joints	► lubricating freely movable joints with ends covered in cartilage
Synovial membrane	► lining inside joint capsule where synovial fluid is produced
Tendons	► strong, non-elastic tissue attaching bone to muscle

Joints are used in every movement.

7 The Importance of Cartilage, Tendons and Ligaments in Sport

Cartilage is a shock absorber. When running, the knee takes a lot of pounding. It is the cartilage that acts as a cushion so that the bones do not rub together and wear away. If the cartilage were not there, pain would occur at the joint due to the friction of the bones rubbing together. This is especially important in activities like long distance running, where there is continued use of the joint. Cartilage damage is common in sportspeople. A frayed cartilage decreases the efficiency of the joint and is extremely painful.

Ligaments attach bone to bone. As there is much movement of bones, ligaments have to be strong and elastic. If there were no ligaments the joint would be unstable. Running, stopping and changing direction all put pressure on the joint. When changing direction at speed it is the ligaments that keep the bones in the right place. If the ligaments are stretched too far then they tear and the joint **dislocates**. After tearing it is unlikely that the ligaments will return to their former strength.

Tendons attach muscle to bone. Without tendons muscle would float around the bone and movement would be impossible. It is this attachment that creates an anchor for muscles to shorten and bring about different actions. Great exertion is required for some actions; therefore tendons are strong and non-elastic. If a muscle is large, or pulls in more than one direction, more than one tendon may be needed to anchor it. A weightlifter moving a maximum weight needs their tendons to hold firm and keep still. That is why they are non-elastic, just like a pole-vaulter pulling on the pole after take-off in order to clear the bar.

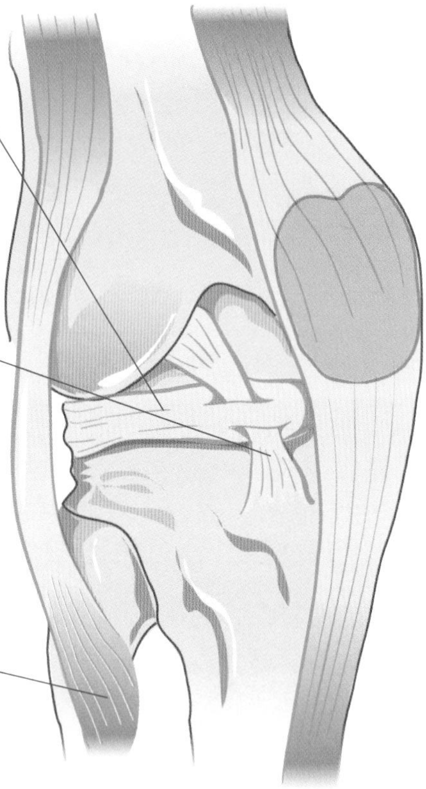

Cross-section of a knee joint showing cartilage, tendons and ligaments.

What to do:

1. Copy the table below. Use the headings cartilage, tendons and ligaments.
2. Put the words from the word bank into the correct column. Words can only be used once.

Cartilage	Tendons	Ligaments

Word bank

flexible at end of bone

elastic sturdy strong

attaches bone to muscle

made of many fibres

size changes depending on the size of the muscle

attaches bone to bone

cushions non-elastic tough

anchor stabilise

Task 5

8 Different Types of Synovial Joint

There are different types of joint at varying places on the skeleton. Each type is distinguished by the variety of movement it allows, its size and the number of bones at the point of the joint.

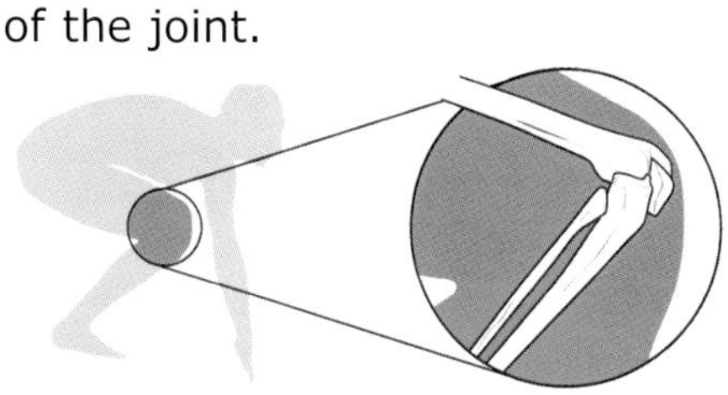

Knee/hinge – movement in two planes forwards and backwards with a small amount of rotation: running, kicking a football, sprint start position in swimming.

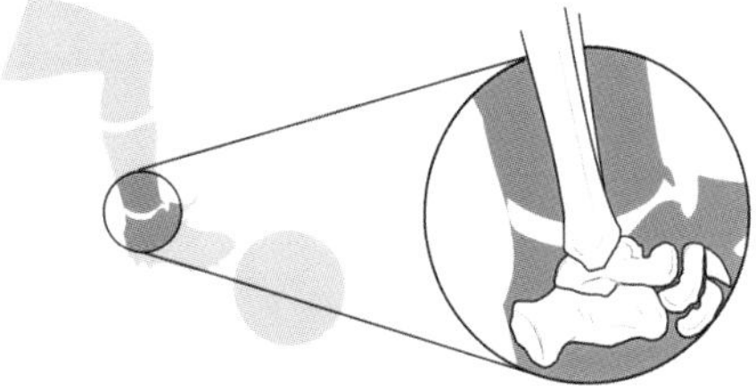

Ankle/hinge and gliding – forward and backward and some sideways and rotation: kicking a ball.

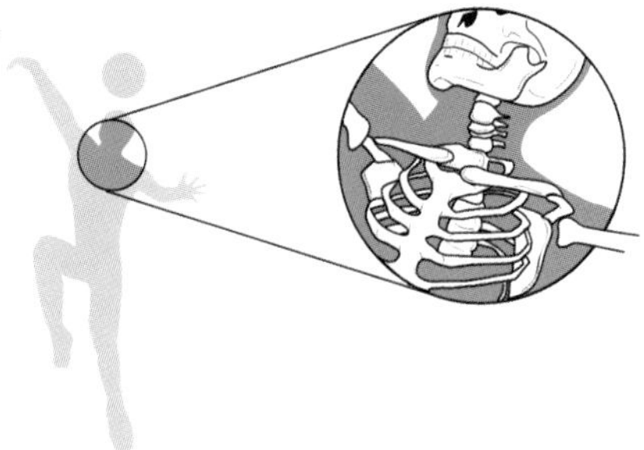

Neck/pivot – rotating and tilting the head: looking for ball, heading a ball.

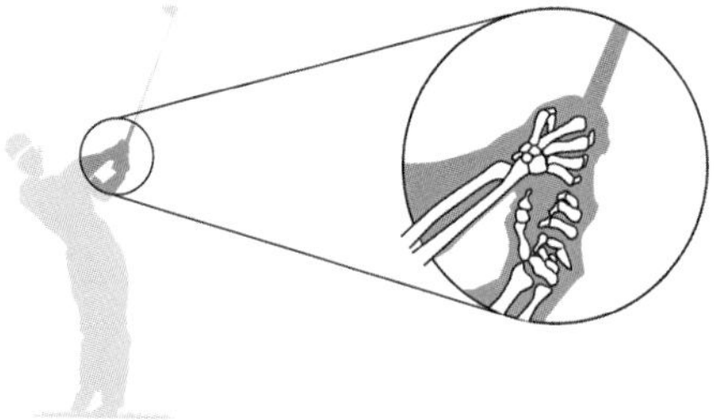

Wrist/condyloid or gliding – forward and backward with some sideways movement: golfer will 'break' their wrists in the back swing.

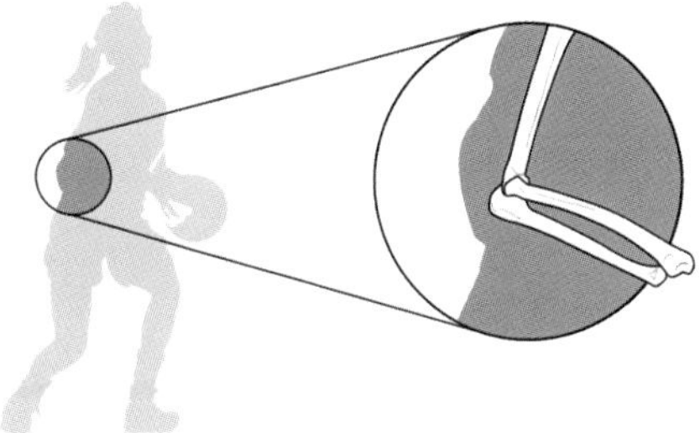

Elbow/hinge – movement in two planes forwards and backwards with a small amount of rotation: preparing to perform a chest pass, breaststroke arm action.

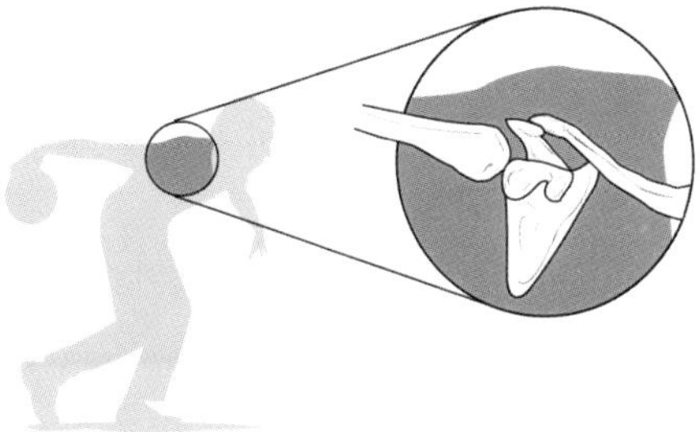

Shoulder/ball and socket – full rotation, allows the greatest amount of movement: arm action in front crawl, tennis serve action, bowling a ball.

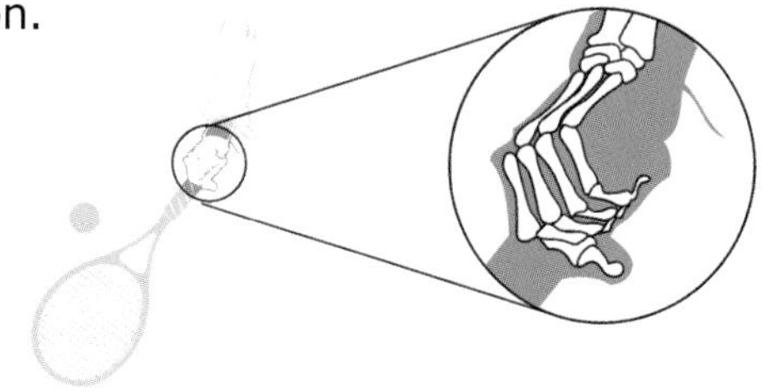

Fingers/hinge – in two directions forward and backward gripping a racket.

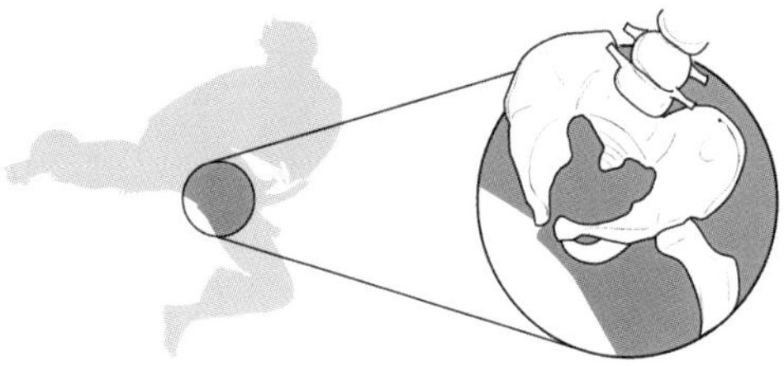

Hip/ball and socket – rotation, allows a lot of movement: breaststroke leg action, trapping a ball on the inner thigh and bringing it down in football, performing a kick in karate.

What to do:

1. Describe how the following type of joints are used in particular sporting actions:
   a. ball and socket b. hinge
   c. pivot.

9 The Range of Movement at Joints

If the centre of the body is where all movement comes from, then working out the different types of movement becomes simpler.

Adduction – this movement brings part of the body towards the centre. In the butterfly arm action, adduction is when the arms pull to the sides in the 's' shape. **Add**uction is **add**ing it to the body.

Abduction – this is the opposite action to adduction. The limbs are abducted from the centre. A goalkeeper abducts their arms when reaching to make a save. A badminton player abducts their arm when preparing for an overhead clear. A way to remember this is that when someone is kidnapped, they are abducted i.e. taken away.

Flexion – closing the angle at a joint. When preparing to throw a ball the angle at the elbow decreases. This movement of flexion gives the arm space to create power in the throw. Catching a ball and bringing it to the body is flexion at the wrist, elbow and shoulder joints. Recovery phase of the sprint leg action is flexion at the knee.

Extension – this is the opposite of flexion. It is when the angle increases between the bones at a joint. In the run-up for a jump the long jumper takes off and extends the take-off leg to generate as much upward lift as possible. This is an example of extension at the hips. Striding the leg forward to take a pace is extension at the knee.

Rotation – the angles do not change but the joint moves in a circular motion. The throwing action of the service in tennis and the bowling action in cricket or rounders demonstrates this type of movement.

James Hickman on his way to winning the men's 400m medley demonstrates adduction of the arms, as he brings his arms back to his torso.

Abduction of the arms happens as Martin Pieckenhagen reaches to save the ball.

Harbhajan Singh shows how flexion occurs as the angle at the joint of both elbows decreases in preparation to throw.

As Yann Domenech's right leg pushes back during take-off, it extends.

Australian Lleyton Hewitt using a rotation movement to serve.

Task 7

What to do:

1. Order the following joints from the greatest amount of movement to the least:

   hip shoulder knee elbow neck

2. Give your own example of a sporting movement for each.
3. Give the correct joint type.

Active Challenge

Point to a joint on your own body for your partner to tell you:

- the name of the joint
- the type of joint
- what movement happens there
- an example of the joint's use in sport.

10 Movement and Levers

A definition of a lever is:

a simple machine that can be regarded as a rigid bar that can turn about a pivot. The relative positions of load, effort and pivot determine the type of lever.

Our limbs and joints consist of a series of levers. Levers enable a weight to be shifted. A small amount of effort enables a larger load to be lifted or moved. In any movement in the body there is always:

- the load = the weight to be moved or resistance
- the force to move the weight = provided by the effort of muscles
- the fulcrum or pivot point = the fixed point around which the movement occurs.

There are three different ways in which weight can be moved. All sporting actions fall into one of these categories.

First order levers

In this order the fulcrum is in the middle and the effort and resistance are at opposite ends. In sport, this comes about in movements like moving the head forward to generate rotation in a somersault for the trampolinist. This order applies to the javelin thrower in athletics. When the thrower's arm is following through, just before release, the elbow is the pivot point, the triceps are the effort and the javelin is the resistance. This order helps to generate speed.

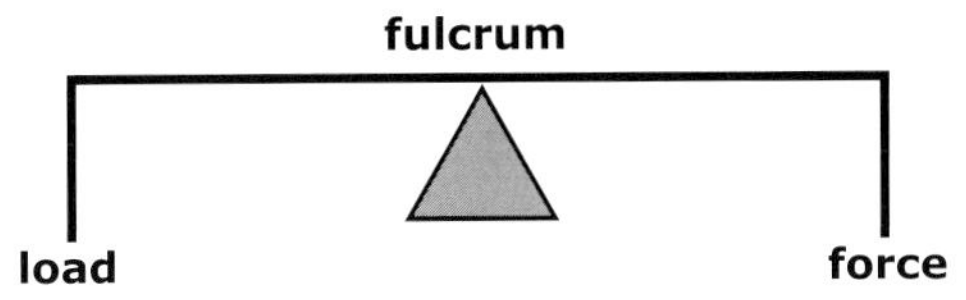

In a somersault the head acts as the force, the shoulders as the fulcrum and the rest of the body is the load or the resistance.

Second order levers

Here the fulcrum is at the opposite end to the effort with the resistance in the middle. Standing on tiptoes is a classic example of this order. In judo the holds and resistance movements are classed as second order levers. This order helps to generate force.

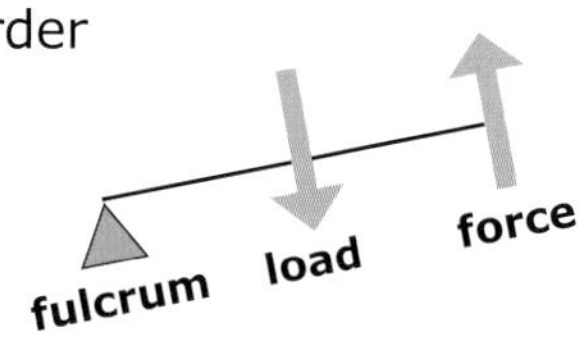

Third order levers

In this order the fulcrum is at the opposite end to the resistance with effort in the middle.

This is common in many actions in sport. When performing the front crawl arm action the swimmer's shoulder joint is the pivot point, the muscle at the shoulder is the effort and the resistance is the water. The tennis shot is also an example of this order of levers. Here the player uses the racket as an extension of the arm in order to generate more speed. The rower's oars also increase the length of the lever in order to make the boat travel quicker through the water by covering more distance with each stroke. This order helps to generate increased speed and distance.

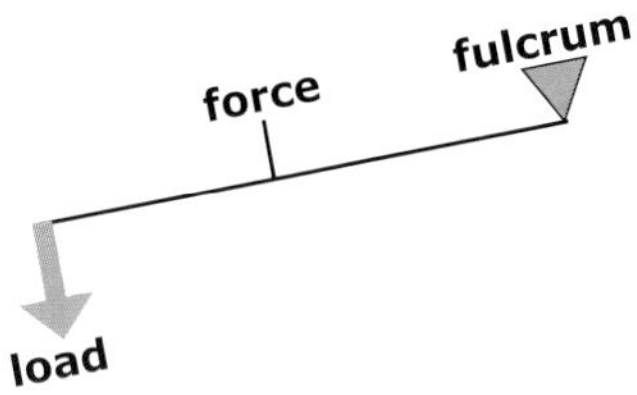

Task 8

What to do:

1. Draw a simple diagram of a sporting action.
2. Label the action with load, force and fulcrum.
3. Write which order lever it is.

Example
Person kicking a football.
Load – football; force – muscles of the leg kicking; fulcrum – standing foot. Third order levers.

11 Effects of Age on Flexibility of the Joints

At different ages the body is capable of different movements. When the young gymnast performing on the asymmetric bars changes her grip from overhand to underhand to swing around the bar, she **dislocates** her shoulders. This relies on the **flexibility** and the softness of the tissues at the joint. As performers get older, tissues become less elastic and therefore their joints become less flexible and incapable of such adaptability. A warm-up that may have taken 15 minutes for a young teenager may take 30 minutes when they are in their early twenties.

If practised in the correct way, flexibility can be increased. To achieve the same standards becomes harder as a person gets older. The less flexible a person is, the more prone to injury they are. The joints will be unable to withstand the shock of forceful contact with the ground. The amount of muscle strength reduces with age, which can lead to instability around joints and a lack of mobility. Later in life arthritis can begin. There is some evidence that arthritis is hereditary. It can also come about because of the rigours of a strenuous sporting life.

12 How Joints Help the Sportsperson

Joints work with muscles to create all movements in daily life and to complete sporting challenges. From the large strides of a long jumper to the small adjustments of the gymnast on the beam, it is joints that allow the range of movement seen. The agility required to dodge around an opponent and keep upright requires many frequent and minor adjustments from the tarsals, metatarsals and phalanges of the feet where they flex and extend to keep balanced. Striding, landing and taking weight could damage the bones if it were not for the cartilage that sits between them absorbing the shock.

In order that joints can achieve their full range they have to be prepared, trained and movements practised. To rotate the arm in the delivery of a javelin throw, a thorough warm-up is necessary, as well as all the previous training and conditioning. These make the joints more flexible, allowing a greater reach in the preparation and follow-through phases of a throw. The extra range leads to more leverage and the possibility of achieving a greater distance.

Task 9

What to do:

1. Link types of movement, joints and sporting actions together. Two types of movement are given to help you:
   - swimmer performing front crawl arm action
   - arm action required when shooting in netball or basketball.

Key Terms:

Abduction ► moving a limb or bone away from the body
Adduction ► moving a limb or bone towards the body
Dislocate ► move bones out of their usual joint arrangement
Extension ► increasing the angle at a joint
Flexibility ► degree of movement around a joint
Flexion ► decreasing the angle at a joint
Rotation ► bone movement in a circular or part circular direction

Summary

A joint is a meeting of two or more bones. There may or may not be movement there. The synovial type of joint is the most important to the sportsperson as the different types give the range of movements to complete all sporting actions.

It is the different sizes of bones and the way in which they are arranged that give them their joint type. In synovial joints there are parts that specialise in helping prevent injury and ensuring smooth action at the joint. These include cartilage, synovial fluid and ligaments. The sportsperson can perform all the movements required for success as long as each joint is kept healthy and strong.

Movement and Performance – Muscles

What you will learn about in this section

1. Three Kinds of Muscle
2. Location and Functions of Major Muscles
3. Link Muscles to Sporting Actions
4. Muscles' Relation to Bone
5. How Muscles Work in Pairs
6. Fast and Slow Twitch Muscle Fibres
7. Muscle Tone and Posture
8. Effect of Training on Muscles

1 Three Kinds of Muscle

Voluntary muscles, also known as skeletal or striated muscles, are the most common muscle type in the body. These muscles attach to the skeleton and provide a person's shape. We can consciously control these muscles and dictate how they move. Their movement happens like this:

- A defender sees an attacker moving into a space.
- A message goes through the defender's nervous system to the brain.
- A decision is made through experience and training as to which muscles will be used in order to mark the opposition.
- The brain sends messages to the appropriate muscles.
- The action takes place.

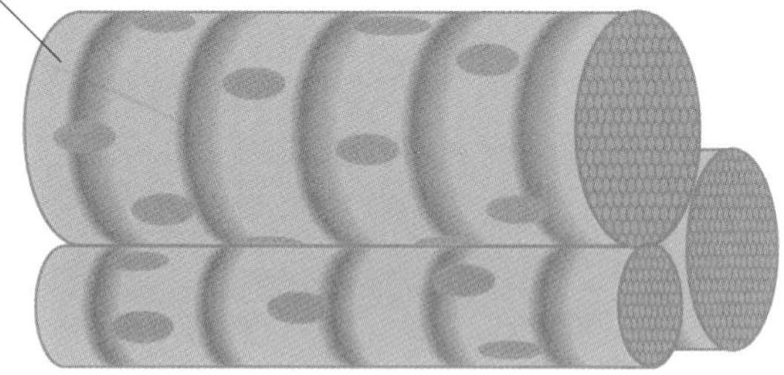

All of this happens in a fraction of a second and this demonstrates why an attacker has a slight advantage over a defender. The defender can compensate for this by learning to read the game and prepare for the most likely course of action from the attacker.

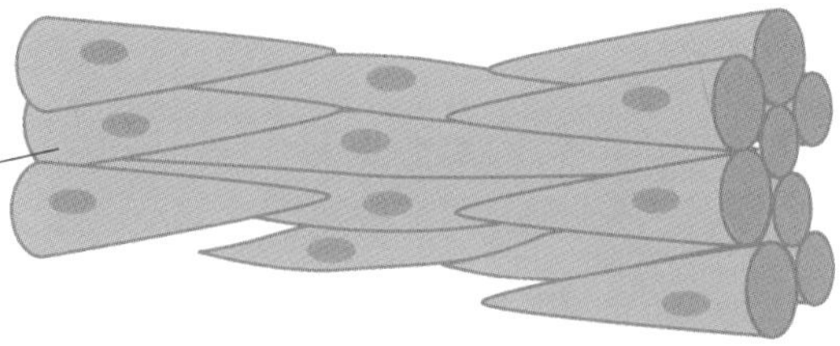

Involuntary muscles, also known as smooth muscles, are not controlled; they work automatically. They carry on functioning throughout life. They are found in the intestines, blood vessels and urinary organs.

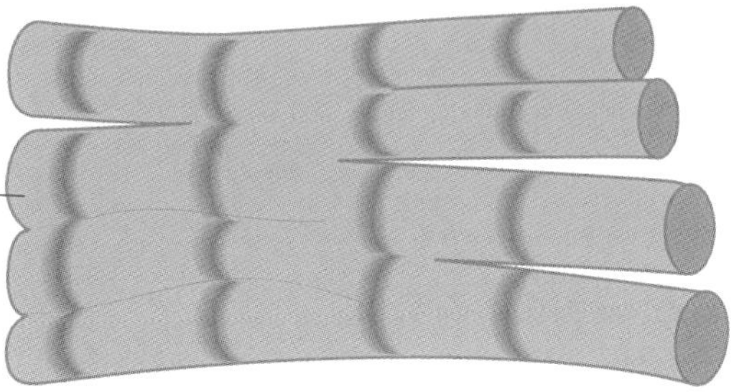

Cardiac muscle is a type of involuntary muscle, as it is not controlled consciously but works automatically. It is special because it is found only in the heart and it never rests or tires during life.

Task 1

What to do:

1. Using the headings **voluntary**, **involuntary** and **cardiac**, put the following words in the correct group:

automatic   striated   involuntary   never rests   controlled
intestines   heart   automatic   most common
smooth   blood vessels   consciously

2 Location and Functions of Major Muscles

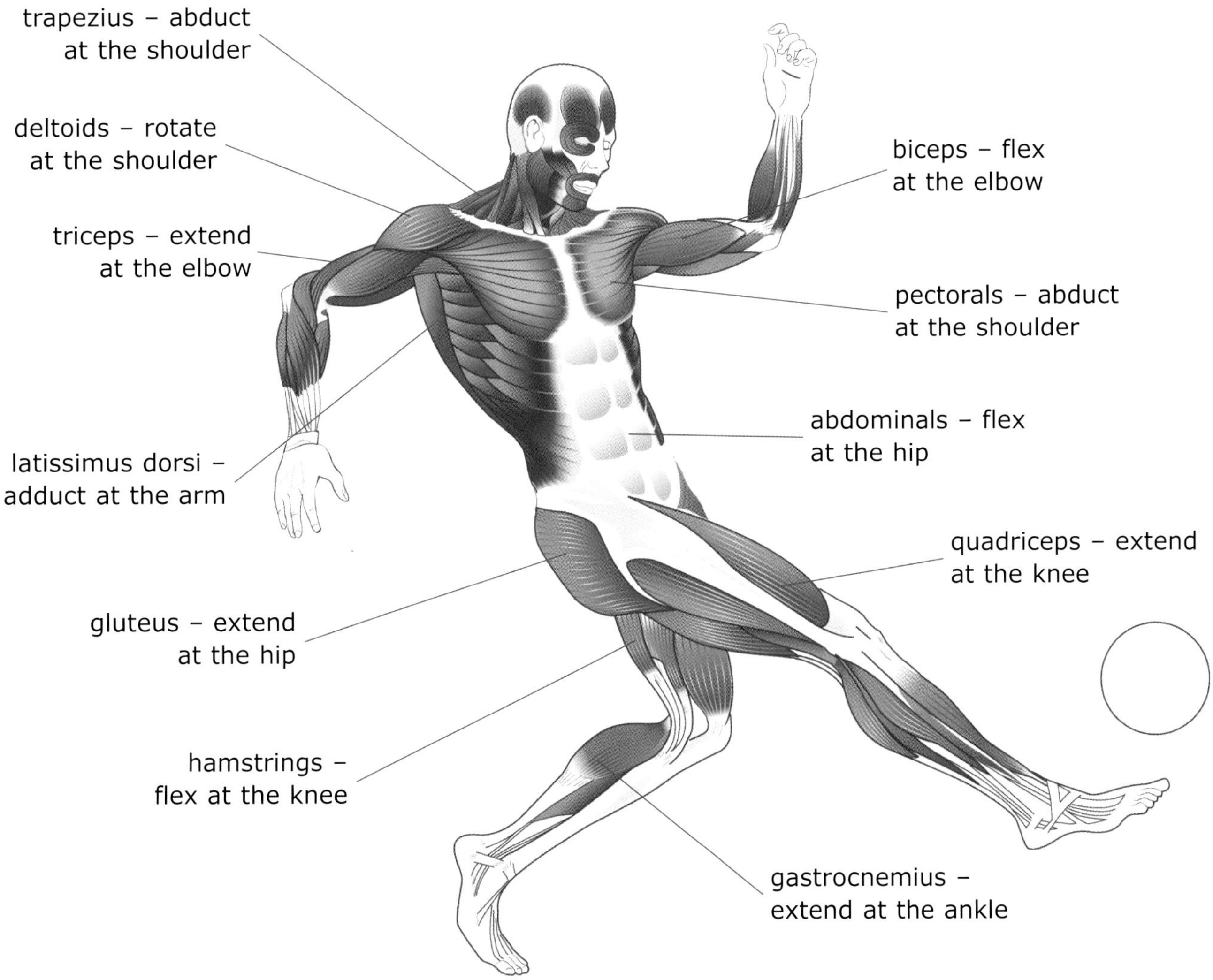

Task 2

What to do:

1. Learn the names of the muscles of the body. Start by trying to memorise the muscles of the upper body. When you feel confident go onto the muscles of the lower body.

> Link the muscles with a bone you already know; this may help you to remember them.

Active Challenge

Work with a partner and take turns testing each other. Point to a muscle in your body and see if your partner can tell you its name. There are 11 types of muscle to remember.

Task 3

3 Link Muscles to Sporting Actions

Voluntary muscle (also called skeletal muscle) is the type that flexes when performing a sporting action, such as pulling quads to extend at the knee to kick a ball.

What to do:

1. Use all of the muscles listed below.
2. Link them with a sporting action.
3. Use the sporting example on the previous page to help you.

biceps, triceps, deltoids, pectorals, trapezius, abdominals, latissimus dorsi, gluteals, quadriceps, hamstrings, gastrocnemius

Example
Abdominals, raise knee so flexing at the hips, used prior to take-off in high jump.

4 Muscles' Relation to Bone

Voluntary muscle is attached to the bone by tendons. The muscle, at the point where it moves, is the **insertion** and the point where it is fixed is the **origin**. When the arm flexes at the elbow the movement is at the elbow, so the fixed point in this example is the shoulder.

In all kinds of sporting actions muscles work in the same way.

The origins are the triceps and biceps at the shoulder.

The insertions are the triceps and biceps at the elbow.

Task 4

What to do:

1. Copy the picture of an arm (on the previous page), showing the muscles clearly.
2. Label all the parts clearly.
3. Add in the origin and insertion of the muscle in another colour.

Key Terms:

Cardiac muscle	only found in the heart, never tires
Insertion	the point where a tendon attaches a muscle to bone where there is movement
Involuntary muscles	work automatically, controlled by the involuntary nervous system
Origin	the end of a muscle that is attached to a fixed bone
Voluntary muscles	skeletal muscles attached to the skeleton, can be made to work consciously

5 How Muscles Work in Pairs

The body is moved by muscle groups, not by individual muscles. Muscles work in pairs. Muscles can only pull, therefore they need to work in partnership so movement can occur. The pulling muscle is called the **prime mover** (agonist). When a muscle pulls, it contracts or becomes shorter. The muscle relaxing is the **antagonist**. When a muscle relaxes it lengthens.

Muscles work in pairs; the quadriceps and hamstrings are working together.

Task 5

What to do:

1. In your own words, describe how muscles work in pairs.

6 Fast and Slow Twitch Muscle Fibres

There are two different types of fibre in muscles. There are **fast twitch muscle fibres** (FTMF) and **slow twitch muscle fibres** (STMF). Each type is better suited to different activities. Every person has a natural combination of both in their body. This amount cannot be changed, although with the correct training improvements can be made to the efficiency of each type. Games and racket sport players will have a fairly even distribution but some will have a higher percentage of fast twitch muscle fibres.

Explosive events like the discus, here performed by Shelley Drew, rely on fast twitch muscle fibres.

Fast twitch muscle fibres

When the nervous system decides an event requires short bursts of energy, the fast twitch muscle fibres are used. These are for the more explosive activities, which need quick reactions. They contract fast and produce a powerful action. They have only a limited oxygen supply and so tire quickly. Under a microscope they are white in colour. They are best used for speed events, throwing and jumping.

Slow twitch muscle fibres

The nervous system can detect when an event is slow and prolonged and will activate the slow twitch muscle fibres. These are more suited to endurance activities. They can contract many times and stay efficient over long periods. They have a very good oxygen supply, which gives them their energy. Under a microscope they are red in colour. They are suited to events that take a long time to complete, such as long distance running, cycling and swimming.

Slow twitch muscle fibres are needed in long-distance events.

Task 6

What to do:

1. Read the paragraphs on the types of fibres in the muscles.
2. Make two columns headed FTMF and STMF.
3. List four main points for each type of fibre.

Active Challenge

In pairs, take turns in naming a sport. Your partner should say whether it needs fast or slow twitch muscle fibres for greatest success.

7 Muscle Tone and Posture

Good and bad posture

Muscle tone is voluntary muscles' readiness to work and be in a prepared state to react. Each muscle has slight tension, waiting to be used. A person's muscles never completely rest; the nearest they come to resting is when a person is asleep. Muscles' state of slight contraction helps with **posture**. The abdominals' toned state helps keep in place the internal organs of that area.

Posture relates to the way the body is supported by the muscles, whether standing, sitting or moving. In some activities where the look of the performer is important to the result, like gymnastics, diving and dance, good posture is vital; it increases the marks awarded to the performer and enhances the performance. When muscles are trained, their tone increases and this can help posture.

There are several advantages of having good posture:

- When breathing, there is more room for the lungs to expand and operate; round shoulders make it hard to breathe properly.
- The heart needs to be given enough space to function properly and beat without hindrance.
- The digestive system works well if it has the space to do its job properly.
- Bone alignment prevents strain and injury – poor posture can strain the bones, tendons and ligaments i.e. fallen arches.
- There is more energy available when the body is in alignment as the muscles do not have to work so hard to keep the body stable. (Like carrying a ladder: if it is vertical it is easy to carry, if it is at an angle more energy is required to carry it.)
- Maintaining good posture can help the shape of a person. In turn, self-esteem is increased if a person feels good about the way they look. A person standing or sitting well can give a good impression to others.

Task 7

What to do:

Part A

1. Look carefully at the picture showing two different postures.
2. Describe what you see.
3. Think about the head, shoulder, stomach and hip positions.

Part B

1. Complete a spidergram relating to good posture using the words from the paragraph on Muscle Tone and Posture.

Key Terms:

Antagonists	relaxing muscles allowing movement
Fast twitch muscle fibres	muscle fibres used in events requiring quick reactions and power
Muscle tone	muscles' state of slight tension and readiness to work
Posture	the way the muscles hold the body when still or in motion
Prime movers	contracting muscles causing movement
Slow twitch muscle fibres	muscle fibres required in endurance events

Muscle strength

A weight lifter, like Belarus' Gennady Oleschuk, seen here at Sydney Olympics 2000, concentrates on developing muscular strength in training.

Strength can be defined as a maximum weight lifted or moved in one try. By repeating strength exercises the size of the muscle increases. A person who would take advantage of an increase in muscle size would be a rugby player in the scrum or any activity where bulk is an advantage. The strength of tendons, ligaments and bone will increase too. Weight training is a method used to improve muscular strength. To do this an athlete would lift heavy weights for a few repetitions.

When the muscles increase in size, this is called **hypertrophy**. If training stops then muscles lose their size; the muscle is said to **atrophy**. When muscles are overworked, they cannot contract, fatigue sets in and the muscles cannot work any more. After intensive stress on a muscle, cramp can often result. This contraction or spasm of the muscle happens automatically due to a build-up of lactic acid in the muscle. Massage and gentle moving of the part help to relieve the pain.

Muscle endurance

A long-distance runner has sinewy muscles that can keep working over long periods.

Endurance is the ability to keep working over a long period without tiring. People who take part in events that take a long time to complete need muscular endurance. These events include long-distance running, cycling and swimming. To improve muscular endurance an athlete will lift light weights many times.

When training for a specific activity the body should be prepared so that it can perform the skills needed throughout the event without losing effectiveness. The body remembers how to perform tasks properly due to a regular training pattern. Regular exercise improves fitness. Activities that increase the heart rate above 75% of its maximum, for 20 minutes, five times a week, will generally make a person fitter.

A person should be able to carry out daily tasks without getting out of breath. Each job requires a different level of fitness to complete the tasks involved successfully. An office worker will be fit to do their job, as a window cleaner will be fit to do theirs.

Increasing the strength around a damaged area such as a joint is important to a **rehabilitating** player. This will give strength to the damaged area and make it less likely to be injured again. A rehabilitation programme, specific to the performer, will be designed according to their needs. Some serious injuries need rehabilitation over many months. Part of the programme would start with moving light weights many times. Gradually, the amount of stress on the injured area is increased; this is achieved by increasing the amount of weight to be moved.

Part of the job of training is to repeat actions needed in the game so that when they are called for, they can be applied to the game. This will train the muscles to repeat actions at the appropriate speed and position.

Task 3

What to do:

1. What happens to muscles when they are trained for strength?
2. What happens to muscles when they are trained for endurance?

Ideas to include are: size, strength, tone and type of exercise.

Key Terms:

Atrophy ► when muscle loses its size because of lack of exercise
Hypertrophy ► when muscle increases in size because of exercise
Muscular endurance ► muscles' ability to keep working over long periods of time without tiring
Muscular strength ► muscles' ability to lift or move a maximum weight in one attempt
Rehabilitation ► recovery from injury

Summary

The body uses three types of muscle. Some can be controlled consciously; others work automatically. The greatest amount of muscle is voluntary muscle, which makes up about 40% of the body. Tendons attach the bone to muscle. Tendons can be different in shape. For instance, the scapula is a flat (plate) bone, therefore the tendon attaching the triceps are broad and flat too.

For movement to take place, the muscles work as antagonistic pairs. There are many pairs of muscles in the body but the ones to concentrate on are the biceps and triceps and the quadriceps and hamstrings. There are two different ways muscles contract. When sudden bursts of energy are needed, fast twitch muscle fibres are used. When moderate effort over a long period is required, then slow twitch muscle fibres come into operation. When you are awake your muscles are in a constant state of readiness to work: this is called muscle tone. This tone helps to maintain good posture. Holding your body, whilst standing, in as straight a line as possible helps internal systems work without hindrance.

Training can make muscles stronger. Training and practice help the body to remember how to complete tasks well. After training for strength, the muscles will hypertrophy. Strength coupled with speed will give the power required to complete explosive events when the fast twitch muscle fibres are used.

Exercising for endurance will help an athlete perform long-distance events. This kind of exercise requires moderate effort and takes a long time to complete. Slow twitch muscle fibres are used in long-distance events.

Training and the Circulatory System

What you will learn about in this section

1 Identifying Parts of the Circulatory System

The **circulatory system** involves the heart, vessels, blood and the **pulmonary** and **systemic circuits**. It is known as the cardiovascular system – cardio meaning heart and vascular relating to blood vessels.

The function of the circulatory system is to:

- transport oxygen and nutrients to parts of the body and remove waste or toxic products from the body – the body relies on these to keep alive. The balance of nutrients also keeps the body functioning properly
- control body temperature – the body is affected by changes of temperature, so keeping it in an acceptable range keeps the body functioning properly
- protect – antibodies in the blood fight disease and platelets help to clot the blood at the source of a cut and prevent other germs entering the body.

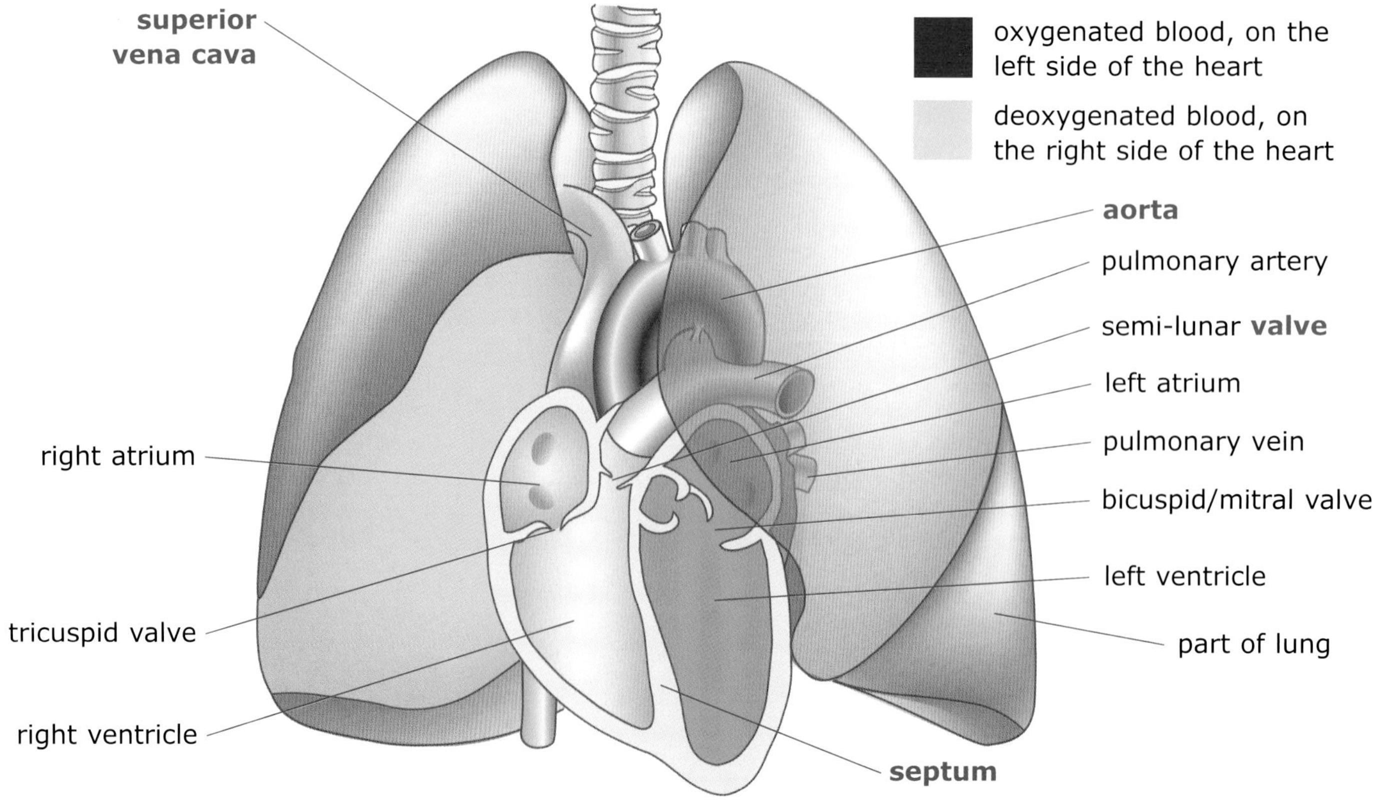

The **pulmonary circuit** carries blood from the heart to the lungs and back again.

The **systemic circuit** carries blood from the heart to the rest of the body and back again.

What to do:

1. Learn the names of the different parts of the circulation system.

Remember the right side of the heart has the pulmonary vein taking deoxygenated blood away and the left side has the pulmonary artery bringing oxygenated blood back to the heart.

2 The Heart as the Pump in a Double Circulatory System

The heart has four chambers. The right side of the body deals with the blood with less oxygen in it – deoxygenated blood; the left side has the blood with more oxygen in it – oxygenated blood. The **septum** divides the left and right sides of the heart so that oxygenated and deoxygenated blood do not mix. The left ventricle wall is thicker than the right side. It is more developed as it pumps blood further around the body.

In the heart, sets of **valves** are positioned to stop the back flow of blood. Between the right atrium and ventricle is the tricuspid valve. On the left side between the left atrium and ventricle is the bicuspid valve. The semi-lunar valves are at the exits of both ventricles as they meet the pulmonary artery on the right and the **aorta** on the left.

The pulmonary circuit is a complete circuit that carries blood from the heart to the lungs and back. It moves deoxygenated blood from the right ventricle via the pulmonary artery and takes it to the lungs. In the lungs, it picks up oxygen and thus becomes re-oxygenated. It leaves the lungs by the pulmonary vein to the left atrium of the heart.

The systemic circuit is also a complete circuit. It carries blood from the heart to all parts of the body and back to the heart. The oxygenated blood is pumped from the left atrium to the left ventricle and into the aorta. It travels around the body to be used by the working muscles. The blood, once used, is deoxygenated. It makes its way back to the right atrium of the heart via the **vena cava** to start the cycle over again.

When the heart beats or contracts it is called 'systole'. This action forces blood through the arteries around the body. When the heart relaxes, it fills up with blood returning from the veins. This is called the 'diastole' or 'diastolic phase'.

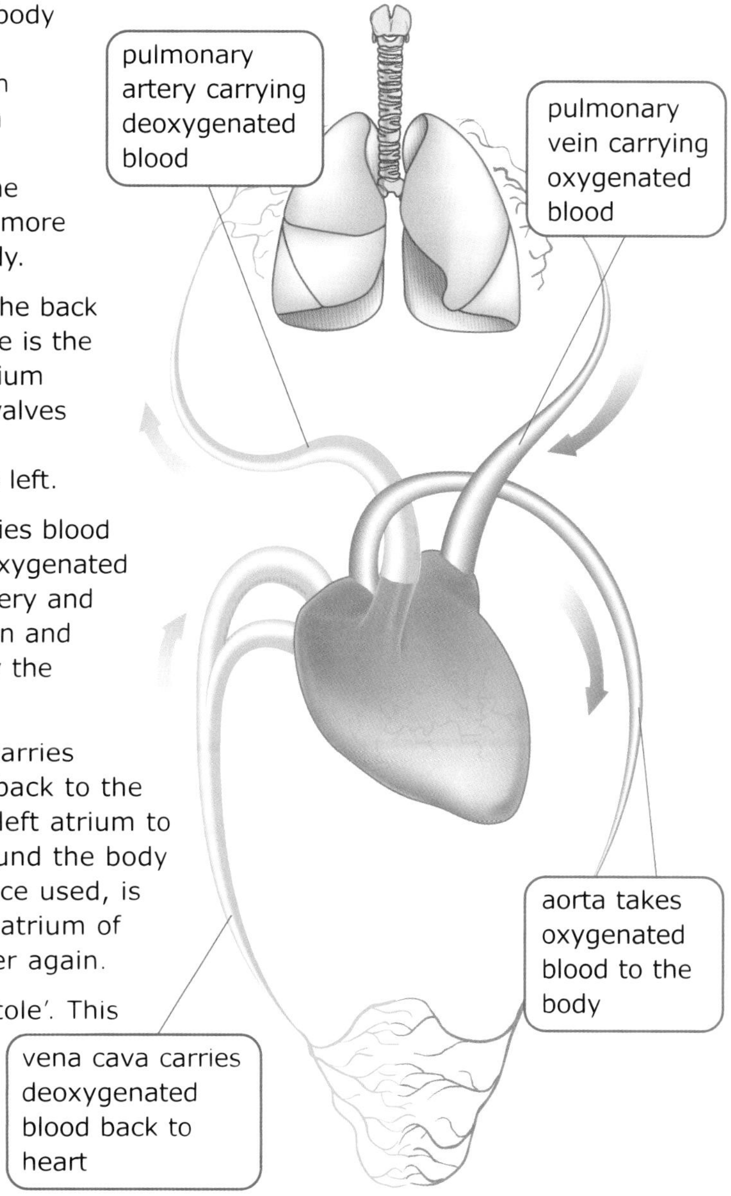

deoxygenated blood

oxygenated blood

What to do:

1. Using the diagram above, trace the pathway of blood.
2. Start at the heart, leading into the pulmonary artery.
3. Colour the systemic and pulmonary systems.

Number parts so they remind you of the order.

Arteries

Arteries carry blood away from the heart. Due to the closeness of some of them to the heart, they have a pulse and work under high pressure. The walls of arteries, therefore, need to be very thick and flexible.

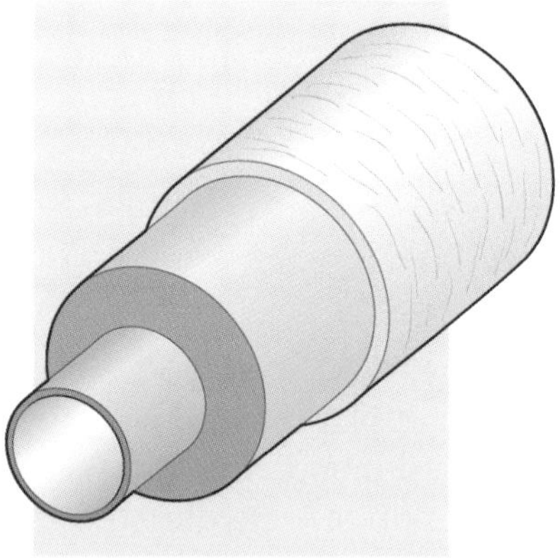

Blood leaves the heart in the aorta, the longest artery in the body. In its transportation of blood, it divides into smaller **arterioles** and then into even smaller capillaries, so that oxygen gets to all parts of the body. The outer layer of an artery is tough and fibrous. The inner lining (**endothelium**) is elastic. The diameter of the inner layer is controlled involuntarily. It automatically changes size according to the amount of blood flowing at any time.

Capillaries

Arterioles feed the capillaries, which are grouped in clusters. Capillaries are the smallest of all the vessels with walls just one cell thick: they are thinner than strands of hair. At one end, they feed muscles, organs and body tissue with oxygen and nutrients. At the other, carbon dioxide and waste products pass through their walls to flow into veins for removal from the body. Blood enters the capillaries under pressure. Capillaries bring blood within reach of every cell. Because substances pass through the walls they are called 'semi-permeable'.

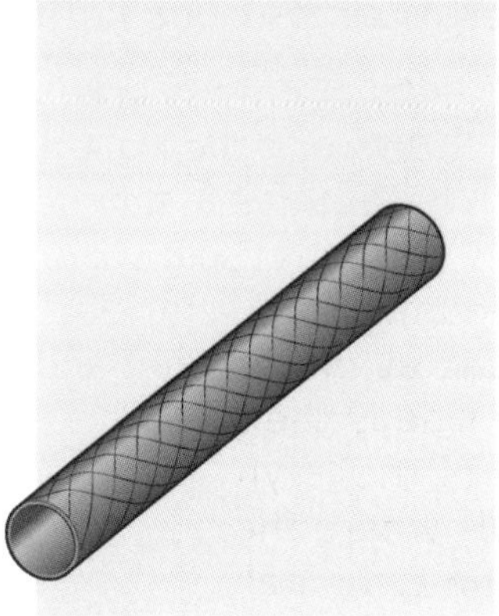

Veins

Capillaries lead into the veins. The walls of veins are thinner than those of arteries. Their function is to bring the dark red, deoxygenated blood back to the heart and they work at lower pressure. They have an inner layer (endothelium) and two tough outer fibrous layers. These are thinner than the arterial layers and less elastic. To help the veins get the blood back to the heart they have valves to stop the blood flowing backwards due in part to gravitational pull. Additionally, pulsating muscles, close to the veins, help to keep the blood moving. This action is called the 'skeletal pump'.

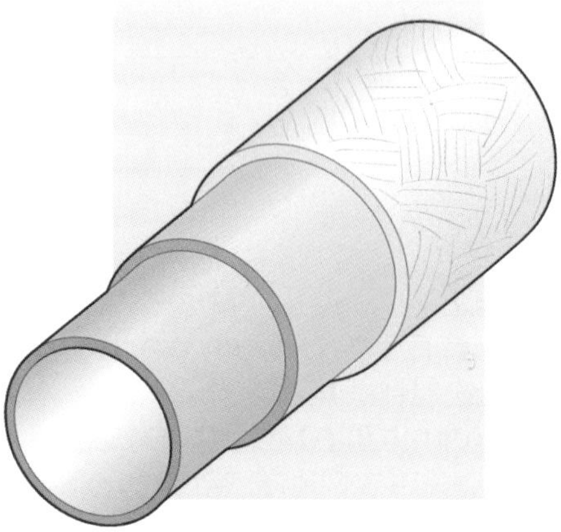

Task 3

What to do:

1. Make a table of information about the three vessels.

Look at the above sections on arteries, capillaries and veins. Think about the similarities and differences.

Key Terms:

- **Aorta** ► main blood vessel leaving the heart
- **Arterioles** ► blood vessels that are sub-divisions of arteries
- **Circulatory system** ► transports blood using the heart and blood vessels
- **Endothelium** ► internal space of the blood vessels; in arteries this changes according to the amount of blood to be transported
- **Pulmonary circuit** ► transports blood from the heart to the lungs and back again
- **Septum** ► wall of muscle dividing the left and right sides of the heart
- **Systemic circuit** ► transports blood from the heart to the body and back to the heart again
- **Valves** ► openings allowing blood flow in one direction only; found in the heart and veins
- **Vena cava** ► blood vessel transporting deoxygenated blood back to the heart

4 Finding a Pulse

There are several places in the body where the pulse is strong and easy to count. These places are where the arteries are easily located. The arteries take blood away from the heart and so work under high pressure: this is why they have a pulse. The pressure gets less by the time the blood reaches the veins and so the veins have no significant pulse.

The two most common places to take a pulse are at the wrist and at the throat. The inside of the wrist on the thumb side is the radial artery. In the throat, on either side of the larynx, is the carotid artery. Two other places where the pulse is strong are at the temple – the temporal pulse and the groin – the femoral pulse.

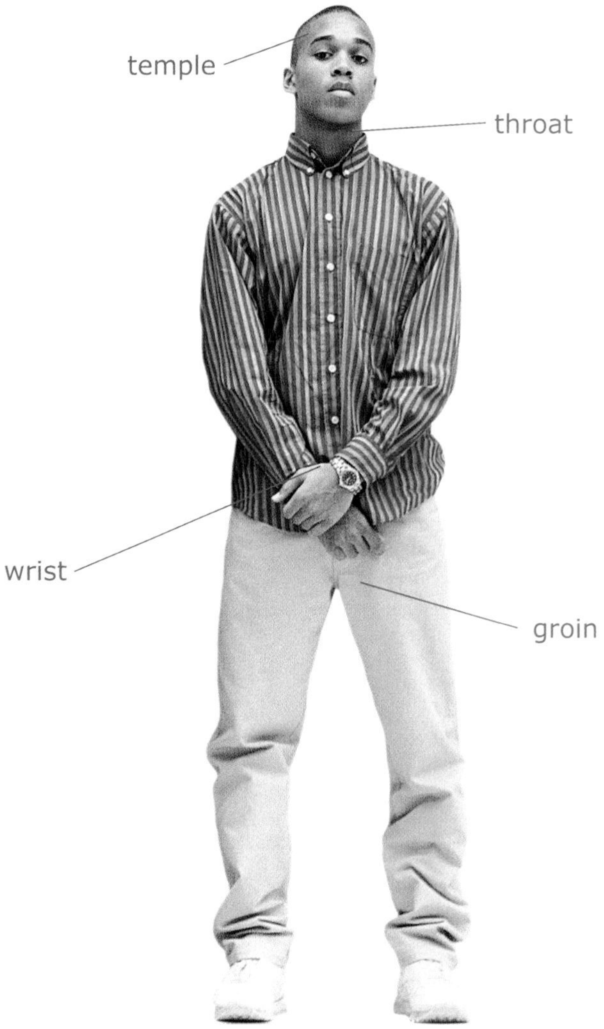

Blood pressure

Blood pressure is the amount of force the blood applies on the sides of the blood vessels. It is used as an indicator of how fit the circulatory system is. A sphygmomanometer is the instrument that measures blood pressure. The reading is given in units of millimetres of mercury (mmHg). One reading is the systolic pressure, the other is the diastolic pressure. On average, the systolic pressure for an adult will range between 100–140mmHg and the diastolic between 60–90mmHg.

The sphygmomanometer aims to check how well the heart (pump) and the blood vessels (pipes) are working. The higher the numbers on the reading the harder the heart is having to work due to the restrictions in the blood vessels. The harder the heart has to work, the sooner it could wear out.

The procedure for taking blood pressure:

- The cuff is wrapped around the arm and pumped up.
- The pressure of the cuff stops the blood supply. This is heard by listening through a stethoscope.
- The cuff is released so the blood starts to flow again. At this point a reading is taken showing the maximum output of pressure of the heart = systolic pressure reading.
- The cuff continues to release until there is no sound of heart beat in the stethoscope. Another reading is taken showing the pressure when the heart is relaxed = diastolic pressure reading.

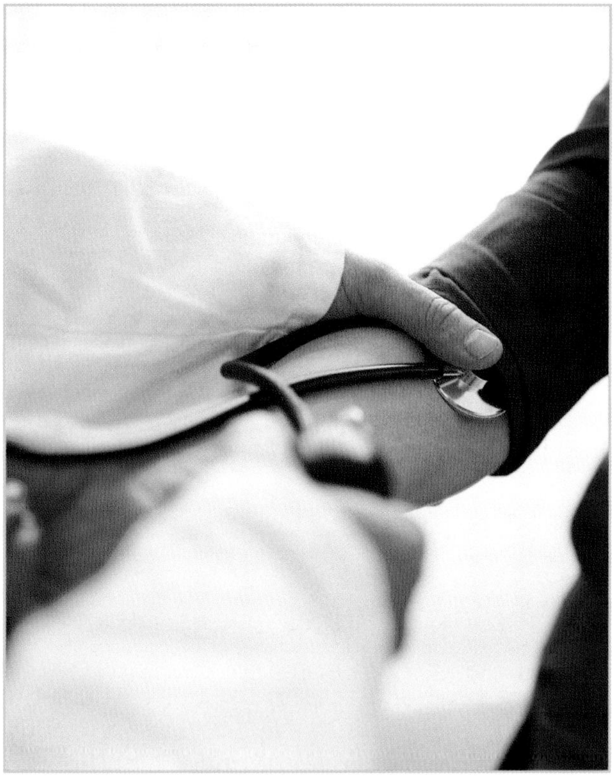

The differing pressures of the cuff around the arm give the systolic and diastolic blood pressures.

Blood pressure is at its greatest when the blood is forced into the arteries by the contraction of the left ventricle. This reading gives the systolic pressure. Blood enters the ventricle from the atrium and then the left ventricle relaxes. When the arteries relax, the pressure reduces, thus giving the diastolic pressure reading.

Blood pressure reading is shown in the following way:

$$\frac{\text{systolic pressure}}{\text{diastolic pressure}}$$

The range of blood pressure can be between 100 over 60 to 140 over 90 for an average person. For younger children the average is about 120 over 80.

When the heart beats, it makes two sounds. One is made when the cuspid valves close, forcing the blood into the arteries from the ventricles; the other is the semi-lunar valves closing, the blood having been forced down into the ventricle.

What affects blood pressure?

There are many circumstances affecting blood pressure. Exercise will make the systolic pressure rise, whereas it will drop during sleep. Age has an effect: if you are young, it is low and the older a person becomes the higher it will be. Children's blood pressure will vary according to their age, gender and height.

Older arteries are less elastic, which means they cannot expand to allow the greater amounts of blood needing to be moved. This is called hardening of the arteries. A man will usually have a higher reading than a woman. If a person is tired, stressed or even at a different altitude their blood pressure will change.

How blood pressure can be reduced

There are several ways to control blood pressure:

- Keep within the guidelines of body weight recommendations.
- Do not smoke as it makes the blood pressure rise and reduces the efficiency of the heart and blood vessels.
- Avoid too much alcohol.
- Eat less salt.
- Avoid stresses and worrying situations.
- Exercise regularly as it will relieve stress, keep the body systems working properly and help to keep your blood pressure within normal boundaries.

What to do:

1. List six ways that blood pressure can be controlled.
2. Where is it easy to count the pulse?
3. Why is it that arteries work under high pressure?
4. Which pressure is the greater, systolic or diastolic?
5. What actions make the sounds of the heartbeat?
6. What should an average person's blood pressure be?
7. Give four factors that affect blood pressure.

5 The Function of Blood at Rest

Red blood cells

These cells - erythrocytes - are small but there are many of them. Two million are produced and destroyed in your body every second! Their main job is to carry oxygen, but they also transport nutrients and waste products, such as carbon dioxide. They are produced in the bone marrow of long bones.

In these cells is **haemoglobin**. Oxygen chemically attaches itself to it to make oxyhaemoglobin. It is in this way that oxygen is transported to the working muscles of the body and carbon dioxide is taken away to the lungs transported in solution in the plasma.

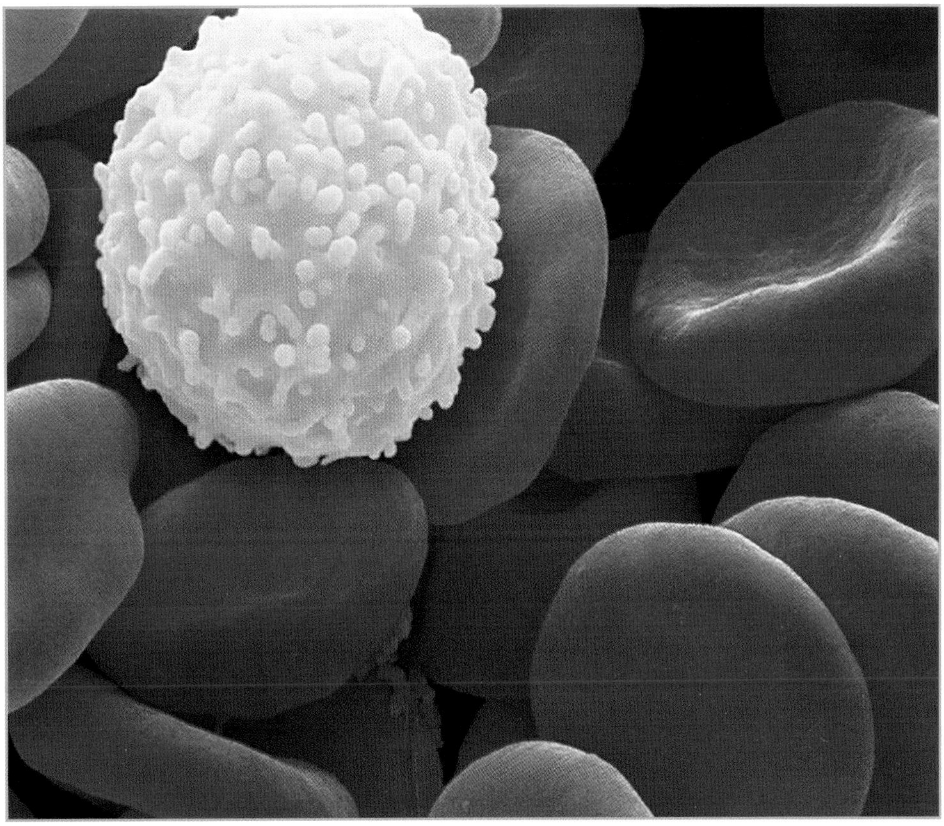

Human blood, showing red and white cells (magnified approx. x3500).

White blood cells

The job of the white blood cells - leucocytes - is to protect the body. There are five types of white blood cells. The main functions of leucocytes are to fight infection at its source, repair damaged tissue and to destroy bacteria. When a cut or graze occurs, the white blood cells gather to stop bacteria entering the body. When a scab forms it is made up of dead leucocytes. There are fewer white than red blood cells in the body. The cells are produced in the marrow of bones and lymph tissue of the body.

Platelets

These are small parts of larger cells. They are in charge of clotting the blood. They clot at the skin surface after a graze or cut. They do the same job internally, on small, damaged blood vessels. Clotting is important to stop blood loss from the body and stop internal bleeding.

Plasma

Plasma is made mostly of water. It makes up 55% of the volume of blood. It helps the blood flow more easily by the use of plasma proteins. The 10% of plasma that is not water contains a mixture of the following: salts, chlorine, amino acids, glucose, antibodies, **fibrinogens** (help clotting), hormones and waste products such as urea and carbon dioxide.

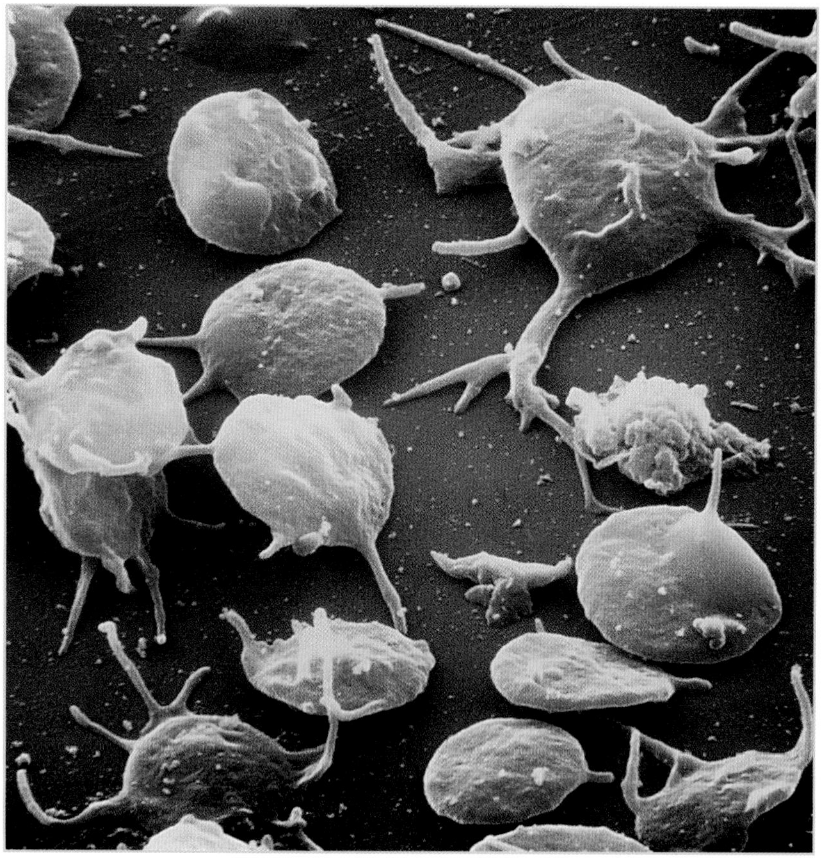

Unactivated blood platelets are oval, whereas activated platelets develop extensions from the cell wall, as seen here (magnified approx. x3300).

Task 5

What to do:

1. From your knowledge of the composition of blood, copy and complete each sentence.
   a. Red blood cells are called
   b. The main function of red blood cells
   c. Red blood cells contain haemoglobin; this helps
   d. White blood cells protect the body
   e. White blood cells are also called
   f. White blood cells are produced
   g. The job of the platelets is
   h. Platelets are smaller parts
   i. Plasma is 90% water and makes up
   j. Plasma contains plasma proteins that help

6 The Effects of Exercise on the Heart

At rest, the heart has a chance to slow down as it does not have to work so hard to circulate the blood. The **resting heart rate** is about 72 beats per minute, although this varies with gender and age. This is sufficient to supply the muscles with the necessary blood and nutrients. Every heartbeat pumps blood out of the heart; this is called the '**stroke volume**'. The total volume of blood pumped out of the heart, calculated over a minute, is called the '**cardiac output**'.

The heart rate increases when extra demands are made on the body. The rate depends on the type of activity. If it is easy, the pulse goes up a little; if the activity is more intense, then the pulse rises further.

Performers can regulate the intensity of their training if they know their **maximum heart rate**. Usually, the heart rate needs to be raised to at least 60% of the maximum to improve cardiovascular fitness levels.

To work out the maximum heart or pulse rate the following formula is used:

220 – age = maximum heart rate

Stroke volume is the amount of blood pumped out of the heart with each beat. At rest, the heart pumps about 85ml of blood. During exercise this could increase to 130ml (nearly a quarter of a pint) depending on fitness levels. This is a lot of blood considering the heart is only the size of a clenched fist.

Cardiac output is the amount of blood ejected from the heart per minute. To work out the cardiac output multiply the stroke volume by the heart rate. As the heart rate and stroke volume increase with exercise so does the cardiac output.

After exercise, the heart returns to its resting rate. The time it takes to do this is referred to as the **recovery rate**. A cool down can help the body gradually return to the resting heart rate. This takes about five minutes depending on the fitness level and type of cool down.

What to do:

1. Create a spidergram showing the effects of exercise on the heart.

7 The Immediate Effects of Exercise on the Circulatory System

Muscles need oxygen to work. This is the key to the circulatory system. In the lungs oxygen combines with haemoglobin in the red blood cells, making oxyhaemoglobin. In this form the red blood cells look bright red. From the lungs the blood transfers oxygen to the working muscles. To supply this demand the heart rate increases. The stroke volume and the cardiac output are both increased during exercise. When exercise starts, the muscles use more energy and so the rates and volume of the heart change. An area in the brain called the 'cardiac centre' controls and regulates how hard the heart works.

Working muscles produce heat

As well as producing movement when they are working, muscles also produce heat. Too much heat is bad for the body and can cause **heat exhaustion**. To prevent the body temperature rising, blood vessels at the surface of the skin open (**dilate**) and heat is transported away from the body. More waste products are made during exercise. These can interfere with the effective running of the body. Salt and water are such waste products. These exit the body via the pores and capillaries at the surface of the skin.

During exercise, there is a greater need for more blood to circulate around the body. The arteries automatically adapt to this demand. Their internal diameter, called the 'endothelium', automatically widens to let more blood through.

Immediate effects of exercise

Active Challenge

Find your carotid pulse at your neck (press your first two fingers to the side of your throat).

Record your resting pulse.

Now jump on the spot for one minute.

Take your pulse again. How has it changed?

Are you showing any other immediate effects of exercise?

8 The Long-term Effects of Exercise

Endurance training, commonly known as aerobic training, helps strengthen the heart. This type of training is progressive, over time. With training the general size of the heart gets bigger, the walls become thicker, stronger and more robust. The resting stroke volume increases and so does the cardiac output.

Whilst everything else is increasing, the heart rate does the opposite. A useful indicator of good fitness is the **resting heart rate**. The slower it is per minute, the more efficient the heart is. It can pump the required amount of blood with fewer beats. Therefore, the slower the resting heartbeat, the fitter the person. With good aerobic fitness, a person will usually be able to keep working efficiently without tiring or losing skill.

Task 1

What to do:

1. Taking regular exercise affects the body in many ways. Using the two headings 'Immediate Effects of Exercise' and 'Long-term Effects of Exercise', make a list of the different changes that happen to the body.

Key Terms:

- **Blood pressure** ► the pressure of the blood against the walls of blood vessels
- **Cardiac output** ► the amount of blood pumped by the heart in one minute
- **Dilate** ► open up or become wider
- **Endothelium** ► internal space of the blood vessels; in arteries this changes according to the amount of blood transported
- **Endurance** ► the ability to keep working over a period without tiring or losing skill
- **Fibrinogens** ► proteins found in blood that helps clotting
- **Haemoglobin** ► found in red blood cells, transports oxygen to body tissue
- **Heat exhaustion** ► fatigue brought on by the body temperature rising
- **Maximum heart rate** ► calculated as 220 minus age
- **Recovery rate** ► the time it takes for the heart to return to resting rate after exercise
- **Resting heart rate** ► number of heart beats per minute when the body is at rest
- **Stroke volume** ► the amount of blood pumped by the heart in one beat

Summary

The contents of blood keep the body alive: the circulation of blood to different parts of the body is vital. Oxygen, nutrients and hormones give the tissues of the body what they need to work. Waste products such as salt, heat, water, carbon dioxide and urea are all removed from the body so it is not poisoned.

When a person exercises, the circulatory system needs to work faster as there is greater demand by the muscles for oxygen. With regular exercise, the body can be trained to make these adjustments quickly and efficiently.

A properly planned personal exercise programme (PEP) should not be too demanding at the start. The PEP will then gradually increase in difficulty or intensity as the person's body adapts to the new stresses. This gradual increase in exercise level will ensure that a person avoids injury and does not place excessive stress on their circulatory system.

Training and the Respiratory System

What you will learn about in this section

1. The Vital Parts of the Respiratory System
2. Role of the Lungs
3. Mechanism of Breathing
4. How Exercise Affects Breathing
5. Aerobic and Anaerobic Activity
6. What Happens to the Body During Exercise and Why
7. How the Respiration System Recovers from Activity

1 The Vital Parts of the Respiratory System

The function of the respiratory system is to get oxygen into the body and carbon dioxide out of the body. This happens through the act of breathing. Breathing in (inhalation) gets the oxygen in, so it can be used by the body to release energy. Breathing out (exhalation) removes the carbon dioxide so it does not build up and poison the body.

The parts of the respiratory system are:

- air passages
- lungs
- **diaphragm**.

Air passages

The air passages are a series of linking tubes. They create the pathway for the air to get to the lungs. Air can enter the body through the mouth or the nose. Air entering the body through the nose, rather than the mouth, has distinct advantages:

- It is warmed, making it a similar temperature to the internal organs.
- There are hairs and mucus in the nose which filter the air, stopping the larger particles of dust and pollen getting into the lungs. The absence of particles allows the **alveoli** to work well.
- The nose moistens the air so it can be absorbed by the alveoli more easily.

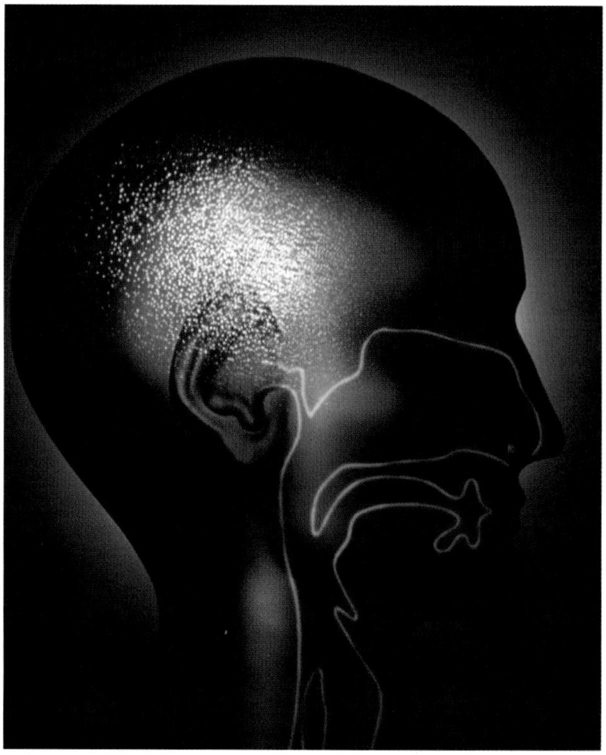

Air passages of the nose and throat outlined in orange.

larynx – air passage to the bronchus; air passing over the larynx produces our voice

trachea (windpipe) – has rings of cartilage along its length to allow the tube to be flexible and to keep the airway open

bronchi – tubes that branch from the trachea to continue the air flow nearer to the lungs

bronchioles – smaller sub-divisions of the bronchi leading to the alveoli

alveoli – tiny air sacs; there are millions in the lungs; gaseous exchange takes place here; this action is vital to sustain life

diaphragm – sheet of muscle dividing the chest cavity and the abdominal cavity

ribs – form a protective cage around the organs in the chest

intercostal muscles – found between the ribs, contracting and relaxing in the breathing process

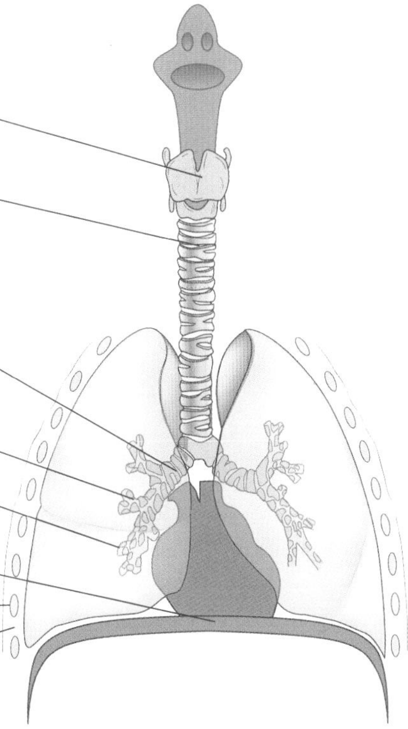

What to do:

1. In your own words, write a description of the following parts of the body linked with the respiratory system: trachea, bronchi, bronchioles, lungs, alveoli, diaphragm, intercostal muscles and ribs.

2 Role of the Lungs

The lungs are positioned inside the chest cavity. The ribs form a cage protecting them. The right lung is bigger than the left lung. This is because it has three cavities and the left only has two.

The action of breathing means that the lungs are constantly moving in and out. To protect the lungs from any friction due to the movement, the pleural membrane forms a complete lining around them. The pleural membrane is smooth and has a moist, slimy mucus.

From the nose or mouth, air enters the trachea and moves towards the lungs. It divides into two branches called the 'bronchi'. These subdivide into smaller tubes called 'bronchioles'. At the end of these are alveoli. These are air sacs with many mini blood vessels called 'capillaries' running from them.

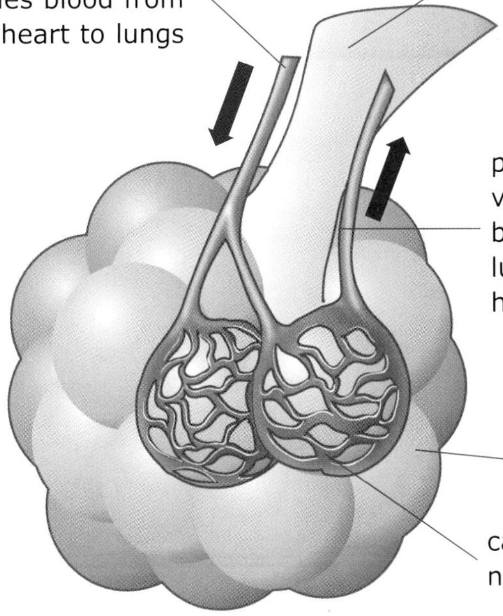

The millions of alveoli allow gases to exchange inside them. Here is a simplified version of what happens:

- Oxygen from the air breathed in enters the circulatory system by being attracted to the haemoglobin in the red blood cells to be used by the working muscles.
- Carbon dioxide, which is toxic or harmful to the system, transfers from the used blood, out of the circulatory system, back into the alveoli, to be breathed out.
- The capillaries, covering the surface of the alveoli, link the respiratory system with the circulatory system.

The exchange of gases is vital for our survival. With training, this exchange becomes more efficient as more alveoli are prepared to make the swap between oxygen (in) and carbon dioxide (out). Regular exercise conditions the lungs to excrete more of the poisonous carbon dioxide from the body. If too much carbon dioxide remained in the body, it would be fatal.

The lungs, at different stages of breathing, have varying amounts of air in them. **Tidal volume** is the amount of air breathed in and out of the body during normal breathing. During exercise, the volume is forced to change. Therefore, it is called '**forced breathing**'. **Vital capacity** is the largest amount or volume of air that can be exhaled (breathed out) after the largest possible inhalation (breath in). **Residual volume** is the amount of air that, even after as much air as possible has been exhaled, is left in the lungs.

Task 2

What to do:

1. Write four sentences on key points about the lungs. Use the following words as headings:
   - Position
   - Protection
   - Exchange of gases
   - Effects of training

3 Mechanism of Breathing

Lungs are not muscle. Lungs cannot move of their own accord, nor are they controlled by the central nervous system. So, how do they move when we breathe in and out? The key to breathing is the diaphragm and the intercostal muscles between the ribs.

When we breathe in – **inspiration** – the following happens:

- our diaphragm pulls down
- our intercostal muscles contract
- air pressure is reduced
- air is sucked through the tubes into the lungs
- our chest expands.

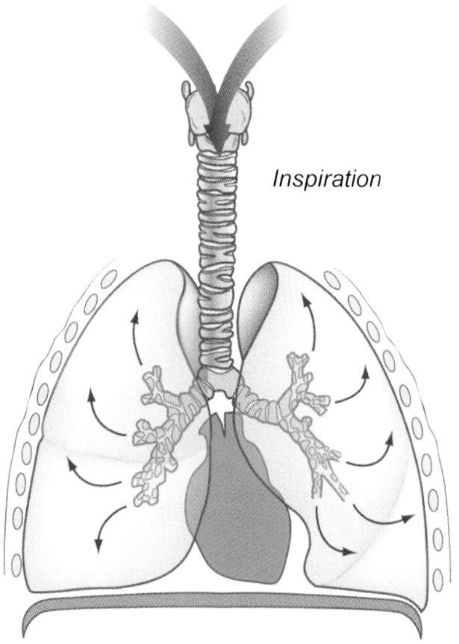

When we breathe out – **expiration** – the opposite happens:

- our diaphragm relaxes into its dome position
- our intercostal muscles relax
- our chest becomes smaller
- pressure increases on our lungs
- air is forced out.

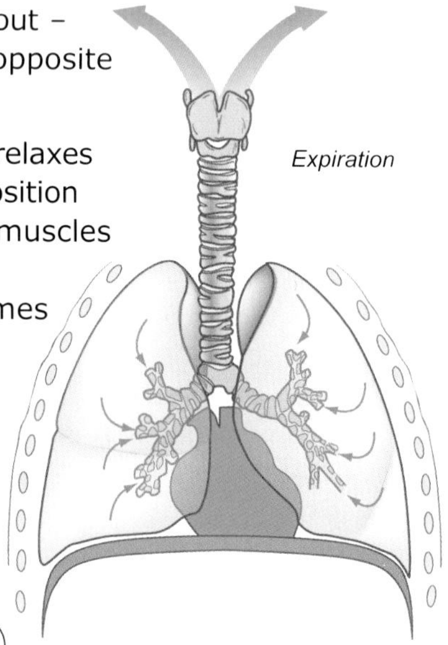

Task 3

What to do:

1. In your own words, describe the action of breathing.

Use the following words to help you: nose, mouth, trachea, lungs, ribs, intercostal muscles and diaphragm.

Behind the scenes

We can feel our chest expand and fall as we breathe in and out. What we are not aware of is the change in the air going into and out of our body. The air we breathe in is different from the air that we breathe out. We now know why we breathe, so let's look at the changes in inhaled and exhaled air.

The parts that make up inhaled and exhaled air are called its 'composition'.

What to do:

1. Make a table showing the composition of inhaled and exhaled air.

Composition of inhaled air

79% = nitrogen
20% = oxygen
trace = carbon dioxide

Composition of exhaled air

79% = nitrogen
16% = oxygen
4%= carbon dioxide

Active Challenge

Exhaled air has more moisture in it. This is because water is a waste product. Some water is removed from your body as you breathe out. Moisture in exhaled air is demonstrated by the mirror test.

Hold a mirror just below your lip and exhale. What do you see?

When you are exercising, how else is water removed from the body?

The respiration and circulation link

There has to be a link between the respiratory and circulatory systems. The oxygen has to go from the respiratory system to the circulatory system and back to the respiratory system again. It follows this order:

- The oxygen breathed in goes through the mouth or nose, down the trachea, into the lungs and into the alveoli (air sacs).
- The oxygen passes through the alveoli walls into the red blood cells, via the capillaries.
- The oxygen joins with haemoglobin to make oxyhaemoglobin.
- The oxyhaemoglobin is used by the working body and is transported by the circulatory system to cells needing to release energy.
- Carbon dioxide is produced as a waste product.
- This is converted into a gas and passes back through the alveoli walls, via the capillaries into the blood plasma.
- Blood takes it back to the capillaries in the lungs.
- The carbon dioxide passes through the capillary and alveoli walls into the alveoli (air sacs).
- It is then exhaled from the body.

Key Terms:

Alveoli	air sacs where gaseous exchange takes place
Diaphragm	muscle that divides the chest cavity from the abdominal cavity
Expiration	breathing out, exhalation
Forced breathing	the change in breathing during exercise when requirements increase
Inspiration	breathing in, inhalation
Residual volume	the amount of air left in the lungs after a maximal exhalation
Tidal volume	amount of air breathed in or out during normal breathing
Vital capacity	amount of air that can be breathed out, after a deep breath in

4 How Exercise Affects Breathing

We have learned how important the action of breathing is. It puts oxygen into the body and removes carbon dioxide. At rest, we take an average of 15 breaths per minute. This is called the 'tidal volume'. This is enough breath for rest but when we start to exercise greater amounts of oxygen are needed and greater amounts of carbon dioxide are produced, which need to be removed. In extreme activity the breathing rate can go up to 50 breaths per minute.

The amount of oxygen a person is able to take up will increase. There is a limit to the increase in each person, which is called the 'VO_2 maximum'. During exercise, the vital capacity will increase because of the demand for greater intake of air. Both the residual volume and the tidal volume increase only slightly.

5 Aerobic and Anaerobic Activity

The body converts fuel to energy and releases it into the body through aerobic and anaerobic respiration. The systems automatically kick in depending on the type and intensity of the exercise performed.

Aerobic fitness

Energy released in aerobic activity needs a sufficient supply of oxygen to the tissues. With enough oxygen present the activity can go on for long periods, as long as the difficulty or intensity does not become too great. This aerobic fitness allows us to keep going at a moderate level. The aerobic system is used in moderate to hard continuous activities that usually take place over a period of more than 60 seconds. The oxygen is breathed in and diffused into the circulatory system. In this type of activity, breathing becomes more regular and deeper. The muscles need oxygen to contract and in aerobic respiration this oxygen enters the body by the breathing process.

Extra air = aerobic

The formula for this is:
glucose + oxygen → carbon dioxide, water, energy

Long-distance runners, such as Paula Radcliffe, need aerobic respiration.

Anaerobic fitness

Athletic field events use anaerobic respiration; Steve Backley demonstrates this in the men's javelin.

When energy is produced anaerobically no oxygen is used in its initial release. Some sports wholly use anaerobic respiration. These are activities where there is a need for a single maximum burst of energy. Athletic field events are good examples of anaerobic exercise. In throwing and jumping events the actions used are explosive. They use one all-out burst of maximum effort to complete the event. The time it takes to complete the attempt is very short, so the energy is produced from the supplies already in the body.

The demand of the muscles for oxygen is so great that the cardiovascular systems do not have time to supply the demand. In anaerobic respiration the energy is provided not by oxygen but by a chemical called 'adenosine triphosphate' (ATP).

ATP can only supply the energy for a short time. If the demand for energy continues for over a minute then another system provides the energy, called the '**lactic acid** system'. This releases energy by breaking down carbohydrates. The side effect of the body using this system is that there is a build-up of lactic acid in the muscles. Lactic acid is a poison and causes cramp in the muscles.

No air = anaerobic

The formula is:
glucose → carbon dioxide,
water, energy, lactic acid

You can tell when a player has just used their anaerobic system from their breathing pattern. After working very hard in the activity their breath may be shallow and gasping. This is an indication that there is an **oxygen debt**, a state in which the body needs more oxygen than it can supply.

A games player will use both aerobic and anaerobic respiration.

This type of energy provision can only carry on for 45–60 seconds. After this, the lactic acid in the muscles becomes too high and prevents muscular contraction. The anaerobic system stops. The body then cannot keep running at its fastest speed or keep lifting heavy weights.

In all games, a combination of aerobic and anaerobic respiration is required. A player while moving and positioning themselves correctly on the pitch according to the play is using aerobic respiration. This is aerobic because the intensity of the exercise is moderate and will continue throughout the game. When the player takes a shot, for example, one maximal contraction is used. For this action, the anaerobic system comes into operation.

Squash players, for example, use both types of respiration. (This contrasts with footballers, who use more anaerobic respiration.) This is due to the need for a maximal effort whenever they strike the ball during a rally.

Task 5

What to do:

1. Study the comments below on the changes in respiration to an athlete in a 400m race. Put them into the order in which the athlete would experience them.
   a. She breathes quickly and respires aerobically.
   b. The oxygen debt is repaid.
   c. Her muscles ache.
   d. Lactic acid forms in the muscles.
   e. She begins anaerobic respiration in her muscles.
   f. She breathes slowly and respires aerobically.

6 What Happens to the Body During Exercise and Why

The effects of exercise and the link between the circulatory and respiratory systems

Task 6

What to do:

1. Make a list of the physical changes that happen to an athlete during exercise.

Long-term effects of training on the respiratory system

Correct training prepares the body in many ways. Endurance training makes the exchange of gases in the alveoli more efficient. The muscles are able to work at a moderate to hard level for longer without tiring. The effect this has on the body is to increase the vital capacity of the lungs. This means that more air is exhaled and so more carbon dioxide can leave the body in one breath and more air can be breathed in, getting more oxygen to the working muscles. Interval training over short distances at fast speeds results in an oxygen debt. By continuing this training new capillaries are formed, heart muscle is strengthened and the delivery of oxygen is improved, which stops the build-up of lactic acid. The overall effect is called an 'oxygen debt tolerance', which the performer develops through this type of training.

7 How the Respiration System Recovers from Activity

As the intensity of the exercise becomes less, the demand for oxygen to fuel the muscles also gets less. Breathing becomes less deep as a result. There are many different factors, which affect the time we take to recover from physical activity:

- time and intensity of the exercise
- physical differences of size and weight
- age
- sex
- fitness level.

Active Challenge

Count the number of breaths you make at rest for one minute.

Perform maximal exercise, such as step-ups, for one minute.

Again, count the number of breaths for one minute.

Time how long it takes breathing to return to rest.

Key Terms:

Lactic acid ► chemical built up in the muscles during anaerobic exercise

Oxygen debt ► shortfall of oxygen to the body after maximal effort/anaerobic exercise, resulting in deep and shallow breathing

Release of energy ► amount and type of energy released used at different stages in different parts of an activity

Summary

A fit and healthy respiratory system is vital. It fuels the muscles and takes away poisonous carbon dioxide from the body. Aerobic and anaerobic systems are used at different times depending on the types of stress put on the body. The respiratory and circulatory systems are linked. The key is the link between the alveoli of the respiratory system and the capillaries of the circulatory system. Training improves the systems.

Principles of Training

What you will learn about in this section

1. Fitness Training
2. How the Principles Help the Performer
3. Details of the Principles
4. The Effects of Muscular Endurance
5. What is Meant by Strength?
6. What Flexibility is

1 Fitness Training

When a coach or athlete designs a fitness training session there are guidelines to keep to, in order to ensure training suits the performer and they achieve the desired result. These are called 'principles of training' and are the rules to follow when exercising, to improve the body safely, through physical activity.

2 How the Principles Help the Performer

Each person has a different reason for exercising. It may be for leisure, competition, professional or personal pride. A person trains to improve performance and their body. When the principles are applied, improvements in cardio, vascular and respiratory condition; fitness, strength, endurance and skill might be expected.

Each of the principles shows the way in which the body is affected by the degree and type of exercise undertaken. If these basic rules are to be adhered to, each stage should be followed and planned carefully. As everyone's fitness level differs, **systematic training** must take into account the **individual needs** of the performer. An understanding of body systems is vital: knowing the existing capabilities of the heart, lungs and muscles sets the degree of difficulty of the training plan. For training to succeed, the degree of difficulty or intensity is set at a personal level. Setting the demands and intensity of the exercise at the right level ensures it is safe for the performer. If the demands are set too low, there will be no improvement; if too high, injuries might occur.

Top-class athletes have a final competition in mind. The training process is systematically planned so they reach a peak of performance to coincide with that event.

Task 1

What to do:

1. Write down the reasons why training principles are important to the performer.
2. What considerations should be made when creating a training schedule?

3 Details of the Principles

There are seven principles, each influencing the training of the performer in a different way. Good training takes into consideration all of the principles and their effects on the body. They are essential to the planning of a systematic training programme so that an individual might improve their fitness. The main principles are specificity, overload, progression and reversibility. The three **FID** (frequency, intensity and duration) components are other significant principles affecting fitness development.

Specificity

This principle requires an understanding of the needs of the game, for example, a goalkeeper will include lots of reaction work in their training. When applying this principle the activity is usually practised at the pace required in the sport. If a person trains too slowly then their skills will only be reproduced at the slower pace and the action will be unable to match the requirements of the game. At a school practice for your team, if you repeat the skills slowly then when you get to the game the other team may be quicker than you are. So, speed up your practices!

The actions in training should copy the actions used in the game. If a person needs good leg strength, simply making them strong may not be enough. A cyclist will train their legs, whilst cycling, in a different way from a long-distance runner; both need muscular endurance but the method of training is different. In order to become a better swimmer a person needs to spend most of their time in the water!

Overload

Muscle strength can be improved by making the muscles work harder than normal. Putting greater demands on the body by exercising can improve fitness. The point where exercise is demanding enough to have an effect on the body is called the 'threshold of training'.

Whether a person is training for muscular endurance or muscular strength, their aim is to train between 60–80% of their maximum. Working between these levels will put enough stress on the athlete to bring about improvement. For older people the threshold of training decreases. Working at 50% of their maximum heart rate will often have a positive effect on their cardiovascular fitness.

There is a combination of three targets (frequency, intensity and duration) that a performer can overload their body with in order to meet the **minimum level of fitness**. Training is adapted by changing any one or more of the FID combinations.

Frequency

Frequency is the number of times exercise is undertaken per week. The more times a person exercises the more often their body is put under stress. Three or more times a week is the recommended number of times extra exercise should be repeated, to reach the minimum level of fitness. Top-class sportspeople would have to train a lot more frequently than this if they are to achieve results good enough for their aspirations.

But remember that the body also needs time to recover from training. Training very hard, every day, may be harmful even for a top-class athlete.

Monday 6–7pm

Wednesday 7–8pm

Friday 8–9am

A person training for general fitness will vary the activities they do. If the intensity of the exercise is 60–80%, fitness will improve.

The pulse increase, when training in the target zone, of a 16 year old

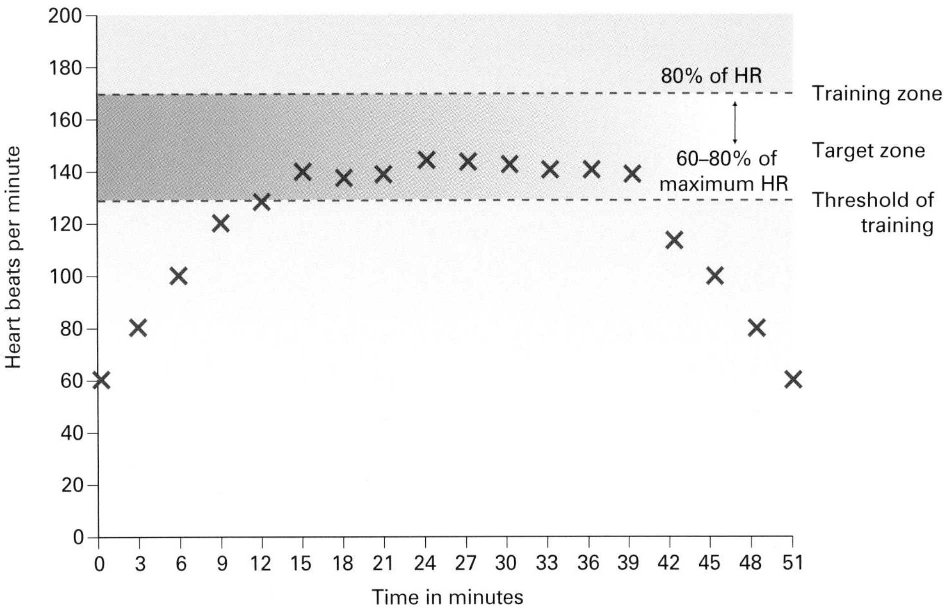

Intensity

This is the level of difficulty of the exercise. For instance, when considering cardiovascular fitness your pulse rate can show you how intensely you are working.

Working in a target zone of 60–80% of the maximum heart rate is the level where fitness will usually increase. When training for strength the intensity is calculated in the same way. A person trains within the target zone by finding the maximum weight they can lift and working to 60–80% of that weight. As the amount of weight lifted increases, with training this adds to the intensity.

After the warm-up, exercising regularly for 20 minutes to 60–80% of maximum heart rate will increase the body's fitness.

Duration

This is the length of time the exercise session lasts. Keeping your pulse at 60–80% of its maximum for 20 minutes is the target. Warming-up is not included in the 20 minutes. The time begins when the pulse is at 60% target.

Progression

Exercising at the same degree of difficulty all the time will only maintain current fitness levels. As training starts to change your body tolerances, the same session will not have the same effect. Your body needs to be put under slightly more pressure to continue to improve. This is the idea behind the principle of progression. The need to increase the amount of difficulty of exercise gradually is reflected by the ease with which you complete tasks for cardiovascular fitness, the same amount of exercise will not bring your pulse rate into the **target zone**. After about five to six weeks there may be a need to change the programme. The resting heart rate decreases the fitter a person becomes; this indicates improvement to fitness.

Reversibility

Just as the body will increase in strength, tone and skill with exercise, it will lose them without it. The body needs to be stressed to maintain and increase strength. After an injury or illness, an athlete may have lost their strength and skill. Although a person can quickly improve their endurance capability, it can be lost three times faster than it can be gained. Remember, if you don't use it you lose it!

What to do:

1. Write three sentences for each of the principles.

> F for frequency
> I for intensity
> D for duration

FID is also known as FITT – frequency, intensity, time (duration) and type.

Regularity

To make the body work harder than the minimum level of fitness, exercise can be repeated more regularly, made harder and last for longer. Training sessions can increase to five times a week. The intensity of the exercise can raise the pulse rate to 70% of its maximum, instead of 60%. The duration of the exercise could be 30 minutes rather than 20 minutes.

By adapting the training programme in this way it more than doubles the FID principles for the minimum level of fitness guideline (20 minutes, three times a week). Increasing training sessions in this way takes the athlete to a higher level of fitness.

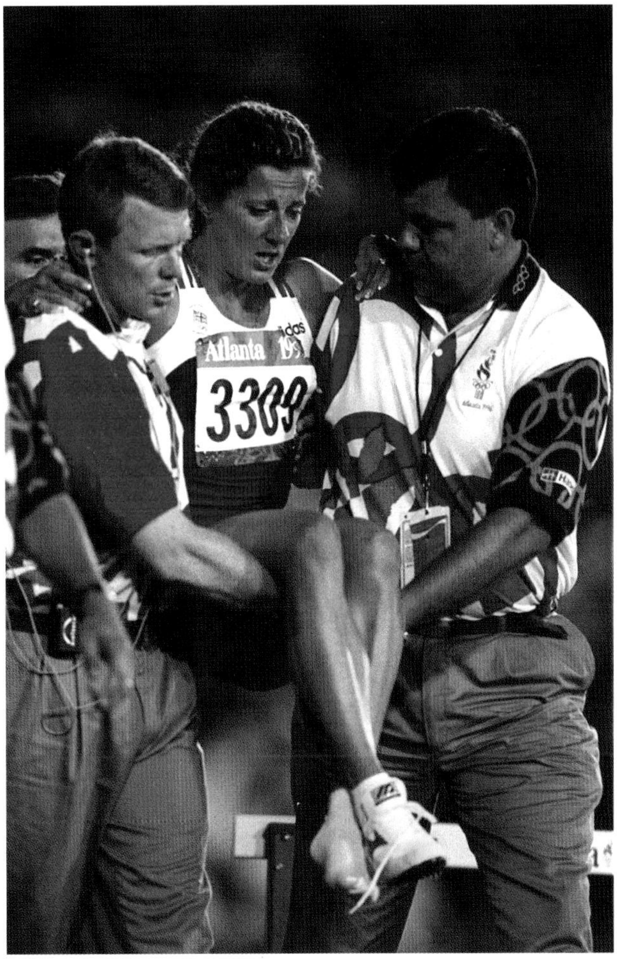

Sally Gunnell suffers an Achilles tendon injury. Injuries can occur at any time. A possible cause can be training too hard for an event.

Moderation

Reaching greater intensities of exercise is a gradual process. All athletes should find their balance between exercises. If they train too little then progress will not be made; if they train too much then injury may occur. Moderation is crucial. Changing the intensity will help to moderate training.

Peaking

The effects of the training will create peaks in an individual's performance. This is when they reach their best possible level of performance. Athletes try to peak at the time of the event. Loss of peak performance may result in poor form and bad results.

What to do:

1. Create a weekly timetable and plot a possible exercise plan.

> Remember to follow the FID principles.

Aerobic and anaerobic fitness

Both aerobic and anaerobic are ways the body uses energy; they depend on the type of activity and the condition of the performer. Each are advantageous to different kinds of activities but also have their limitations.

Aerobic energy is used in any activities taking a long period of time to complete. The exercise is moderate to hard and the amount of oxygen available is dependent on the respiratory system. For this kind of activity, which includes long-distance running, cycling and swimming, the heart and lungs need to be in good working order and trained for endurance.

Anaerobic energy is used without the presence of oxygen. The kinds of activities included are those requiring short, sharp, maximum bursts of energy. No athlete can keep working at this rate for long – up to 45 seconds is about the limit. Events like sprinting, javelin, long jump and shot-put suit this kind of energy.

Active Challenge

In pairs, prepare two questions with answers ready to ask another pair on the principles of training.

Round-up of ideas

All the principles are important when devising a training programme. The individual needs of the performer are taken into account and an exercise programme is set out solely for their capabilities.

When training for a specific event, specificity is a key principle. A swimmer will mainly swim; a runner will mainly run.

To gain from any training, overload must be applied. Muscles and body systems need to be subjected to stress. This is training above the threshold of training. The threshold is 60% of the maximum heart rate.

Once the performer is used to the exercise programme, then the principle of progression is applied. When applying progression the changes are planned systematically. This will make each change at the correct level and not injure the performer.

Applying the principles of FID is vital to the success of the exercise programme. The regularity of exercising leads to improvements in fitness. Generally, the more frequent the exercise, the better the results that will follow. A person working towards more than the minimum level of fitness would train five times a week for 30 minutes at a time, with their pulse rate above 60% of its maximum. A serious sportsperson would need to ensure that their pulse was above 80% of its maximum when training for endurance. Moderating the number of training sessions strikes the balance between training too much – and causing overuse injury – and too little, when insufficient stress is put on the body to show progression. Once training has stopped then reversibility may occur. This is when the muscles **atrophy** – or weaken – due to lack of work.

4 The Effects of Muscular Endurance

A definition of muscular endurance is:

'the muscle's ability to keep working over a long period of time without tiring'.

People with naturally good muscular endurance are able to keep exercising for long periods of time. They tend to be attracted to endurance events or play in a team position requiring endurance ability. Such activities include long- and middle-distance running and outfield players in team games, as they need to keep working and be effective throughout the game. Most sports require performers to have an element of stamina.

In order to improve muscular endurance the duration of an activity or exercise needs to increase. This can be applied to working on a weight training programme, using machines. The performer, by lifting lighter weights and increasing the number of repetitions, will train the muscles for endurance. So, by decreasing the intensity but increasing the duration the muscles are trained for endurance.

Developing muscular endurance

Strength endurance tests include sit-ups (like crunches), push-ups, chins and dips. There are other tests for different parts of the body. Performers, working for a lengthy period, need muscular endurance so they can keep their skill level high throughout the game.

Push-ups

How it works

- The performer adopts the front support position.
- Arms are extended, shoulder width apart.
- Partner places hand 10cm from the ground beneath chest.
- One repetition is when chest touches the hand, then arms fully extend.
- The activity is repeated as many times in a minute as possible.
  (When testing young people, the front support position can be adapted to kneeling.)

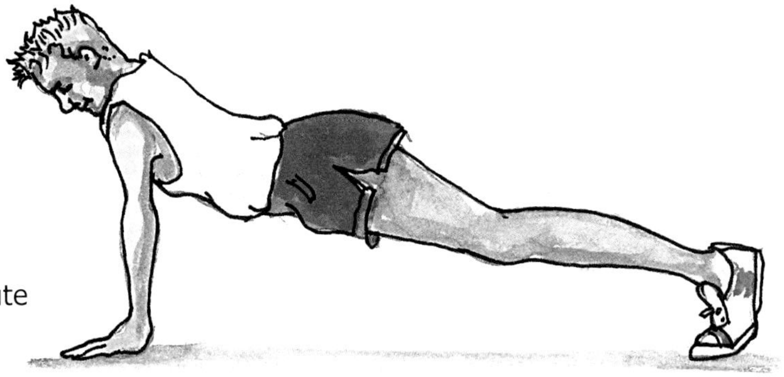

The push-up position. This can be adapted so that the performer kneels and performs push-ups from that position.

Sit-ups

How it works

- Performer lies on their back.
- Knees bent at a 90° angle.
- Feet flat on the floor.
- Partner has arm across performer's legs but is not holding their legs down.
- Performer's arms are extended.
- One repetition is: curl trunk forward until hands touch partner's forearm and return.
- The activity is repeated as many times as possible in one minute.

Equipment needed

- indoor area
- mat for safety
- stop-watch
- recorder and recording sheet

Push-ups results table

Rating	Male (18–25)	Female (18–25)
excellent	>50	>31
good	35–50	21–31
average	19–34	11–20
below average	4–18	0–10
poor	<4	

Sit-ups results table

Rating	Male (18–25)	Female (18–25)
excellent	>49	>43
very good	44–49	37–43
above average	39–43	33–36
average	35–38	29–32
below average	31–34	25–28
poor	25–30	18–24
very poor	<25	<18

CAUTION! All results shown are for adults.

5 What is Meant by Strength?

Strength can be defined as:

'the ability of a muscle (or muscle group) to apply force and overcome resistance'.

A sportsperson uses different types of strength depending on the type of action required. Some sports can depend on one type of strength, but most rely on a combination of the different types. The type of strength needed for the activity needs to be identified and developed through training. There are three main types of strength:

- static strength
- explosive strength
- dynamic strength.

Static strength takes place when the muscle length stays the same. It is used for stabilising parts of the body or holding the body steady so that movement can take place elsewhere. Rugby players in a scrum and gymnasts in a balance use this type of strength. Static strength does not develop power or muscular endurance and the cardiovascular and cardiorespiratory systems are not improved. Only few sports require this type of contraction alone.

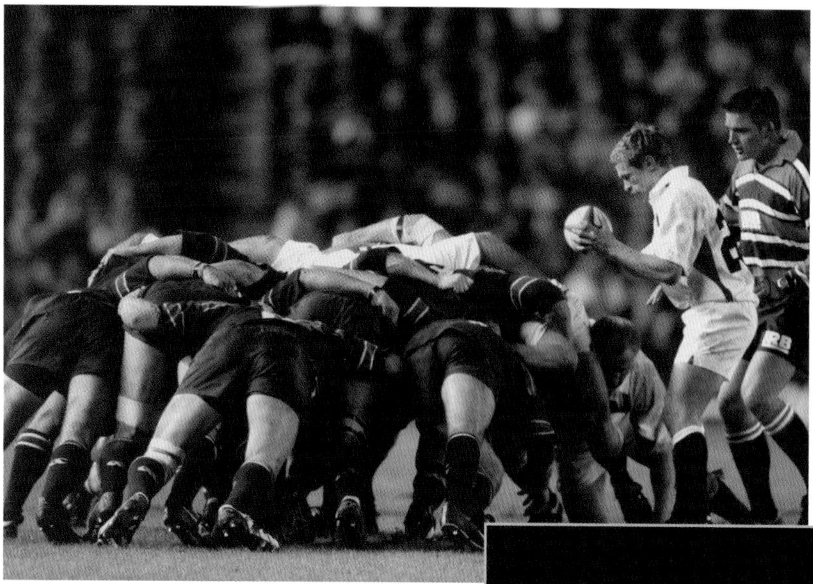

Examples of static strength.

Explosive strength comes about when a burst of maximum effort is used, like in athletic field events, striking a ball in tennis and kicking a penalty in football. This type of strength is a maximum burst of energy that is anaerobic.

Dynamic strength uses prolonged, moving muscular contractions. Rowing is a good example as it shows the rhythmical pulling action of the oars and the prolonged period of activity. Middle- and long-distance runners and games players also benefit from this type of strength. Training for dynamic strength develops cardiovascular and cardiorespiratory systems and increases power and endurance. As this type of strength is used in events taking a long period of time they use aerobic energy. For the athlete there is a greater possibility of injury as the body is moving whilst the contractions are taking place.

A basketball jump and a tennis shot are examples of explosive strength.

Rowing is a good example of dynamic strength.

Active Challenge

Decide, with a partner, two sporting examples each for static, explosive and dynamic strength.

Muscular strength can be improved by systematically increasing the frequency (number of sessions per week) and the intensity (weight lifted or distance run) of an activity, but decreasing its duration (number of repetitions). Using the example of weight training, strength would improve by systematically increasing the weights lifted, which would limit the number of repetitions the performer could complete. So, by increasing the intensity (weight lifted) and decreasing the duration (number of times the weight is lifted) muscular strength is developed.

Developing muscular strength

Muscular strength can vary in different parts of the body.

The vertical jump test and the standing broad jump test measure leg strength. The pull-up test measures arm strength. Games players need to be able to jump for a ball in a challenge or to play a shot.

Vertical jump test

How it works

- Performer stands sideways to a wall.
- While standing with feet flat, performer reaches up with their arm nearest to the wall.
- The height where the stretched fingers reach is measured.
- Standing slightly away from the wall (for safety), the performer jumps vertically as high as possible using arms and legs for maximum height.
- They touch the wall at the highest point possible (by chalking the fingers a clear mark is left to measure).
- The distance between the two measures is recorded.
- The performer has three attempts.

Equipment needed

- indoor area
- measuring tape
- chalk
- recorder and recording sheet

Vertical jump test results table		
Rating	Male (cms)	Female (cms)
excellent	>70	>60
very good	61–70	51–60
above average	51–60	41–50
average	41–50	31–40
below average	31–40	21–30
poor	21–30	11–20
very poor	<21	<11

The difference between muscular strength and endurance

Muscular strength and muscular endurance are similar, but not the same. Strength is the ability to shift a weight and muscular endurance is the ability to shift weight repeatedly, or over a long period of time. When an activity takes place over a long period it uses muscular endurance; for short, explosive events muscular strength is necessary. Team games use a combination of both types.

6 What Flexibility is

Flexibility can be defined as:

'the range of movement around a joint'.

Flexibility, also referred to as mobility and suppleness, has an important part to play in many aspects of physical activity. In the warm-up session it loosens and prepares the muscles to move in the correct way and so reducing the chances of injury in the activity. Performers with a good range of flexibility are less likely to experience overstretching injuries.

Performing a thorough series of flexibility exercises increase the range of movement around the joint and so can improve performance. The coach or performer identifies the areas needing most flexibility and concentrates on working them. A hurdler needs good hip flexibility to quickly and efficiently clear the hurdle in the shortest possible time. A sprinter will benefit from an increased stride length and so cover more ground each stride if their hips are flexible.

The more flexible the body is the better shapes it can adopt. In events reliant on form and style like gymnastics, trampolining and diving, good flexibility is vital as it can earn better marks for the performer.

When performing flexibility exercises the muscles of the body are trained to work together. Pairs of muscles (agonistic and antagonistic) practise working in unison with each other aiding the development of skilful movement.

There are various stretching and mobility exercises used to improve flexibility. Static stretching are stretching exercises where there is no movement but the body is held in the same position for about 10 seconds.

Active stretching are slow stretching exercises performed unassisted. The athlete applies their own muscular force (internal muscular force) to stretch the opposing muscle. These are the safest form of mobility training.

Passive stretching are exercises performed with a partner. The performer relaxes their muscles and the partner applies force (external muscular force) to stretch the desired muscles.

There are instances when good flexibility alone is not an advantage to the sportsperson and can lead to injury. A rugby hooker, for instance, with exceptionally flexible shoulders would not be able to hold their position in the scrum and perform effectively. Flexibility works as long as there is strength development as well. The strength of the muscles, tendons and ligaments makes sure the joint is not extended into a dangerous position.

What to do:

1. Describe and draw diagrams showing two of your own examples of stretches helping to increase a performer's flexibility.

Testing flexibility

Players need to move the joints to their full range without hurting themselves. In football, tackling effectively needs flexibility. The sit and reach test is the most common test for flexibility.

Sit and reach

How it works

- Person sits, straight legged, with feet touching the start of the measuring block.
- They reach forward and place hands on the block to be measured.
- If they reach as far as their toes this measures 0cm, beyond their toes it is +0cm and if it is not as far as their toes it is -0cm.
- Recorder measures the distance along the block that the hands reach.

Equipment needed

- indoor area
- wooden block or bench
- measure

Sit and reach results table (cms)		
Rating	Male	Female
super	>+27	>+30
excellent	+17 to +27	+21 to +30
good	+6 to +16	+11 to +20
average	0 to +5	+1 to +10
fair	-8 to -1	-7 to 0
poor	-19 to -9	-14 to -8
very poor	<-19	<-14

A person performing the sit and reach test.

Key Terms:

Atrophy ► when muscles atrophy, they weaken and lose their strength and size because of lack of exercise

Body composition ► the amount of bone, muscle and fat making up the body

FID ► frequency, intensity and duration

Individual needs ► personal requirements for training

Minimum level of fitness ► the resulting fitness level when someone exercises over a period of weeks, three sessions of 20 minutes, raising the heart rate to 60–80% of its maximum

Moderation ► achieving a balance in training and not over-training

Principles of training ► ideas behind effects of training

Regularity ► repeating exercise sessions in a week to bring about improved fitness

Systematic training ► planning a programme for an individual based on present level and desired outcome

Target zone ► level of effort applied keeping within aerobic levels

Training zone ► high level of effort moving the body systems to the anaerobic level

VO_2 maximum ► amount of oxygen exhaled from the lungs after one maximum inhalation

Summary

People deciding to train need to think carefully about the type and intensity of the exercise they are to do. The training programme should be designed specifically for the individual and the activity. Age, ability, gender and experience will all play a part in making the programme unique. A clear awareness of the reason for training will influence the type of activities included. For the minimum level of fitness to take place, a person needs to participate in three exercise sessions per week each lasting for twenty minutes and increasing the heart rate to 60% of its maximum. For higher levels of fitness the frequency, intensity and duration should increase.

Different sports require distinct types of fitness. Long-distance events and players in the outfield for most games need aerobic fitness. Developing aerobic fitness allows a person to work for the whole game without losing form. Anaerobic fitness is needed in athletic events and for single actions within games play, such as a single penalty kick or forehand drive in racket sports. Most games events need an element of muscular endurance. This allows the muscles of the body to keep working for a long period without tiring. The various sports require different types of muscular strength. Explosive strength is used in events such as shot put and javelin; static strength is employed when holding the body still and dynamic strength is utilised in moving actions over a period of time, such as the leg action in cycling.

Many sports require the body to move the joints into extreme positions. The training programme should concentrate on the specific movements and develop the best range of actions. Having good flexibility often prevents injury but in some sports, too much flexibility can be dangerous.

Specific Training Methods

What you will learn about in this section

You will learn about circuit training, weight training, interval training, fartlek training, continuous training and altitude training. For each method of training you will learn:

1. About the Training Method
2. What the Training Develops
3. How the Method Works
4. The Exercises Involved
5. How the Training Principles Apply

There are many training methods open to the performer. Each method works the body differently. The reason for training and the type of activity being trained for will steer a performer to a particular training method. When training over a long period, varying the methods used will reduce the risk of overuse injury and keep the athlete interested and fresh for each session.

1 About the Training Method: Circuit Training

Circuit training is a series of exercises completed for a certain amount of time after one another.

2 What the Training Develops

Circuit training can be useful in different ways. Depending on how the circuit is set up, it can develop power, strength, flexibility and endurance. At a basic level, it can improve the general fitness of the heart and lungs as long as the rests in between the activities are kept short. It can be adapted to incorporate skills for a particular game. Top-class performers, however, do not benefit much from circuit training as it does not allow them to achieve a high enough level of skill.

Circuit training can develop aerobic and anaerobic respiration. When using large muscle groups at each station (moving the whole body), aerobic respiration is in operation and this will develop the cardiovascular system. If exercising small muscle groups (such as the biceps and triceps) in turn at the stations, this is anaerobic, which builds strength.

3 How the Method Works

A circuit is made up of several activities. Each activity is given its own space in the gym or sports hall; this space is called a 'station'. Each activity is completed as many times as possible; these are called 'repetitions'. There is a set time for each activity; this is usually between 30 and 60 seconds. In this time as many repetitions of the activity are performed as possible. When all exercises at each station are completed, the circuit is finished. By repeating the circuit or adding exercises, the session increases in intensity. For general fitness the sequence of exercises works different muscle groups at each station. For beginners one circuit is usually enough.

4 The Exercises Involved

Active Challenge

Cover the numbered list below without reading it. With a partner, study the picture. Try to name some of the exercises in the circuit. Make additions to the list of exercises from your own experience.

1. Step-ups
2. Skipping
3. Sit-ups
4. Benchlifts
5. Bench activities
6. Leg raises
7. Push-ups
8. Squats
9. Star jumps
10. Shuttle runs

Circuit training in school.

5 How the Training Principles Apply

A circuit can be set for individual needs. Each person doing the circuit can have their own targets. This means that beginners and fitter people can work at the same time because they can work within the same time limits, but they each complete a different number of repetitions. Completing a circuit can be competitive and motivate people to work harder and achieve more repetitions. Even with inexpensive equipment, a successful general fitness circuit can be set up.

What to do:

1. List the advantages and disadvantages of circuit training.
2. Look at the circuit training picture. Change four exercises from general fitness to skills using a named sport.

Choose skills from a sport. Are the skills repeated in the same way? Place them in the circuit.

1 About the Training Method: Weight Training

The training involves shifting weight to increase the strength of muscles, using a programme of repetitions and sets.

Weight training machines are always set up and fully adjustable.

2 What the Training Develops

A person setting up a weight training programme needs to think about the following questions: What is the reason for doing the training? Is it for aerobic or anaerobic development? Which parts of the body are to be exercised? The answers to these questions will shape the whole programme.

Lifting heavy weights with few repetitions develops strength and power. This will build up strength, increase muscle size and use anaerobic respiration.

Lifting lighter weights many times develops muscular endurance. This way of adapting weight training can help a person who is rehabilitating after injury. By moving light weights, the muscles gradually get used to working and taking weight again in a safe and controlled way.

3 How the Method Works

Organising a weight training programme:

Assess – the performer's strength and fitness. Once the maximum a person can lift is known, the programme can start to develop.

Weights – light for aerobic and endurance, heavier for anaerobic strength and size.

Number of exercises – the usual range is between 8 and 12.

Repetitions – complete 12–17 repetitions at 60–70% of maximum lifting ability for an anaerobic beginner. Use many repetitions for lighter, aerobic work.

Number of sets – a beginner might complete 1 set for anaerobic, building up to 2 sets after 2 weeks. More repetitions are completed for aerobic training.

Rest between sets – about 2 minutes.

Number of sessions per week – 3–4 sessions should show an improvement with up to 48 hours between each session.

Training to get the best results – speed of exercise: to lift and lower takes 2 seconds.

Safety factors – use of straps, adjustments to the seats, setting the correct weight and correct technique are essential for safe weight training.

Review – when the body has adapted to the stresses of the programme, changes are made. The strength of the performer is re-tested. If the programme has been set at the right level, the performer will have increased in strength.

New programme – changes are made to the programme. As a result, a combination of weights, repetitions and sets increases slightly.

Examples of weight training cards

% of maximum lift	Repetitions
60%	17
65%	14
70%	12
75%	10
80%	8
85%	6
90%	5
95%	3
100%	1

Good for beginners.

Complete 1 set of above (starting with easiest).

After 3 weeks, increase sets.

Weight training repetitions – the performer works through the order from 60%–100% in a session.

Lift 70% of max.

8 repetitions

3 sets completed

Good for novice.

Level of effort required means weights are lifted properly.

Little risk of injury.

Simple sets – the performer works at the same intensity throughout the session, completing 3 sets of 8 repetitions.

160kg x 1 rep
150kg x 2 reps
140kg x 3 reps
130kg x 4 reps
120kg x 5 reps
100kg x 10 reps
start

Good for experienced lifters.

Pyramid sets – the performer starts at the easiest weight working their way to heavy weights but with fewer repetitions.

4 The Exercises Involved (Two Ways of Training)

Machine weights

Using machines, rather than free weights, can be a safer way of weight training. They are technically designed to move in the correct way and are adjustable for different sizes of user. They are safe as they are steady and do not vary position apart from the designed range. This also has the effect of not training the stabilising muscles that may be needed for a sport. They usually have supports and belts to make sure the body is prepared in the correct position to shift the weight. They are always set up so are ready to use. Users starting a weight training programme find them easy to work. One drawback is that extra weights cannot be added to the machines. This limits their use for the advanced performer.

A variety of exercises in the gym.

Free weights

Free weights can be used in a weight training programme. The use of such weights is specialised and needs lots of training so the performer works safely. Many top sportspeople use free weights. A person training with heavy weights must always use a spotter; this is a person who helps steady the performer and is ready to catch the bar or assist if the performer is struggling.

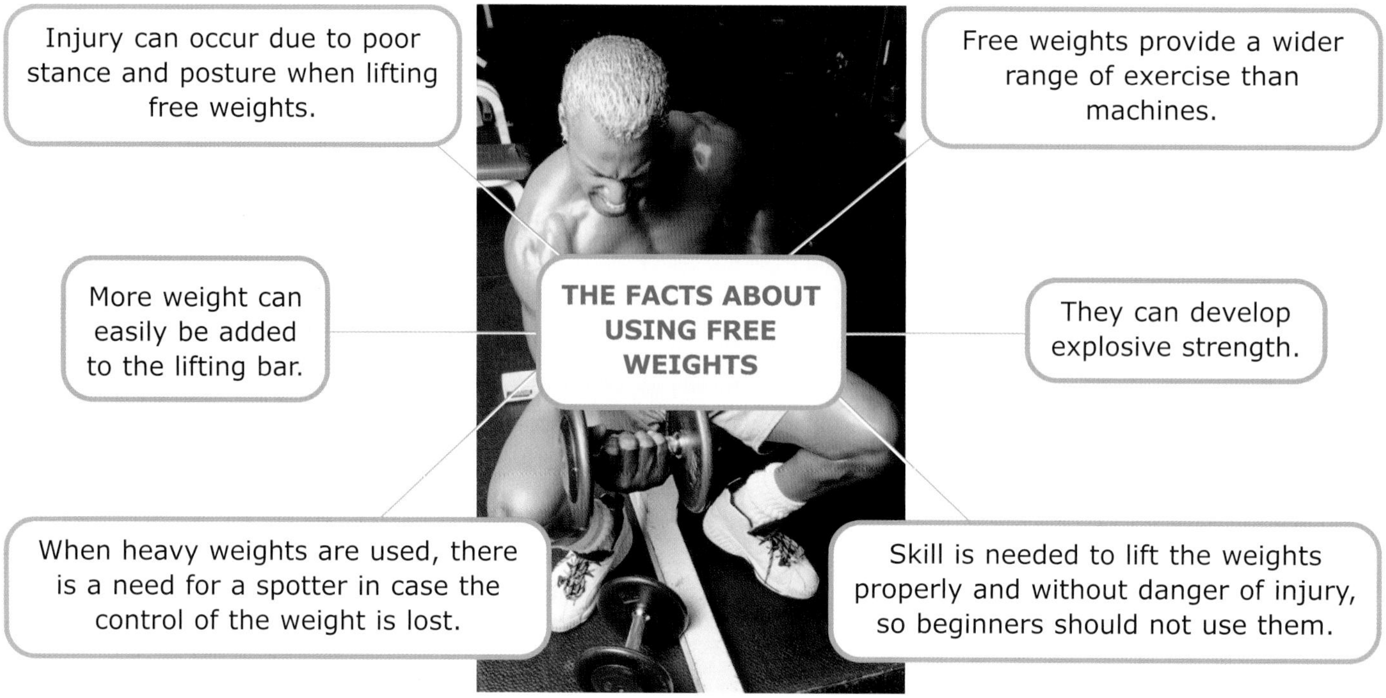

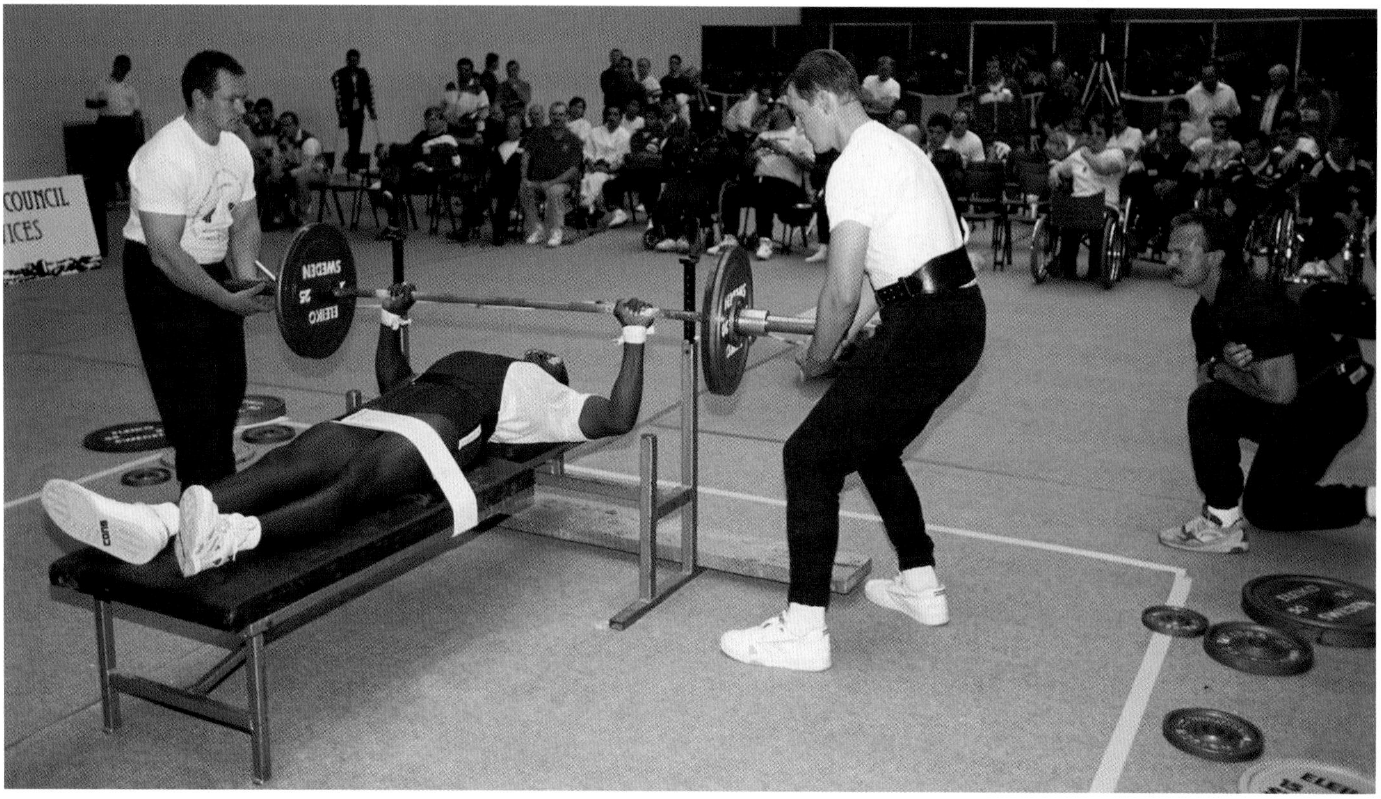

Spotters help make free weight training safe, as shown here at the British Disabled Powerlift Competition.

5 How the Training Principles Apply

With both types of weight training method, regular training improves the muscles' ability to move the weight. As the body adapts, the progression, overload and FITT principles are applied and the weights, repetitions and sets are gradually increased. This allows improvement of the muscles to continue. Lifting 60–80% of the maximum weight a person is able to lift will keep the performer within the target zone. Each session should last for no longer than 45 minutes.

A weight training card helps the performer to train safely and see progress

NAME	PERSONAL TRAINER		DATE PROGRAMME STARTED	
VISITS	1 2 3 4 5 6 7 8 9 10 11 12 13 14			
WARM-UP OPTIONS	JOG 5 MINS	CYCLE 5 MINS	EASY ROW 5 MINS	STEPPER 5 MINS
THEN	STRETCHES:	ARMS/SHOULDERS	LEGS/HIPS	ABDOMINALS
EXERCISE	**STARTING POINT**	**PROGRESSION 1**	**PROGRESSION 2**	**PROGRESSION 3**
TRICEP PULLDOWNS				
SQUATS				
HIP FLEXORS				
LATERAL PULLDOWN				
HAMSTRING CURLS				
HIP EXTENSORS				
BENCH PRESSES				
SEATED LEG EXTENSIONS				
COOL DOWN OPTIONS	WALK/JOG 5 MINS	EASY CYCLE 5 MINS	EASY ROW 5 MINS	
FINISH	WITH STRETCHES			

What to do:

Answer these questions:

1. What makes each weight training session different?
2. How do free weight training sessions compare to machine weight training sessions?

The training principles change the sessions: say how they do this. When comparing each type, think of the special features each method has.

1 About the Training Method: Interval Training

This method of training involves times of work followed by times of rest.

2 What the Training Develops

This method can be adapted to develop different types of fitness. Short bursts of pace, using anaerobic respiration, needed in games play, use short interval training. Prolonged moderate to hard pace, using aerobic respiration, needed in middle-distance running events, uses long interval training.

Interval training is suited to individuals working on their own, small groups of people and to larger numbers like teams of players. Many sportspeople can benefit from interval training. The sessions can be adapted to practise the skills used in a particular game. Whether a runner, swimmer, footballer or netball player, interval training can be adapted to your sport.

The work is intensive and should be performed with accuracy and at competition pace. The times of rest allow performers to regain energy so they do not become too tired and can no longer carry on training. The times of work are repeated to form repetitions. Four or five repetitions make up a set. There may be four or five sets in a session.

An example of an interval training activity

Time limit for activity →	Complete 4 sets of the following	Time limit for return ←
6–10 seconds	dribble and shoot →	
	jog, return and rest ←	60–180 seconds
6–10 seconds	dribble and shoot →	
	jog, return and rest ←	60–180 seconds
6–10 seconds	dribble and shoot →	
	jog, return and rest ←	60–180 seconds
6–10 seconds	dribble and shoot →	
	jog, return and rest ←	60–180 seconds

3 How the Method Works

Interval training can be adapted for different types of athlete and event. The working periods copy those in the event. The rest periods allow time for recovery in the same way that there would be quieter times during a game.

Long interval training

Work time is 15 seconds to 3 minutes. Games players and middle-distance athletes benefit from this type of training. The training copies the events in the need for bursts of maximal effort within the 15-second and 3-minute time spans. Even the best athletes cannot work at full pace for longer than 60-second periods so, when using this method, performers work at 80–85% of their maximum.

The resting times match the working times so the longer they work the longer they rest. The resting times are important to enable a performer to recover and continue the session. When working in larger groups it is more difficult for everyone to keep together due to the longer time limit and the variation in ability.

A 4-minute-mile runner could use interval training in the following way: repeat 10 x 60 second $\frac{1}{4}$ mile distances with 2 minutes rest between each run.

Short interval training

This training works on short bursts of maximal effort. The working times may be as short as 15 seconds. The performer aims to work all out for the whole of this time. Sprinters and racket sport players use this method to match the short bursts of maximal effort used in their events. A sprinter goes all out to reach the line as fast as possible and a squash player hits the ball with a burst of maximal effort. Due to the effects of the intensive effort on the body, rests of 2 minutes are necessary. In this time, the body has a chance to recover enough to carry on training.

4 The Exercises Involved

You will have used interval training in school already. Shuttle runs, dribbling relays, lay up shot drills and swimming 25m are all examples of exercises used for interval training. In a games or athletics lesson, you will have used shuttle runs. As you complete your shuttle run, that is one repetition. You rest while your teammates complete theirs. You may complete four repetitions before you are stopped; those make up a set. The teacher may give you another chance to complete the shuttle run after resting and so you will have then completed two sets.

Swimming, athletics and many games, such as football, use interval training. Here, Michael Owen practises his dribbling skills.

5 How the Training Principles Apply

As the periods of work and rest imitate the game, the principle of specificity is applied. To keep the performer improving when using interval training, the principle of progression is used. There are several ways to do this:

- the amount of recovery time may shorten and competitive pace work be increased
- the intensity or difficulty of the work may increase; this could be increasing the distance covered or amount of time run
- the number of repetitions or sets completed may increase.

Task 3

What to do:

1. Choose and name a sport.
2. Design a 30-minute interval training session for that sport.

If designing a session for long interval training, include 5 repetitions and 4 sets. If using short interval training, use more repetitions and sets.

1 About the Training Method: Fartlek Training

Fartlek is a Swedish word meaning 'speed play'. It involves exercise, often running, varying in time, distance and effort.

2 What the Training Develops

Due to the changes of intensity of the exercises, it trains both aerobic and anaerobic fitness. The athlete becomes increasingly capable of meeting the changes of pace in a competition or game.

3 How the Method Works

Speed, distances covered and the amount of time spent exercising change. In general, the session has work of varying intensity taking place over a minimum of a 20-minute period.

Fartlek can be an introduction to interval training and sometimes both can be combined to form a programme of exercise, owing to their similar content. This would suit a games player. The content of the session is flexible. The repetitions in the sessions, therefore, are made different to add interest to the training. Rest periods or less strenuous exercise give time to recover so training can continue.

0–15 minutes	*warm-up*
15–35 minutes	*sprint 10 seconds on flat*
	jog on flat
	sprint 10 seconds uphill
	jog/walk downhill on flat
	run 150m on flat for 1 minute
	jog
	sprint 80m on flat
	jog
	sprint 20m uphill
	jog downhill on flat
	sprint 10 seconds on flat
	jog/run downhill on flat
	sprint 10 seconds uphill
	jog/run downhill on flat
35-45 minutes	*cool down*

As an athlete's fitness improves the session will be planned to include increased intensity.

4 The Exercises Involved

Sprints, jogs and runs make up the session. These may have times set for them or may be for a certain distance. The session can be continuous with periods of intense work followed by easier work, which gives the body a chance to recover. Sometimes the session can include periods of complete rest.

In Sweden, where this method originated, athletes use the surrounding hills and forests to train in. Many areas large enough to run in can be used to vary the training session such as in a park, at the beach and in the countryside. Fartlek training can be adapted to running, cycling and swimming.

5 How the Training Principles Apply

The principles of FITT adapt to keep the performer improving.

Heart rate of a 16 year old whilst fartlek training

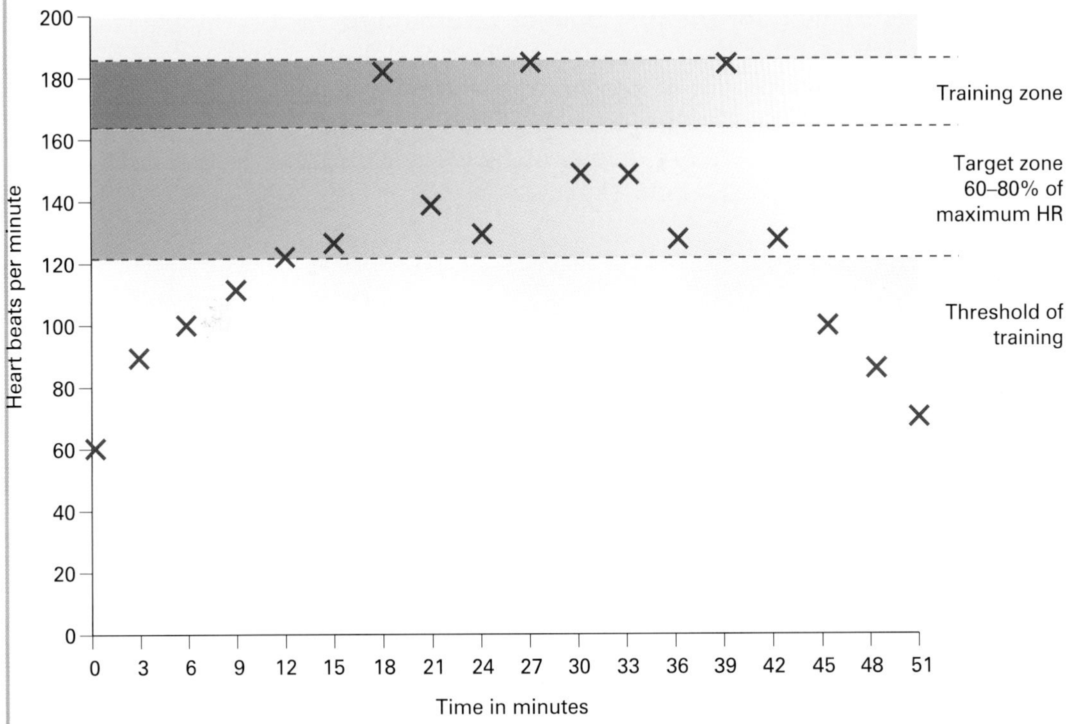

The heart rate rises and falls regularly in a fartlek session.

What to do:

1. From your understanding of fartlek training, copy and complete the paragraph below.

   The word fartlek means __________ __________ in ______________ where this training method originated. Athletes can use ________________, ________________, and ________________ to run in. By using the natural changes in the countryside and beach the demands on the athletes ________________. Uphill work increases the ________________ of the exercise and the heart rate will rise. Sprinting to set markers trains ________________. Periods of slower running help the athlete to ________________ so that training can continue and the athlete uses ________________ respiration.

1 About the Training Method: Continuous Training

This method exercises the body at a moderate rate, keeping the pulse at a constant level between 60–80% of maximum.

2 What the Training Develops

This training works the body aerobically and keeps the pulse at a high rate. Its effect is to improve the cardiovascular and respiratory systems. It can be adapted for both the health and fitness performer and the top athlete.

3 How the Method Works

After a gradual warm-up, the person training works their body at a moderate level throughout the session. The heart rate is above 60% of its maximum but below 80%. By keeping in this zone the work is aerobic and can carry on for a long time.

Continuous training suits a person who is training for the first time or returning to exercise after a period of non-activity, such as after injury. A person who specialises in long-distance events can use this type of training out of season to maintain a good level of cardiorespiratory fitness. At the start of the season, continuous training can adapt as a gentle way to re-establish the cardiorespiratory levels. At this level, the work is moderate but can be adapted to be harder at a later time.

The use of a variety of machines, such as rowers, treadmills and exercise cycles can adapt to continuous training.

4 The Exercises Involved

The types of activity that suit this training include cycling, swimming, exercise classes (aerobics), running and jogging. Many sports centres and gyms have specialised machines that adapt to continuous training. Treadmills, exercise cycles, rowing machines and steppers all lend themselves to this type of training. The activities are a good way of developing general fitness and can be adapted to suit both individuals and groups of people. If running is the exercise chosen, then it is inexpensive to start: changing the place of training is easily arranged, adding interest to the session.

5 How the Training Principles Apply

After several training sessions, the body will have adapted to the strains of the exercise. Checking the pulse rate during exercise will show if it is in the 60–80% zone, showing that the heart has become stronger as a result of the exercise. The speed of the exercise should be increased, in order to get the pulse rate into the target zone and continue to have an effect on the performer.

For the more advanced performer, greater stresses and demands are made on their body. By keeping in the training zone of 80–90% of their maximum heart rate and working for 15–20 minutes, the training will be effective. An endurance athlete, like a marathon runner, would use this method as part of their training programme.

Marathon runners use continuous training within their training programme. Francis Naali of Tanzania won the men's Marathon at the Commonwealth Games 2002.

What to do:

1. Write six facts about continuous training.
2. How can the training method be adapted for beginners and more competitive performers?

Think about: How hard does the body work? What effect does the exercise have on the heart? What types of activity can adapt to this method? Who would use this method of training?

1 About the Training Method: Altitude Training

This method needs the athletes to travel to areas where the altitude is higher than they are used to and to train there.

2 What the Training Develops

At high altitude there is less oxygen in the air, so for the body to carry enough oxygen for its needs it produces more red blood cells. This increased capacity of blood to carry oxygen is then available in the body to use aerobically, by the athlete when he or she returns to a lower altitude. This improves the athlete's level of endurance and therefore improves performance for long-distance events, until the red blood cell level returns to normal.

3 How the Method Works

For the first few days at altitude athletes experience some side effects when training. They find it difficult to complete sessions and tire quickly. This is because with the change in air pressure not as much oxygen mixes with the haemoglobin; therefore, there is not as much oxygen carried to the working muscles of the body. Due to the reduced amounts of oxygen available, the athlete's aerobic ability is affected. For a short time, athletes find they cannot complete the same amount of training as they did at sea level. But as the number of red blood cells increase, their performance improves. Endurance athletes who have recently been at high altitude are able to carry more oxygen in their blood when they return to lower altitude levels, and this helps their performance.

4 The Exercises Involved

When athletes train in areas of high altitude, they complete their specific training scheduled for their event.

Some athletes partake in altitude training several times a year.

5 How the Training Principles Apply

As with all training programmes, when the body adapts to the sessions then the FID principles apply. This may be that more sessions are performed in a week, sessions may last longer or the type of work completed may make the heart rate beat faster.

What to do:

1. Write three statements a person may make about the following training methods:
   a. fartlek training b. altitude training c. interval training

You could use speech marks as though a person is actually saying the statements.

Key Terms:

Altitude training	training in places where the height above sea level is much greater than athlete is used to
Circuit training	a series of exercises completed in order and for a certain time
Continuous training	aerobic exercising, at a moderate to high level, with no rests
Fartlek training	'speed play', changing speed, distances and times of exercise in the same session
Interval training	mixing periods of hard exercise with rest periods
Weight training	progressively lifting heavier weights to improve strength or lifting weights more often to improve stamina

Summary

The method of training can be a personal choice or it can be sport specific. Some methods suit certain kinds of event or game. People exercising for leisure can make any choice they want. People needing specialised training must choose the method that will improve their body systems and skills to the best of their ability. In this case, knowledge of the requirements of the sport is essential. By combining the knowledge of the sport and the abilities of the individual, an appropriate programme can be designed.

Individuals need their own programme of exercise as everyone is different and has their own reasons for training. Testing a person's capabilities first gives a clear idea of the level of training needed. By applying the FID principles, both beginners and top athletes can be catered for. The key is to work the heart above the threshold of training. Working in the target zone will help general fitness; working in the training zone is for more serious athletes.

The principles of training create guidelines for improving the body. Plan progression carefully by reviewing the improvements made by the athlete. Systematically plan new programmes, increasing the intensity of the exercise when old levels have been adapted to. Remember, training at the correct levels will improve the body but it will reach a stable state from time to time and progress will stop temporarily.

Physiological Factors

What you will learn about in this section

1. Fatigue
2. Drugs in Society and Sport
3. Drugs and the Sportsperson
4. Performance-enhancing Drugs
5. Banned Method
6. Drugs Testing
7. Individual Differences
8. Measuring the Body to Decide the Somatotype

1 Fatigue

When the body tires it becomes less effective. A sportsperson, tiring in a game, will be unable to maintain the standard of play they started with. The aspects of skill-related fitness will become less effective: for example, passing a ball will be less accurate and tackles could be mistimed. As well as a decrease in the level of skill performance, the quality of decision making gets worse. Both of these combine to lower overall performance and increase the likelihood of dangerous play.

The body needs rests in order to recover. If a fatigued performer continues, then there is a possibility that they may have to stop completely. Any athlete at any level of sport can suffer the effects of fatigue. A player may know they should stop, but desire and determination keeps them going without realising their change in form. In these cases it is up to the coach or manager to be aware of the signs of fatigue and be prepared to stop training, stop the event or substitute a team member. By following a rigorous training programme the effects of fatigue can be offset.

Task 1

What to do:

1. Fatigue affects the skill of a performer. Give four examples of different sports and the skills affected.

Your answer should include: name of the sport, skill component and sporting action affected.

England's Andrea Whitcombe collapses with exhaustion after winning the silver medal at the Commonwealth Games 1998.

Drugs are chemicals consumed, inhaled or injected into the body to artificially change its natural qualities. Some drugs are accepted in society, some have an age restraint on their use and others are illegal.

Each type of drug affects the body in a different way. Drugs can be used to develop the body in a desired way but they can also change the mental approach of a person. Some are addictive and people get into the habit of depending on them. When a body is manipulated in such an artificial way, there is usually a price to pay. Undesirable side effects may occur quickly but there may also be long-term health risks and possible shortening of life expectancy.

Socially acceptable drugs

Cigarettes

Cigarettes are legal but are becoming less socially acceptable. It has been recognised that smoking can contribute to long-term illness (such as coronary heart disease).

When a person smokes, they take harmful chemicals into their body. The worst substance is tar, which collects in the lungs and is believed to be directly related to cancer. Tobacco contains nicotine, which is not a banned drug but some would say that it has an addictive quality. Nicotine affects the body by stimulating the brain to release noradrenaline, which is usually released in times of stress.

Smoking raises the pulse rate and so makes the heart work faster for no reason. The smoker's blood vessels contract, raising the blood pressure and causing a sensation of cold. Smoke contains carbon monoxide and when this enters the blood stream it reduces the red blood cells' ability to transport oxygen. As a result, fitness levels are reduced.

In endurance activities where the good condition of the cardiorespiratory systems is required smoking can be a major hindrance as it can affect the necessary blood flow around the body.

Bowler Phil Tufnell is shown smoking and drinking after the Ashes Test Match.

Alcohol

Alcohol is a socially acceptable drug but is banned in most sports as it has an unfair or detrimental effect on the performer. It can act as a sedative, slowing reactions and impairing judgement. It is dangerous if combined with a sport relying on judgement at speed, such as motor racing.

Socially unacceptable drugs

Drugs that are seen as socially unacceptable are those that are illegal to possess or use; there are many such drugs and they have various effects. A few are detailed below.

Cannabis

This drug is known as a depressant. It has the effect of making a person's reactions slower and their judgement poor. There is no use of this drug for the sportsperson.

Ecstasy

This drug is a stimulant. It increases a person's self-esteem, making them feel confident and good about themselves. It can cause slight hallucinations and after taking it a person will lose their ability to carry out regular tasks properly. It is of no use to the sportsperson as it affects a person's awareness, impairing their judgement.

LSD

This is classed as a hallucinogen. It affects a person's ability to make decisions as they see life in a bizarre way. It can cause flashbacks of strange experiences. It has no use to the sportsperson.

What to do:

Copy and complete the following sentences.

1. Smoking can affect the good ________________ of the blood around the body and can cause ________________ problems in later life. Cigarettes contain ________________ which has an addictive quality.
2. Alcohol is a __________ __________ drug. In sufficient quantities it can ________________ and combined with sport it can be dangerous.
3. Cannabis is a ________________ and affects ________________ as well as slowing people's reactions. These effects are of __________ __________ to the sportsperson.
4. Ecstasy is a ________________, which can cause hallucinations. It stops a person ________________ and is of no use to the sportsperson.
5. LSD is a hallucinogen affecting a __________ __________ and view of life. It is of no use to the ________________.

Task 2

3 Drugs and the Sportsperson

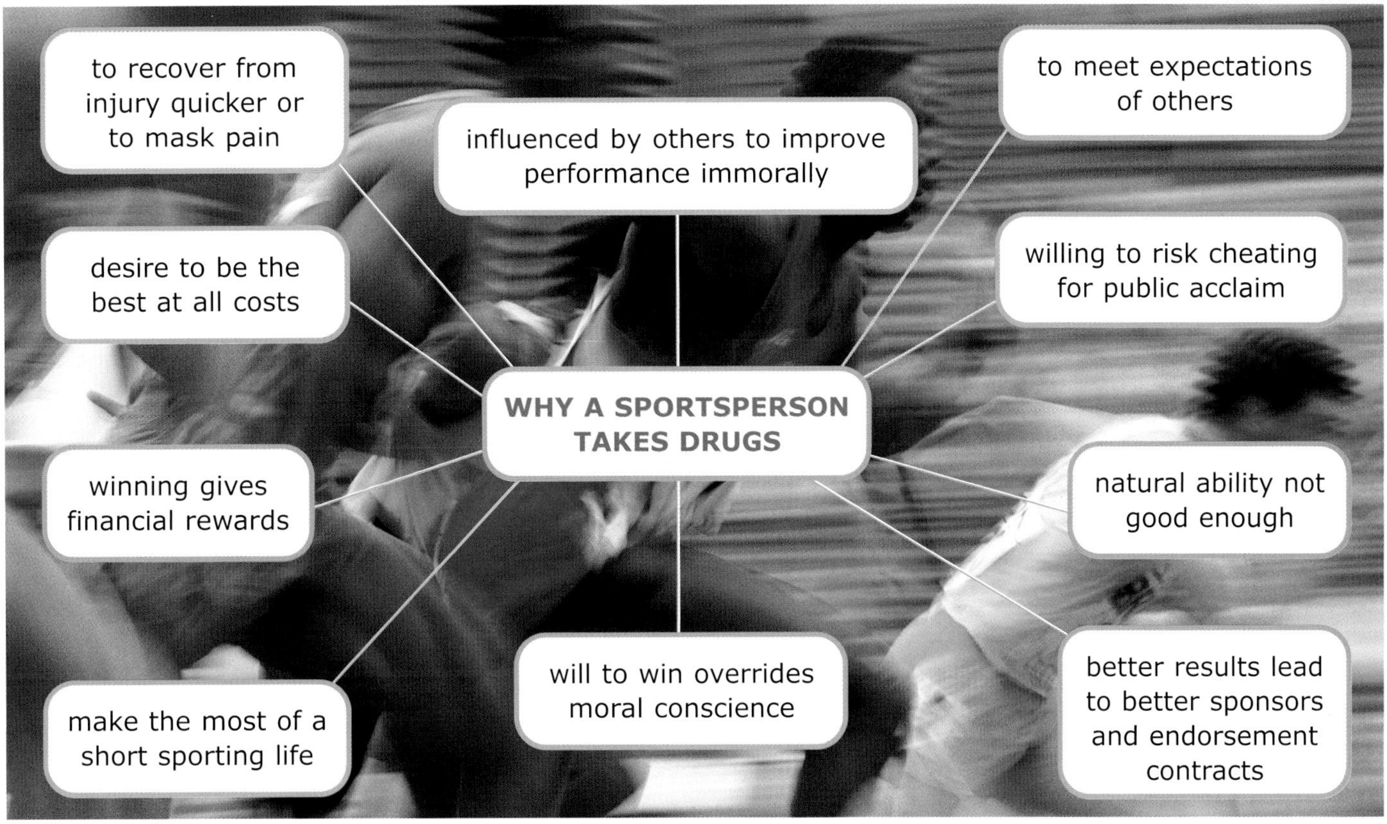

4 Performance-enhancing Drugs

The rewards for winning can be great in sport. Some athletes are tempted to cheat in order to win. This undermines the integrity of the sport and so the governing bodies of different sports have clear drug-testing policies to try to keep their sport 'clean'.

Each sport has its own list of banned substances, which are published to make it clear to performers and their coaches what cannot be taken during training and competition. The effects of taking different drugs are wide and varied: some help to hide pain, like methadone (an opioid analgesic); others develop the body artificially, like anabolic steroids.

The governing bodies work to try to keep a good name for sports and look after the interests of the athletes. The International Olympic Committee (IOC) medical commission works to: 'protect the health of athletes ... ensure respect for both medical and sport ethics ... enforce equality for all competing athletes.'

IOC guide to classes of prohibited substances and methods of doping

Prohibited classes of substances:

A. stimulants
B. opioid analgesics
C. anabolic agents
D. diuretics
E. peptide hormones, mimetics and analogues.

Prohibited methods:

A. blood doping
B. pharmacological, chemical and physical manipulation.

Classes of drug subject to restriction:

A. alcohol
B. cannabinoids
C. local anaesthetics
D. corticosteroids
E. beta blockers.

Anabolic agents

- Most commonly used drugs in sport – mimic testosterone, a male hormone.
- **Examples of drug** Testosterone, nandrolone, stanozolol, boldenone, clenbuterol.
- **Effects** Increases muscle mass and develops bone growth, increases strength, allowing the athlete to train harder. Has a quick effect so there is a rapid improvement. Increases aggression, so seen as good for competitive contact sports. Prevents muscle wastage and are an aid to rehabilitation.
- **Side effects** Has the greatest effect on women: deepens voice, increases facial hair, causes irregular periods and possible infertility. Men grow breasts, can become impotent and develop kidney problems. Mood swings, anxiety, aggression, face can swell up, high blood pressure, heart attacks, strokes. Increased risk of muscle injury and liver disease.
- Injected into the blood stream.
- Recent research indicates long-term users show signs of addiction.

CJ Hunter, the 1999 world shotput champion, served a two-year ban after testing positive for nandrolone on four separate occasions. He registered close to record levels, 1000 times above the legal limit.

Stimulants

- Second most commonly used drugs.
- **Examples of drug** Amphetamines, ephedrine, cocaine, caffeine.
- **Effects** Reduces feelings of tiredness so a person can train for longer, stimulates the central nervous system (CNS) and makes people more alert.
- **Side effects** User is irritable, unable to sleep, has high blood pressure, irregular heartbeat, faster heartbeat.
- Some are addictive – amphetamines.

Stimulants improve reaction time.

Opioid analgesics (including narcotic analgesics)

- **Examples of drug** Heroin, methadone, pethidine, morphine, codeine.
- **Effects** Reduces the sensation of the CNS. Helps pain relief, so athlete is back from injury sooner, hides the pain.
- **Side effects** Loss of concentration, loss of balance, loss of co-ordination making sport dangerous. Using these drugs can make an injury worse and may cause a long-term problem related to the first injury.
- Usually, injected into the blood stream.
- They are addictive.

Diuretics

- **Examples of drug** Furosemide, triamterene, chlortalidone. Mannitol is prohibited if intravenously injected.
- **Effects** Speeds up work of kidneys by producing more urine. Reduces fluid retention, which causes rapid weight loss; used in sports where there are weight categories. Sportspeople use diuretics to 'make the weight'.
- **Side effects** Dehydration and possibly dizziness, muscle cramps, headaches, nausea, fatigue. Kidney illness can develop.

Naseem Hamed trains hard to make the weight, whereas a few athletes are tempted to use drugs.

Peptide hormones, mimetics, analogues

- **Examples of drug** Human growth hormone (hGH), erythropoietin (EPO), synthetic substance that copies natural hormones of the body.
- **Effects** hGH develops muscle, makes the body use fat and helps reduce tiredness. Recovery from injury and training is quicker, increases red blood cells and so helps the endurance athlete.
- **Side effects** EPO thickens the blood, inhibiting circulation, which can lead to a heart attack or stroke, and hGH acts like anabolic steroids.

Beta blockers

- **Examples of drug** Atenolol, nodolol. Some beta blockers are available on prescription to treat angina and have a similar effect to alcohol. Their use in sport is subject to certain restrictions. They are completely banned in some sports.
- **Effects** Users maintain a slow heart rate and low blood pressure, used as a relaxant, useful in tense situations. They also have the effect of steadying the hand, important to competitors in target sports. The calming effect can also help in high-risk sports where speed is involved.
- **Side effects** Reduces the heart rate so much that there is a danger that it may stop.

Beta blockers are banned in snooker. Here, Peter Ebdon bridges to make a shot.

Active Challenge

With a partner, study the information on banned substances for several minutes. Now test each other on the categories, names and effects they have on a sportsperson.

Masking agents

These are drugs taken to hide the presence of another drug. Some **masking agents** do not appear on the list of banned substances for particular sports, so their presence is legal. The masking agent hides the presence of a banned substance, which would otherwise disqualify the performer. Substances used for this effect are epitestosterone, probenecid and diuretics which mask the presence of anabolic steroids.

5 Banned Method

Blood doping is a banned method of improving performance that does not involve the use of drugs. For endurance athletes, the ability of the blood to carry oxygen is crucial to their performance and blood doping aims to improve this. The more oxygen delivered to the working areas of the body the better the results.

Blood can be used from the competitor or from another donor. Two to three months before the competition, blood is removed from the competitor. This gives time for the natural blood reserves to be replenished. The plasma and red blood cells are separated. The plasma is immediately re-injected and the red blood cells are put in cold storage. This blood is then injected back into the body, one week prior to the event. The extra blood in the body has the effect of increasing the amount of red blood cells present and therefore improving the oxygen-carrying capacity, benefiting the athlete's aerobic endurance. An athlete can improve performance by 20% from accurately using this method.

With blood doping there is a threat of blood clots and the blood pressure in the body increases and overloads the circulatory system, putting an unusual and dangerous strain on the heart. There is also the problem, when injecting, of transmitting infectious diseases such as hepatitis and Aids.

Task 3

What to do:

1. From the information on drugs, create a matrix using the following headings:
   Type of drug
   Drugs in this category
   Which athletes may use it?
   Effect on the athlete
   Side effects/dangers

6 Drugs Testing

All top-class sportspeople are tested for drugs. For example, after each of the 2002 World Cup matches in Korea and Japan, random drugs tests were carried out on players from each of the teams. In national athletics, drugs testing is carried out at several different times:

- in a national event
- in an international event
- at random
- on achieving a world record time or distance, even in training
- on those achieving the first three places in an event
- in training (this is to guard against the athlete who takes performance-enhancing drugs in training but weans themselves off them by the competition date).

Drugs-testing procedure

- An athlete is chosen for the test.
- The athlete chooses a chaperone, of the same sex, for the test who stays with them at all times. The athlete also chooses a witness, usually their coach or manager.
- The athlete gives a urine sample, witnessed by their coach or manager, and then pours samples into small bottles labelled A and B.
- These samples are then correctly labelled, packed up and locked with a special seal.
- The drugs-testing officials completely oversee the whole procedure.
- The samples are then sent to the laboratory for testing. Sample A is tested. Any competitor who refuses to be tested is treated as though they gave a positive sample.

Procedure for positive results

- Governing body of the sport and the competitor informed.
- Governing body investigates the matter. At this stage, the competitor is asked for their account and sample B may be tested.
- An official hearing is arranged by the governing body at which a legal team may defend the competitor.
- If guilty, a penalty is imposed, which varies depending on the type of drug and the sport. Generally a first offence leads to a two-year ban and a second offence has a life ban imposed.
- Any medals or awards achieved at the time of the sample, or after, are taken away from the competitor.

The problem for athletes is that certain banned substances are found in common foods and medicines. Tea and coffee contain caffeine; flu, headache and asthma tablets all contain some banned substances. It is important that the coach checks anything taken by the performer as any illegal substance in the athlete's body, however innocently taken, is treated as a performance enhancer.

Accused athletes have the right to defend themselves against allegations. Diane Modahl, a British athletics champion, was banned for four years, in 1992, after it was claimed she tested positive for a banned performance-enhancing substance. The suspension was lifted after she won a lengthy legal fight to clear her name.

Procedure for negative results

If no drugs are found then no action is taken and the sample B is destroyed. The governing body of the sport and the competitor are informed.

Task 4

What to do:

1. State the three reasons why the IOC bans performance-enhancing drugs.
2. Make a brief list of 12 stages of a drugs test. Include in the list what happens in the case of both a positive and negative test.

7 Individual Differences

There are many differences in people's physical shape and size.
The following are the main factors creating the individual shape of a person:

- height
- weight
- body fat
- muscle girth
- bone size.

Depending on the combination of these different components, a person may be influenced to participate in a certain sport or even to play in a particular position within a team due to the suitability of their shape and size.

Somatotypes

This is a method of identifying people by their body shape. WJ Sheldon devised this method in 1940; he originally adapted his findings to criminology. Professor Tanner studied sportspeople from the 1960 Olympic Games and applied Sheldon's ideas to sport. There are three extreme categories of body type; each type is determined by the amount of fat, muscle and bone making up the body.

Identifying the three types

The three somatotypes are:

Endomorphic – tendency to put on fat, soft roundness of shape, short tapering limbs, small bones, wide hips.

Mesomorphic – high proportion of muscle, bone, large trunk, heavy chest, broad shoulders and narrow hips.

Ectomorphic – lean, fragile, delicate body, small bones, narrow at shoulders and hips.

Each type has a 1–7 score; 1 is low and 7 is high. Each person is measured to find their personal mark. A non-sportsperson may have the following combination 4, 3, 3 (4 – medium endomorphy), (3 – low mesomorphy), (3 – low ectomorphy).

Sport attracts extremes

There are very few people with the extreme examples of body type. Most people have a combination of all three. Sportspeople have more mesomorphic (muscle) and ectomorphic (thinness) than endomorphic (fatness) characteristics. A top-class sport, however, will attract the best extremes of body type suitable to that game. Basketball, for instance, will attract players who are all very tall and thin with sinewy muscles, falling into the ectomorph and mesomorph categories.

Each sport is different and suits people of a certain somatotype.

What to do:

1. Put the following into the correct category for somatotype:
   a. basketball player
   b. hockey player
   c. rugby player
   d. gymnast
   e. swimmer
   f. marathon runner
   g. shot putter.
2. For each of the above sportspeople write a sentence on how they might describe themselves.

You may need to do some research to find out about the sports mentioned. Use your judgement to decide the somatotype by using the photographs above to help your decisions.

The three body types are the extremes; many people have a combination of different body types. When working out a person's type, their age, gender, height, weight, size of bones, amount of fat on the body and size of muscle are all taken into consideration.

Measuring somatotype is used to find the shape category of a person using size, composition and build. Knowing their somatotype can steer people into a sport to which they are naturally suited or show areas of the body that need to change in order to reach maximum success rate in an activity.

Fat ratio of the body

The fat layer is just below the top layer of skin on the body. Fat is a good insulator and can be of benefit in activities in cold climatic conditions. The amount of fat people have on the body varies with age and gender. Babies and women have thicker layers than men. Both sexes can increase their fat ratio as they get older. Men increase the amount around their middle; women the amount on their thighs and buttocks.

Measuring fat

A **skin-fold calliper** is an adjustable instrument that measures the amount of fat at different places on the body. The method is to place skin and underlying layers of fat between callipers; a dial gives the reading of the thickness of the flesh. There are four main measurements to take:

- Biceps – at the front of the upper arm
- Triceps – at the back of the upper arm
- Supra-iliac – at the front of the body above the hips
- Subscapula – at the bottom point of the scapula (shoulder blade).

In all cases take care not to include muscle in the callipers.

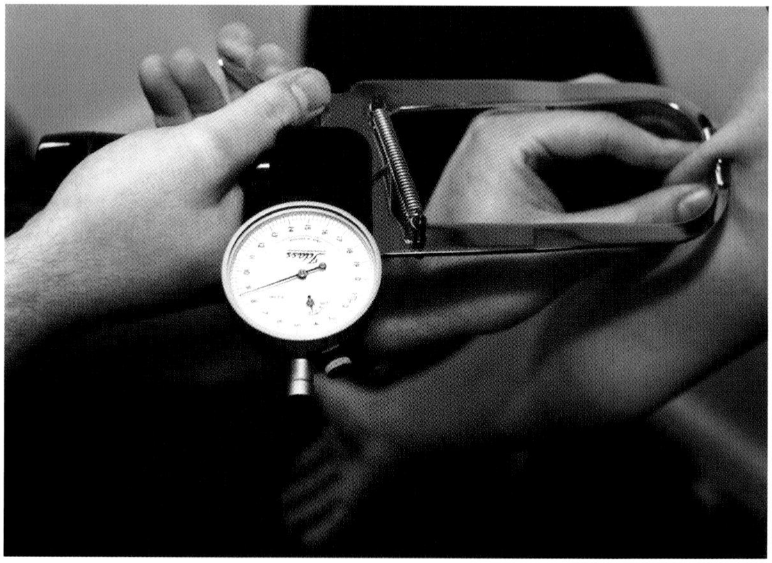

Skin-fold calliper being used to measure the amount of fat at the biceps area.

Measuring bones

Measuring bones gives the size of bones in relationship to the muscle and fat levels of the body. The places to measure are the elbow and knee joints.

For the elbow:

- Flex the biceps until the joint is at right angles.
- Use a condyle calliper to measure across the elbow at the widest point. This is a condyle measurement of the humerus.

Active Challenge

Using the same method as above write how you would take the condyle measurement of the femur.

Measuring muscles

This measurement is taken, in centimetres, of a muscle while it is flexed and at its widest point. The muscles measured are the biceps (upper front arm) and gastrocnemius (back lower leg, commonly known as the calf muscle).

Taking a biceps girth reading:

- Hold the humerus horizontally.
- Flex the biceps so arm is at right angles.
- Take measurement around widest part in centimetres.

Taking a gastrocnemius girth reading:

- Stand with feet slightly apart.
- Flex gastrocnemius by standing on toes.
- Take measurement around widest part in centimetres.

Active Challenge

Measure your partner's flexed biceps.

Age

Training improves control over the body and so it may be argued that the longer a person has participated in an activity, the better they become. This is not always the case: certain activities, like gymnastics, are better performed when younger. This is because the body at this time is more flexible and more able to complete complex moves. Some sports, however, may need more experience, better-developed muscles and stronger bones to achieve good results. Training will improve the body systems, but the type and duration of training should be geared to the correct age group or the exercise can be dangerous and harmful to the exerciser.

Ageing affects the body in the following ways:

- Arteries become less elastic, reducing blood flow to the working muscles, making it difficult for the blood to reach the working areas.
- Less oxygen is carried to the body as the cardiac output is reduced, so tiring the exerciser.
- Muscles get smaller, so strength is lost.
- As a person becomes older there is an increase in the development of slow twitch muscle fibres and so reaction time is affected.
- Body fat builds up due to exercising less and eating the same or more. The extra weight tires the performer quicker.
- Joints become less flexible and so it becomes increasingly difficult to perform with the correct technique.

Key Terms:

Blood doping ► method of increasing the oxygen-carrying capacity of the blood

Drugs ► substances (other than food) which have a physiological effect when taken into the body

Fatigue ► extreme tiredness resulting in the body's inability to complete a task

Masking agent ► a legal substance for a sport, hiding the presence of an illegal one

Performance-enhancing drugs ► substances that artificially improve personal characteristics and performance

Skin-fold calliper ► a device that measures the thickness of a fold of skin with its underlying layer of fat

Somatotype ► particular body type or shape of an individual

Summary

Taking drugs has an effect on the body and mind of a person. Some of these effects are useless to the sportsperson. However, through research, some drugs are seen to have a beneficial effect on performance. Some sportspeople are tempted to break the rules of the governing bodies as they see only the rewards of their drug abuse. By taking drugs the health of the performer can be seriously endangered. Regulations and procedures are put in place by the governing bodies of each sport to help and guide the performer to make an ethical choice. The sporting authorities want athletes to be safe, sport to have a good name and competition to remain fair.

Somatotype

This is the shape and body composition of an individual. The tissue ratio can be changed by adapting the type of diet consumed and exercise undertaken. However, extreme diets can badly affect the health of an individual. Certain somatotypes are better suited to some sports than others; shape may encourage a person to make a natural choice to take part in a particular activity.

Psychological Factors

What you will learn about in this section

1. Response to Training and Competition
2. Motivation
3. Personality and Sport
4. The Role of Aggression in Sport
5. The Importance of Feedback in Learning
6. Open and Closed Skills

1 Response to Training and Competition

The feelings of stress, tension and pressure can all affect the performance of a player. However, experiencing these psychological feelings can have a positive effect by helping some players bring an edge to their performance. Often, the bigger the competition or game, the greater the effect on the individual or team.

Stress is similar to tension. Positive thinking sportspeople will turn what can be seen as a negative feeling into a positive one by declaring this as the 'buzz' they get. Being stressed can have the effect of making the performer more alert and able to react better to situations. Although, too much stress can lower levels of performance. For example, a tennis player may be so affected that they are unable to play successful shots, which in turn affects their confidence. A downward spiral of worse play can then follow.

Tension can happen at any time before an event: minutes, hours, days before it is scheduled. This may badly affect training or performance. Some players, however, need this tension in order to bring the best out of their play. When a lot is at stake, like the final of a major competition, the importance of the occasion may make or break a player's performance.

Before a match, players feel tension; this can give an edge to their play.

Pressure on a player may come about due to the particular game, the other team, the crowd or the particular play in the match. Keeping calm and being able to adapt to the pressure is a sign of a champion. It can give the edge to a player, making them more determined. Others may crack under the pressure, as it is just too much for them to handle. In a game example there may be little time left and a team needs to hold onto a 1–0 lead, so they are said to soak up the pressure of the other team's efforts.

Anxiety results from worrying about an event. Too much worry can make a player perform badly. However, if a player felt nothing about the game then they may have a poor game; some players need to feel some anxiety to put an edge to their play.

Boredom, generally, leads to poor performance, lack of concentration and the performer having little or no focus in the event. It is important, therefore, to keep the training sessions fun, different, lively, challenging and relevant. The competition should challenge the player or team at the appropriate level – if it is too easy, then concentration will be lost and players may not take the game seriously; too hard and the struggle may seem too much and players may stop trying.

When competition comes around a player will feel excited. It is important that they keep control of the level of excitement so it does not have a negative effect on success. For many competitors, having the right mental approach is where an event is won or lost. Competitors need to spend time **focusing** on the event and **visualing** the dersired outcome. The external pressures on a person to do well are great and the tension and anxiety of the moment need to be controlled.

Task 1

What to do:

State the positive and negative effects on the performer that may result from an important game. Think about the following:

- crowd
- opposition
- the importance of the game
- personal desire to do well.

2 Motivation

Players can be motivated in many ways. They know why they are competing – personal pride, will to win, need to be a winner, want to be the best. These are all internal or intrinsic motivating factors. There are also external or extrinsic motivators. These are outside factors making people do well. For the top-class performer they can take the form of financial reward, public acclaim, winning the best competitions, fame or a better lifestyle. For school or club players having results announced in assemblies, receiving certificates, achieving awards and winning trophies all have a motivational effect.

Goal-setting

When a player or coach sets out a plan, it prepares the participant for performance both mentally and physically. The plan sets out stages for physical achievement in certain time limits. If the goals are met then they can have a positive effect on the performer's mental approach. A player can gain confidence about their performance, which reduces the amount of anxiety for a competition – linked with the thought of failure – this will help them perform well.

A coach may use the following method to motivate the performer in training:

SMARTER

S – goals must be **specific**

M – training targets should be **measurable**

A – goals should be **adjustable**

R – goals must be **realistic**

T – training targets should be **time-based**

E – goals should be challenging and **exciting**

R – goals should be **recorded**

What to do:

1. Write three sentences on each of the following:
   - How players motivate themselves in a game.
   - How the coach helps the performer.
2. List ways your school rewards efforts in sport and list how professional sportspeople are rewarded. Some rewards may be similar so underline them.

3 Personality and Sport

People all have different personalities and playing a sport can sometimes bring out the best or worst in a person's personality. At one extreme there are introverts, those people who are always quiet and rarely add to a conversation; then there are extroverts, people who hog the limelight and are invariably the centre of attention. Different sports can attract both personality types (introverts and extroverts).

The introverted personality could lend itself to individual sports, as this type can be self-motivated. Extroverts like to be in the company of others and are often leaders, so team games may suit them. There may also be roles within a team suiting extroverts rather than introverts. Being a captain can suit an extrovert as they are required to give instructions and call the play to their teammates.

Extroverts are often leaders. Here, Roy Keane shouts to his teammates.

Active Challenge

Discuss with a partner possible sports, or positions in a team, favouring introvert or extrovert characters.

4 The Role of Aggression in Sport

In most sports there is an element of aggression required in order to win. This is very evident in sports where there are two teams, or opposite players, in competition against each other. Aggression in sport takes two forms – indirect and direct.

In contact sports direct aggression is essential.

Indirect aggression

This type of aggression comes about when there is no actual contact with the opposition. When playing volleyball or tennis the aggression comes when an object, in these cases the ball, is forcibly propelled into the opposition's court in such a way as to seek the best advantage.

Direct aggression

This relates to sports where there is bodily contact between the players. Tackling in rugby and throwing an opponent in judo use this type of aggression. In these examples the force, produced by the players, is made directly on the opponent's body.

Active Challenge

Make a list of sports where there is direct and indirect aggression.

5 The Importance of Feedback in Learning

In order for participants in sport to improve performance they have to adapt to the feedback gathered from previous competition and training. Without a response to feedback, little or no improvement can be made. There are several ways feedback can affect the performer.

Intrinsic feedback

This type of feedback is made by the performer themself. It is made in the brain in direct response to the performer's own movement. They judge how well the skills or play is going. It is a continual assessment made at the time of the event and is based on how well the players feel or sense they are performing.

Extrinsic feedback

This is a form of external feedback given to the performer while the activity is being undertaken. It deals with how the player's sight and sound is affected. It may be the sound of a ball being struck, telling the performer how hard the shot will be and so influencing the movement in the game. It may be the sight of the direction of the ball influencing the position of the feet on the field of play.

Knowledge of results

This is feedback made at the end of the game, reviewing the success of the outcome or particular parts of the play. It can be made verbally by a coach or teacher, or even by looking at a video of the event. Detailed analysis can pinpoint areas to work on in preparation for the next game. Analysing the unsuccessful parts of the performance gives negative feedback and analysing successful performance gives positive feedback. By adapting to this feedback the training programme may change so that next time in the activity the weaknesses are not so marked and the strengths emphasised.

Point Won	Serve	Baseline	Net
Player A	18	25	7
Player B	17	32	6

An example of feedback that may be given showing points won during a game of tennis.

What to do:

1. Make a list of examples, from different sports, of the three types of feedback – intrinsic, extrinsic and knowledge of results.
2. Add to your list the name of the sport, the type of feedback and the form it takes.

6 Open and Closed Skills

Skills can be divided into those that have only one outcome and those where the outcome is unpredictable. Games generally use open skills but there are times when closed skills are necessary for success.

Open skills have many solutions and influencing factors. In general team play, the skills required are open. This means that the player has to adapt the skills to suit the situation. The player must have a good command of basic skills and be able to adapt them to the conditions, opposition, weather and the weight of the oncoming ball.

Open skills are those where there are many outcomes to play. An attacker attempting to dribble the ball around an approaching opposition has to use open skills. The player has to perform the dribble whilst watching where the opposition is, how fast they are approaching, how near they are to the goal or other teammates to pass to and adapt the dribble to available space.

Closed skills have necessary skills to put into practice to gain success. There is no interference with the skill. The weather, other players and a moving ball, for instance, are not an issue for success.

Closed skills have one outcome. These skills can be seen in gymnastic vaulting. The gymnast has practised the skill, the floor is a regulation standard, there is no change in the environment and there are no other people influencing the execution of the skill. There are certain times in team games where there is the need for a closed skill. Taking a basketball free throw is an example. The player is always the same distance away from the basket, the basket is always the same height and there are no environmental influences.

Indoor tennis demonstrates closed skills as there are no external influences on the shot. Here, Venus Williams is playing an indoor game of tennis.

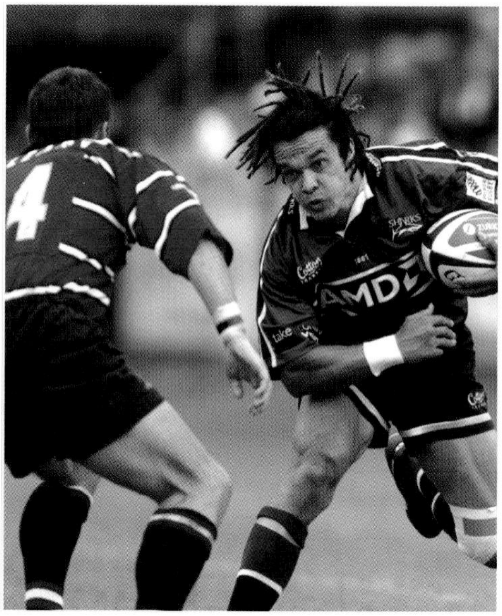

Rugby player Vaughan Going avoiding an oncoming tackle from Darren O'Leary shows an open skill.

Task 4

What to do:

1. Describe fully three open skills and three closed skills. Link them with a game and say at what point of the game they would occur.

Key Terms:

- **Closed skill** ► skill unaffected by external factors
- **Extrinsic feedback** ► external information gathered by the performer, based on what they see or hear, at the time of the action
- **Focusing** ► blocking out other thoughts and concentrating on the performance only
- **Intrinsic feedback** ► internal information gathered by the performer at the time of the action about how they feel the performance is going
- **Mental rehearsal** ► going through the activity in the mind
- **Open skill** ► skill which is affected by external factors and where there are many possible outcomes
- **Visualise** ► create positive mental pictures of the successful attempt prior to actual execution

Prior to an event athletes focus and block out all noise as they listen for the starting gun.

Summary

There are many personality types in sport. A person may choose a particular sport, event or position in a team because it suits their character. For a performer to do their best both body and mind should be trained to compete. In an important competition, spectators or the opposition may all play a part in making the challenge more difficult. By controlling thoughts before and during the event the player can use certain techniques, such as visualising, to help keep their physical performance at a peak. A person training can be kept motivated by knowing the plan and seeing where on the plan they are. It is important to use the feedback after training or after a big event to readjust the schedule for improvement in the future.

For games players to do their best the correct skills training should be followed, starting with basic individual skills, moving on to team play and then practice with the opposition. The top performers need to be able to adapt their skills to the situation at hand. Most team game sports involve open skills where this adaptability is vital although there are times in a game where a closed skill, like a penalty shot for instance, is necessary. Some sports, such as gymnastics, totally rely on the ability to repeat closed skills consistently and to a high level of technical accuracy in order to succeed.

Technological Developments

What you will learn about in this section

1 Equipment
2 Materials
3 Improved Facilities
4 Safety Factors
5 Teaching and Training Aids
6 Information Communication Technology (ICT)
7 Technological Advances

Technology is the link between science and sport. By identifying the different aspects of a sport and seeing possible routes for its improvement, scientists use their expertise to advance the activity in some way. Technological improvements, however, are limited by the rules laid out by the governing bodies of the sports.

1 Equipment

Pole vault

There is no restriction on the length of the pole or the material it is made from. Throughout the history of the event poles have been made from wood, bamboo, glass fibre and, most recently, carbon fibre. All the changes have brought about marked increases in the heights achieved. The transition between bamboo and glass fibre brought about the most improvement.

Javelin

The rules for javelin are strict and clear. They control the length, weight and where the central mass should be. The controls have to be strict as the distances thrown had increased by so much that by 1984 the full length of the stadium was reached, putting the spectators in a dangerous position. The result was that the javelin had to be redesigned to underperform. This was done by moving the centre of mass forward so the javelin would land sooner.

South African Okkert Brits won a gold medal for the pole vault event at the 2002 Commonwealth Games.

Cycling

Many improvements to the equipment have been made in cycling. Track bikes have no gears, breaks or free-wheeling. To stop, the rider just has to gradually slow down, naturally. The bike is made up of parts made from aluminium or carbon fibre. The frame design has a teardrop shape making it more aerodynamic and faster. The new wheels are flatter and more aerodynamic (they have no spokes) and can sometimes be solid discs.

Netherlands' Leontien Zijlaard on her way to winning gold at the Sydney Olympics 2000.

Russia's Raisa Obodovskaya won a gold medal at the World Cycling Championships in 1968.

Look at the differences technology has made to track cycling.

Tennis rackets

Modern rackets, for all racket sports, now use graphite rather than wood or aluminium as they used in the past. The high-tech, lightweight, carbon-fibre rackets were developed for tennis. The resulting play was so fast that serve domination made the rallies too short and less entertaining. To combat this, a bigger, slower tennis ball has been introduced. The bounce of these tennis balls gives an extra 16 milliseconds of reaction time from a 150mph service. This has the effect of increasing and lengthening the number of rallies in the game and so increases the entertainment value. Some rackets combine a large 'sweet spot' or contact point with a smaller head, so that it can move through the air quicker and therefore generate more power in the shot.

2 Materials

An athlete is always looking for ways to improve their performance. In recent years clothing for different sports has been developed to enhance performance where possible. One-armed tennis tops reduce the restriction of the racket arm, body suits for swimming reduce water resistance and new suit designs for sprinters and javelin throwers all contribute to performance-enhancing sportswear. The standards are so high that the athlete must attempt to gain as much advantage as possible within the rules laid out by the governing bodies.

The Lycra Power® material used in sports clothing can be a great aid to the performer. The elastic quality of the material acts as a spring to the working muscles, allowing them to achieve the same results but by not working so hard and so tiring less quickly. It is claimed that performance can be raised by as much as 12% when using this Lycra product in some sports.

Ian Thorpe wears a Lycra® swimming suit.

Footwear

The type of footwear for each activity is a specialised piece of equipment. Changes are made to improve the fit, traction, durability, cushioning, lightweight performance and specific action of the event. There have been 78 different patents for football boots since 1990, each attempting to help the players with ball control, comfort, support, power and accuracy in the kicks and shots. New features are valuable commodities and have patents on them. Two such features include 'elastomer', which deforms on contact with the ball, giving greater ball control, and stiffened raised inner soles, ensuring the total force from a powerful shot can be transmitted to the ball.

3 Improved Facilities

The current trend is to build facilities especially for a certain sport. Previously the sports had to adapt to the buildings they used. Facilities now have the correct playing surface, specialised safety areas (like landing pits for gymnastics) and outdoor areas are often all-weather, making the facility available all year round.

The Manchester Velodrome is the best facility in the country for track cycling. It will hopefully improve the current national standards by attracting greater interest and participation. The 250m track has been especially designed with high banks; the exit curves are steeper than those on entry to maximise speed allowing the riders to use gravitational pull when travelling at top speeds.

A new era of stadium was seen in the Japan and Korea World Cup in 2002. The architects of Sapporo Dome Stadium came up with a truly remarkable feat of engineering. A roof was built that could open and close, to let light into the stadium, and the pitch was built outside, in the sunlight. The pitch is moved into the stadium only when matches are being played. The pitch is elevated by a cushion of compressed air and moved into the stadium prior to a match. The stands then rotate so that they are as close to the pitch as possible.

The pitch of the Sapporo Dome Stadium is stored outside and is moved into the dome for matches.

4 Safety Factors

Safety in sport is extremely important for both the participants and the spectators. For the public, older facilities have been upgraded and new stadiums provide seats for all spectators, making watching the event safer. Often new facilities are built away from the towns, so road access is easier and safer too.

Landing areas In athletics, the higher the jumps the athletes achieve, the better the landing areas have to be. A safe landing area gives the athlete the confidence to perform their activity in the knowledge that their landing will be safe.

Gymnastics requires safe landing areas too. In training, the performers attempt new tricks and moves so they need to be confident that landing areas are safe so that they will not injure themselves when they fall. Specially designed pits, filled with foam cushioning, give the gymnast this confidence.

Safer footwear Improved stud design on rugby and football boots help the player to stop and change direction with a lessened risk of tearing knee ligaments.

Shoulder pads for rugby Research has been done at Limerick Rugby Club by using a special scrum machine. This machine is an inflatable bag that the players push against and the forces generated are measured. This assesses how wearing padding can make players tackle harder and more confidently, safe in the knowledge that they have less risk of injury.

5 Teaching and Training Aids

Studies and developments are being made all of the time to improve the teaching and coaching aids in sport. These combine the skills of design, science, engineering, sport and safety together. Each sport has its own group of training aids focusing on a particular aspect of the game. In volleyball, for example, the skills of blocking, digging and spiking all have training aids designed to develop these areas. Vertical jumping is important in volleyball when blocking and spiking so equipment is made to increase that skill.

Not all training aids need to be very advanced. Here, boxing champion Sugar Ray Leonard hits the hand pads as his trainer offers resistance.

Video cameras

Recording a performance on video and replaying the action can help give feedback to the performer. Aspects of the game or activity such as positional play, technique and effectiveness can be played back at normal speed, in slow motion or freeze-framed to focus directly on certain parts of the play.

Active Challenge

Think of the teaching aids you have seen used in sport. This might be in school, a club or from the television. Discuss them with a partner.

Heart rate monitor

Heart rate monitors give an instant feedback on the intensity of the exercise. This can help the coach plan the training programme and the information provided can boost the athlete psychologically. The coach can download the reading and study the printed-out tables and charts at a later time. Interpreting the information that the monitors provide can guard against fatigue and prevent overtraining. For the triathlete, the monitors can record the different heart rates in the three disciplines of their sport, which again can be used to adapt training programmes. Some monitors can show calorie expenditure in relation to the exercise; this is useful for planning dietary requirements for the athlete.

6 Information Communication Technology (ICT)

Websites

Top clubs, governing bodies and sports organisations have websites. These provide up-to-date information on their sport, including results, training methods and new innovations.

CD-ROMs

These are readily available on a variety of sports and help with training and coaching skills of the game.

Computer links improve performance

New technology allows a training session to be recorded via video and then played back on a laptop. This allows immediate feedback to the player on their performance and technique.

7 Technological Advances

Hawkeye

This technology is used in televised cricket. It gives an image of the crease and the line of the ball's flight. It shows where the ball would have actually gone in relation to the stumps. It is also used to show the line of the stumps so if the ball pitches in the area (coloured red on the screen) it shows whether a delivery is eligible for a leg before wicket (LBW) decision.

Referees' two-way radios

In the USA, American football referees have a radio receiver, which they use to communicate with other officials and then announce publicly to the spectators the decision made. Similar innovations were tried in the Premiership in 1999, but with little success.

The offside trap

In Norway, companies have been developing systems to help the assistant referee with offside decisions, as it was found that many were wrong. The ex-Arsenal player, Kenny Sansom, has been involved in encouraging the Football Association to trial the system at England Youth level. The system is called Reference Point System (RPS) and uses prismatic lights to show the players' positions.

LCD

On a racing bike an LCD box fixed to the handlebars records the amount of power and effort used by the cyclist. After the training or race it is linked to a laptop computer and the information is downloaded to help assess the performance.

Timing devices

Timing of athletic events has become more sophisticated as the difference between the athletes becomes less.

- In the 1972 Munich Olympics timers could measure one-hundredth of a second and were linked to the start and finish.
- At the 1980 Winter Olympics first- and second-placed competitors could be split by one-hundredth of a second.
- At the Sydney Olympics 2000, sophisticated digital and computer linked equipment ensured accuracy in competitors' times and results.

Sophisticated photographs can decide the finishing positions of competitors.

Active Challenge

Discuss as a group changes that you know have been made to equipment in sport. Start with the examples from the text, then think of some of your own. Debate what is good and bad about technological developments.

Summary

As new, specialised facilities are built, more athletes have the benefit of using them. The best facilities often attract the best coaches and so higher standards can be achieved. New products help to boost past results so better times are run, further throws are achieved and greater distances are jumped. It can be the case that some skills are lost due to advances in technology. Long-distance runners can use pacing monitors in order to keep to their race plan. Devices like these reduce the need for pacing skills and can make the event too clinical.

Sometimes the technology can be the factor that helps the athlete to win. Some say that the same technology should be available to all, at the same time, ensuring that the ability, skills and hard work of the performer are the reasons for victory.

Risk Assessment and First Aid

What you will learn about in this section

1. Minor Injuries
2. Common Injuries
3. Major Injuries
4. Head and Awareness Problems
5. Dangers from the Environment

There are minor and major risks of injury involved with most sports. There is less risk of injury in sports where teams stay on their side of a net, like volleyball and badminton. The risks increase in contact sports where players invade the territory of the other team. The rules and nature of the sport may present safety problems. The weather may play a part in increasing the risk or technical problems may occur.

The following pages contain the procedures for dealing with a series of injuries. Only trained and qualified first aid and medical personnel should deal with serious injuries.

Expert training cannot always prevent injury.

The nature of the game can cause injuries.

1 Minor Injuries

All people who take part in sport will occasionally suffer from minor injuries. They are easy to deal with and treat: using a combination of ice, antiseptic wipes, plasters and dressing is enough. It is important to treat injuries quickly to prevent them from becoming worse.

The minor injuries ready reckoner

Bruises	Cuts	Abrasions/Grazes	Blisters
soft tissue skin damage	soft tissue skin damage	soft tissue skin damage	soft tissue skin damage
How it happens			
impact with equipment, floor or player	studs, collision with sharp object	skin rubs against rough surface	continual rubbing of skin against another surface
When it might happen			
during a tackle, landing or interception	during a tackle	fall, sliding tackle, on Astroturf, friction with other objects on ground, against a wall (squash)	badly fitting boots, running on hard surfaces
Where it could happen			
muscles of the body	on the surface of the skin	on the surface of the skin	on heels from shoes rubbing, hands rowing or drawing bow in archery or using asymmetric bars
Effect on the body			
blood vessels damaged beneath the surface = bruise, colour goes blue/purple to green/yellow	bleeding	pain at injury, grit can often enter the wound, top layer of skin removed	thin bubbles of salty liquid form under the skin
What to do			
put ice on the injured area, reducing swelling	clean and dress with plaster, add bandage if a bad cut, if worse go to hospital	clean wound and dress	keep the blister intact, as this is a natural, sterile covering; below the blister there is another layer of skin forming to replace the upper one; if blister is likely to be damaged a dressing should be applied that more than covers the area
How to avoid			
avoid collisions and wear protective clothing	wear protective clothing, check equipment, check players for jewellery and long fingernails	wear protective clothing	wear correctly fitting footwear; wear in new boots, spikes or trainers gradually; wear thick, correctly-sized socks; check feet and dress to prevent skin damage

Task 1

What to do:

1. Write a paragraph about each of the following injuries:
   a. bruise
   b. cut
   c. blister
   d. graze.

> Use the headings from the table on page 135 to help you make sentences.

2 Common Injuries

These injuries are more complex than minor injuries. Although some can be dealt with using basic first aid, some injuries may need expert treatment. Strains and pulls affect the soft tissues of the body; tennis or golf elbow affects the joints.

Use the RICE procedure to treat soft tissue injuries. Each initial stands for part of the treatment.

Rest the injured part.

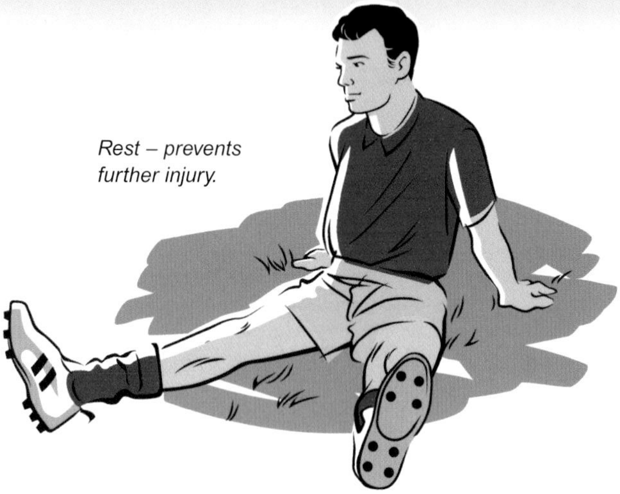

Rest – prevents further injury.

Ice – apply ice to the injured part to stop the swelling and help the pain.

Ice – applied for 10-minute periods stops swelling, pain and flow of blood to area.

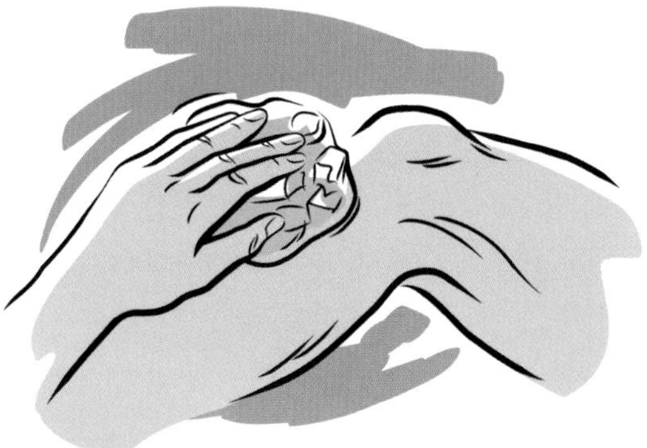

Compression – put a bandage around the injured area for support and to stop swelling.

Compression – the bandage is just tight enough to reduce internal bleeding and swelling.

Elevate – lift the injured part to restrict the blood flow to the area and reduce swelling and painful throbbing.

Elevation – raising injured area above level of the heart lowers internal bleeding and stops swelling and throbbing. In some instances raising an injured part slightly is enough to reduce any pressure on it.

Strain (pulled muscle) – soft tissue injury

How it happens – overstretching of the muscles

When it happens – twist or wrench of the muscle

Where it happens – muscles of the body

Effects on the body – may be weakened as a result

What to do – use RICE

How to avoid – warm-up thoroughly; but it is difficult to avoid when an activity requires the performer to contract and relax a muscle quickly

Sprain – soft tissue injury

How it happens – ankle or wrist joint twisted suddenly

When it happens – changing direction or landing badly

Where it happens – at the ankle or wrist joint

Effects on the body – tears ligaments at a joint and is extremely painful

What to do – use RICE; if more severe can look like a fracture or dislocation so treat as such and have an x-ray

How to avoid – improve the strength of the area; sometimes it is difficult to avoid

Tennis elbow – overuse injury

How it happens – too much use of the tendons

When it happens – playing tennis or golf; playing with a racket with the wrong-sized handle

Where it happens – at the elbow joint

Effects on the body – **inflamed** elbow joint

What to do – use RICE or seek medical advice

How to avoid – choose the correct-sized equipment; moderate the amount of play

What to do:

Write out the following paragraphs, filling in the gaps as you go.

1. Strains and sprains are examples of ______________ __________ ___________. Strains are to do with _______________ and sprains are to do with _____________ and ___________. Each occurs when rigorous over____________ and twisting take place. __________ too far to reach a ball in tennis or ____________ at speed in basketball can cause these problems.
2. Both injuries are treated using the RICE procedure. The initials stand for ______, ice, ___________ and elevation. The reason to rest the injured part is so that no further___________ is done. By putting ice on the injury it _________________ the ________________. ________________ the part also stops the swelling as does elevating the injured part which stops the ______________ too.
3. Tennis and golf elbow affect the ______________ attaching the muscle to the bone at the elbow. This can be caused by playing the sport _______ __________ and by using the _________________ equipment. Again, RICE is the treatment for this injury.

These injuries require expert treatment. Some need surgery, others need special **convalescence**. Such injuries happen when stresses on the body are too much for it to handle. This might be because of changing direction at speed, the impact of another player or collision with equipment. Shock can often result as a reaction, of the casualty or a bystander, after witnessing a major injury.

Applying pressure to the cut reduces the loss of blood.

Deep cuts

If there is a large or deep cut to the skin, hospital treatment may be necessary. Pressure should be placed on the cut in an attempt to stop the loss of blood. The area of the cut should be elevated. If the blood is pulsating, like the beat of the heart, it indicates that an artery has been damaged. This is a serious condition and an ambulance should be called immediately.

Torn cartilage - soft tissue injury

A torn cartilage happens when a joint is twisted excessively. A player is prone to doing this when changing direction or pivoting at speed. A common area for this injury is at the knee joint. When it happens it is extremely painful when the joint is moved. Treatment for this is RICE. An operation may be necessary in severe cases. Due to the nature of the game this injury is common in footballers. It is hard to avoid an injury of this kind, especially in competitive matches.

Dislocation - hard tissue injury

A **dislocation** occurs when the joint is moved outside its designed range. A forceful blow can move the joint out of position. All major joints are vulnerable. When it happens the joint looks deformed, it may be very painful and the person will have no control over the movement in that area. In these cases the person should be made comfortable, the joint immobilised and medical help found quickly. Do not attempt to put the joint back into place. Strength training exercises for the muscles and tissues around the joints will help prevent this happening.

Fractures - hard tissue injury

Fractures occur when an excessive impact or force is put on the bone. This can happen with a blow or a twist. When a bone is fractured, the limb becomes immobile and there is extreme pain. The area is tender and there may be swelling, leading to bruising. The fractured area immediately looks deformed. Fractures are difficult to avoid, as they are a result of spur of the moment accidents. Keeping to the rules of the game and not tackling recklessly reduce the risk of injury.

Open/compound fracture

The broken end of a bone comes through the skin. This causes complications as there is a risk of infection from germs entering where the skin is damaged.

Closed/simple fracture

The break of the bone is under the skin.

In rugby, because of the upper body impact of tackling and falling on an outstretched hand a fracture of the clavicle is a common injury. When this happens the casualty may automatically cradle the arm on the injured side under the elbow. They may lean their head to the injured side too.

The impact of two legs meeting with force in a football tackle can cause a fracture. The tibia and fibula (lower leg bones) are the most common leg bones to fracture. If both are broken, the limb will rotate and have an angle at the point of the fracture. If the tibia (shin bone) is broken then there is a possibility that the fracture will be open.

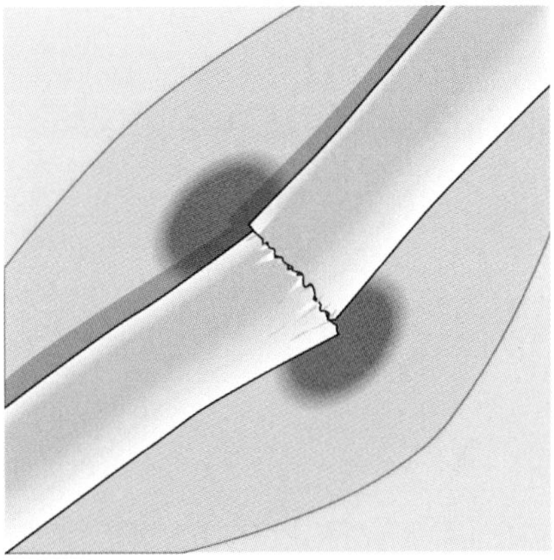

Closed fracture of the tibia.

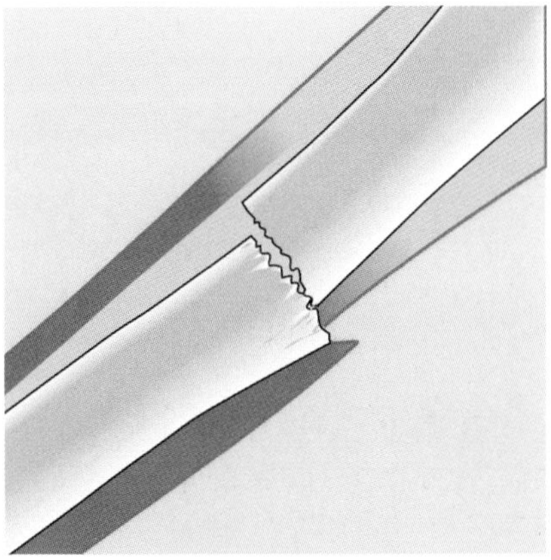

Open fracture of the tibia.

Medical help should be sent for immediately and the casualty should be made comfortable and kept warm without moving the injured part.

There are several types of fracture, each differing due to the age of the bone and the type of impact, blow or pressure placed on it.

Greenstick

A pressure or impact buckles or bends a bone but only partially breaks it. This fracture is common in the developing bones of young children, whose bones are quite springy.

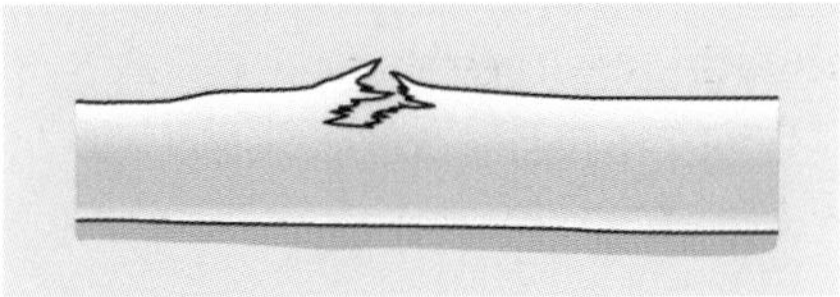

Transverse

This fracture is the result of a direct blow made at a right angle to a bone, resulting in a break straight across. The name relates to the direction of the break in the bone.

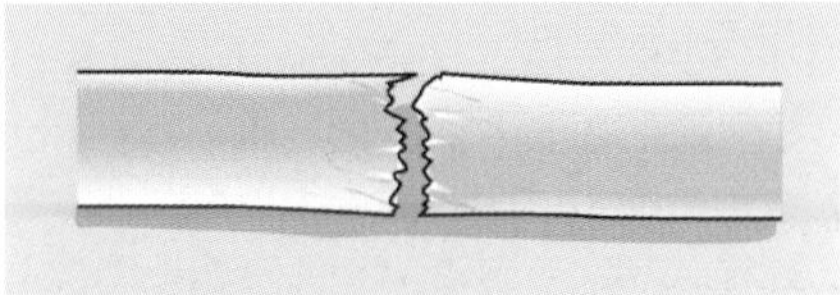

Impacted

In this fracture the two ends of bone are firmly shoved together causing it to fracture. The ends of the bone are misaligned, but pressed together.

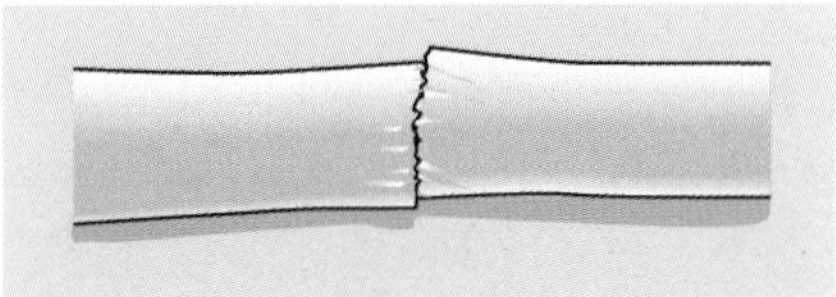

Comminuted

Here an impact causes a bone to splinter, resulting in more than two pieces of bone at the site of the injury. This fracture is usually the result of a direct blow on a bone.

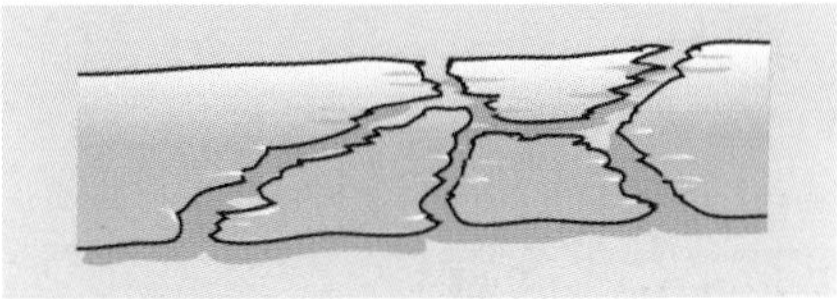

Oblique/Spiral

Here the direction of the fracture is diagonal to the length of a bone. It happens when there is a twisting movement along the bone's length, for example if a foot is trapped and the leg twists.

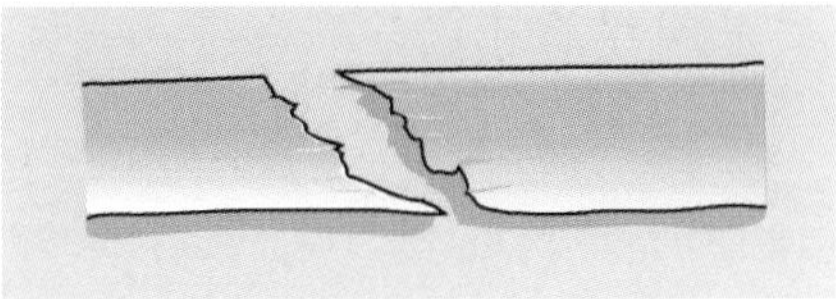

Active Challenge

With a partner, think of sporting occasions where participation might result in the above fractures happening.

Key Terms:

Compound/Open fracture ► break of the bone when the skin is broken
Convalescence ► period of time when body is rested to aid recovery
Dislocate ► joints moved out of their normal arrangement
Inflamed ► reddened and swollen
Simple/Closed fracture ► break of the bone when the skin is not broken

Shock – primary

How it happens – in reaction to a traumatic event
When it happens – after witnessing an emotional or traumatic event
Where it happens – at the site of the incident
How to avoid – avoid known causes

Shock – true shock

How it happens – in reaction to injury
When it happens – after serious injury, usually bad cut or fracture
Where it happens – at the site of the accident
How to avoid – difficult to avoid
Effects on the body – pale complexion, quick pulse, cold and clammy skin, **nausea**, thirsty, feeling faint, restlessness, quick gasps for air, aggression, possibly unconsciousness
What to do – send for medical help, lay person down, lift legs higher than head as this helps the flow of blood to the brain, loosen tight clothing, keep a good air flow around them, keep checking breathing and pulse; if unconscious put in the recovery position

Task 3

What to do:

1. Create a matrix for the medical conditions torn cartilage, dislocation, fracture and shock.

Use the minor injuries ready reckoner to help.

4 Head and Awareness Problems

There are several causes of unconsciousness. In sport, too much stress on the body systems can cause a heart attack or a stroke, which lead to losing consciousness. There may be an impact on the head or blockage of the windpipe. Any blow to the head is serious. Concussion may result and the effects may only become evident some time after the incident. Medical advice is always necessary.

Recovery position

The purpose of the recovery position is to make the casualty comfortable, safe from falling and further injury, able to breathe clearly and safe from choking. It is used on unconscious casualties.

- The chin is lifted to keep airway clear; hand supports head.
- The arm and leg are bent to make position stable.
- The chest is flat on ground, so breathing is easier.

Unconsciousness

How it happens– a blow to the head, heart attack, fainting, stroke, shock, asphyxia
When it happens – impact with another player, raising the pulse too high, blocking or compressing the windpipe
Where it happens – affects the whole body
Effects on the body – a state of unwakening sleep
What to do – send for medical help and place in the recovery position
How to avoid – wear protective equipment and take care in the sport

Emergency procedures

If the casualty has lost consciousness, a sequence of actions should be followed to deal with the situation. Send for medical help. In the time it takes for this help to arrive, put the 'DR ABC' sequence into operation.

Danger

Are you or the casualty in danger?

Response

Is the casualty conscious?

Airway

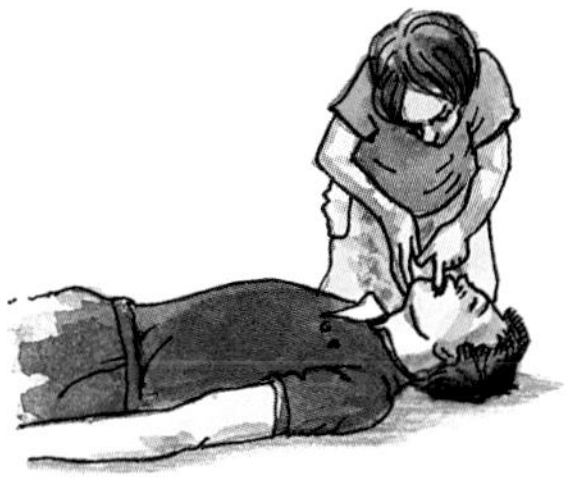

Is the casualty's airway open? Check there is no blockage of the airway. This may be vomit from the person or another obstacle. Clear the mouth if there is a blockage.

Breathing

Is the casualty breathing? **Look** for the rise and fall of the chest. **Listen** for sounds of breathing. **Feel** for breath on your cheek or condensation on a mirror. If not, apply MMV. If breathing, place in the recovery position.

Circulation

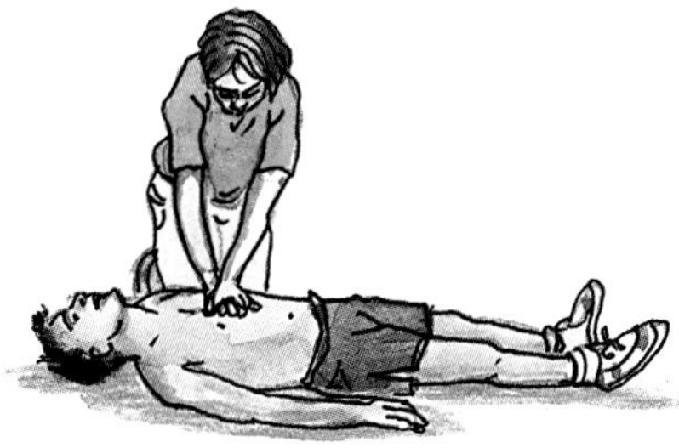

Can you feel the casualty's pulse? If there is a pulse, place in the recovery position. If not, administer CPR.

Active Challenge

With a partner, study the illustrations above. Now test each other on the meaning of and procedure for DR ABC.

Concussion

How it happens – blow to the head

When it happens – games play, physical contact sports, from slipping and falling

Where it happens – head or jaw

Effects on the body – shallow breathing, pale complexion, confusion, dizziness, sickness

What to do – place in the recovery position, stay with victim and seek medical advice; rugby players who have suffered from concussion have a period of time when they cannot compete

How to avoid – care in sport, wear safety and protective equipment

5 Dangers from the Environment

The weather can cause a major problem if a team is not equipped to deal with its changes. Its effects are obvious in adventurous sports, like mountaineering and sailing, but problems can occur even in regular team games situations. The answer is to prepare for possible changes and adapt plans to suit the situation. It is better to prevent the problem happening than have to deal with it.

Hypothermia – extreme environmental injury

How it happens – a rapid drop in the inner core temperature of the body (lungs, heart, brain) below 35°C. The loss of heat from the body is related to the size of the individual and the environment. Generally the bigger a person is, the slower the heat loss. The colder and windier the air the greater the heat loss. Therefore, children will tend to lose heat more quickly and suffer from hypothermia more quickly.

When it happens – activity in a cold, wet and windy environment when the energy required is more than the energy available.

Where it happens – any cold environment, hostile mountain areas, sea, river or lake.

Effects on the body – shivering, pale complexion, dry complexion, pulse rate could be slower than normal, shallow breathing, behaviour may be irrational, state of confusion, lack of energy leading to unconsciousness.

What to do – if the casualty is responsive try to make them more mobile, but stopping inactivity will have to be matched by energy intake. If the victim is unresponsive send for help and then take them to a sheltered spot and keep their body from the wet ground. Immediate action is necessary to heat the core of the body: replace wet clothes with warm, dry ones; cover the head; provide a sugary, warm drink; give quick energy food like chocolate. Check pulse and breathing regularly. If available, put the victim into a warm bath, not more than 40°C, to warm the body back up gradually.

How to avoid – when the weather is colder, put on layers of warmer clothes. Be aware of the wind chill factor, which often causes hypothermia. Always take the proper equipment and know the safety procedures. Keep an eye on all members of the party to prevent this happening. Long-distance swimmers can use grease to keep the cold out.

Hypothermia starts as shivering.

The sufferer may become abusive.

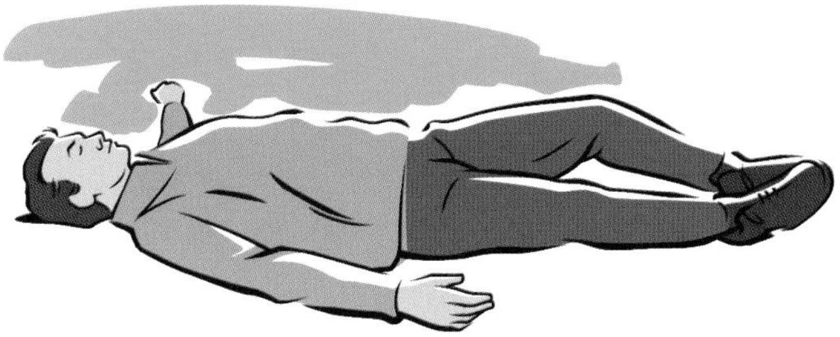

As more heat is lost, the casualty loses consciousness.

Dehydration – extreme environmental injury

How it happens – when there is a rapid loss of water from the body

When it happens – training hard, sweating, breathing out water vapour or passing water and not replenishing the water lost

Where it happens – more common in a hot climate or during an endurance event

Effects on the body – tiredness, sickness and dizziness

What to do – replace lost fluid and salt

How to avoid – keep replacing water loss by drinking regularly, particularly when exercising

What to do:

1. Work with a partner and create a crossword using words that indicate a major injury.

   A list of clues are provided to help get you started.

   1. This happens if the knee is twisted excessively. 4, 9
   2. The C in RICE. 11
   3. The bones do this if they are moved out of their normal arrangement. 9
   4. A place where two or more bones meet. 5
   5. The injured part is ____________ to stop further damage. 8
   6. Type of fracture. 8
   7. A fractured bone may have _______ around it. 8
   8. Immediate action for a fracture – send for an _______ . 9
   9. Can happen as a reaction to witnessing an injury. 5
   10. The pulse can ________ when suffering from shock. 7
   11. A casualty is placed in this when unconscious. 8, 8
   12. A state of unwakening sleep. 15
   13. The C in DR ABC. 11
   14. Can result from a blow to the head. 10
   15. The V in MMV. 11
   16. Condition resulting from rapid heat loss. 11
   17. What a long distance swimmer uses to stop the cold. 6
   18. Condition resulting from lack of water in the body. 11

Key Terms:

Concussion	► injury to the brain that may cause the victim temporarily to lose consciousness
Dehydration	► having an unusually low water content in the body
Emergency procedures	► series of actions to be followed in a crisis
Hypothermia	► condition of the body when its core temperature falls below 35°C
Nausea	► feeling of sickness
Unconsciousness	► state of unawareness, an unwakening sleep

In any competitive sport injuries can occur. Wolverhampton Wanderers' goalkeeper, Mike Stowell, collides with Manchester City's Gareth Taylor.

Summary

There are many injuries that are caused by sport: some in training and some in the game itself. In general, soft tissue injuries, minor cuts and bruises for example, happen frequently and, if treated early, clear up quickly, but if left they can become more serious. Such injuries can usually be treated immediately with basic first aid.

Hard tissue injuries – torn cartilage and broken bones – need specialised medical treatment and a period of rehabilitation so the injury is given time to heal fully and the body will need to return gradually to fitness.

Shock may occur as a reaction to witnessing or suffering an injury. This condition can show at the time of the injury or hours afterwards.

Head injuries should always be treated seriously however minor they seem at the time. Blows to the head may have no immediate effects but could, after time, cause concussion.

Players or performers are sometimes not aware of an injury or condition gradually affecting their bodies, like heat and cold. Knowledge and experience of the event and the effects of the environment are crucial to the well-being of the performer, and preventative measures can be taken to counter the dangers.

Safety and Risk Assessment

What you will learn about in this section

All players have a responsibility to prepare well for their chosen event. By listening to their coach and completing their training programme, they learn the rules and **techniques** of the activity. From experience, they build up an understanding of the risks and hazards of the chosen sport and can learn to avoid them in the competition. The rules help to keep the play safe and prevent unfair play.

1 How to Prepare for Safety in Sport

In contact sports there are rules that keep similar age groups together and that separate the sexes at certain ages. This is an attempt to make the competition even and safe by keeping the experience and strength of the players at a similar level. Different factors are taken into account to ensure a **balanced competition**. These include:

- grading
- skill level
- weight
- age
- sex.

An even match ensures a good competition. France's Christine Cicot and Great Britain's Karina Bryant during the 2000 Olympic Games.

2 Assess the Risks for Self and Others

With any game, competitive activity or adventurous pursuit, there are potential dangers. Participants should be prepared properly for the event and trained for skill, strength and tactics. Coaching, training and experience build up knowledge and an awareness of the sport makes the game safer to play. Some dangers are easier to spot than others. In body contact sports, the risk of injury is plain to see. In racket sports there are dangers too. In squash, for example, the confined area could lead to collisions with the opposition and a squash ball just fits in the eye socket!

Warming up before an event is vital to train the mind and prepare the body and so reduce the risks. Warm-ups in the winter may have to be extended and extra clothes worn to get the body in the correct condition for competition because of the colder temperatures.

Changes in the environment may cause extra risks. Working in the winter will change the way a training session is conducted. The daylight is gone more quickly, so the timing of training may change or be moved indoors. New safety considerations must also be taken into account, as working surfaces may become wet and icy making them slippery to train on. Athletes should be aware of the need to change their footwear to combat the conditions or the session needs to be moved indoors.

In the winter, the standard and condition of facilities may drop; for example, maintenance of **throwing cages** may not be scheduled out of season. Landing areas may not be kept and dug over properly. For athletes training for throwing events, especially shot and discus, wet weather makes the equipment slippery and hard to control.

In hotter weather, **dehydration** is an issue. The good weather may encourage people to train more frequently and overuse injury may occur.

Active Challenge

With a partner, choose a sport. Think of as many risks as possible related to that sport. Use examples from television, personal experience and incidents told to you.

3 Coaching and Training

Coaching is essential to all levels of sport. The coach is responsible for giving the performer an understanding of the game. The skills learned will be within the laws of the game and prepare the player for competition. The correct techniques are learned, not only for success but for risk prevention: this is especially important for tackles and lifts.

Training improves the body so it is strong enough to deal with the stresses of the event. This reduces the possibility of fatigue, which often leads to injury. Coaching trains the performer to complete skills in a technically correct way. Body alignment is important in take-offs and landings, especially in activities like gymnastics, trampolining and volleyball, to reduce the risk to the bones and tissues of the body. Knowledge and experience of how to control the equipment for the activity comes about through training. A hockey stick used without training can become a danger to all on the pitch, not just the opposition.

Using the correct techniques can reduce the risk of injury.

4 Dressing Safely

The clothing for team events not only gives a feeling of unity to the group but can also play its part in safety. Each sport has a unique type of clothing, which has developed due to the nature of the game. It may allow protective guards underneath or be close fitting so it does not catch on equipment. Importantly, it provides free movement so the full range of skills can be performed in each sport.
Clothing should:

- be in good order
- not catch on equipment
- ensure the performer can keep a clear view ahead
- not flap in the opposition's face and hinder their performance
- allow free movement to perform the skills of the game.

Sports equipment and clothing should be checked regularly. Repairs should be made so that there is nothing to act as a hindrance or danger to anyone. The correct design of equipment should be used for the job. Specialised equipment should always be worn properly. Loose straps and poorly fitting helmets can be a danger.

Footwear to fit the event

Footwear is a specialised part of sports gear; each sport has its own design. Some sports have several different technical designs to suit a variety of conditions. The correct footwear helps in many ways: it gives support, protection, grip, greatest or least amount of movement and is an aid to performance and streamlining.

The condition of studded footwear should be smooth so that studs do not cut into another player. Checking studs is the job of a referee at the beginning of the game and referee's assistants can be seen checking the studs of football substitutes. There are specific rules set out in certain sports in which some footwear may be seen as dangerous. It is therefore essential to keep footwear in good order.

What to do:

1. Study the pictures above. Notice that each sport has a different kind of footwear.
2. Say which sport is shown in each picture.
3. Give a reason why the footwear has been developed in that way for each sport.

Look at the differences in the sole, strapping, material and weather conditions.

Protect and be safe

Each activity needs its own protective equipment. Each item of protection guards against a different kind of injury. These injuries could take the form of: impact of another player, the playing surface, the ball, external conditions, forces put on the body by lifting, friction caused by repeating the skills of the event.

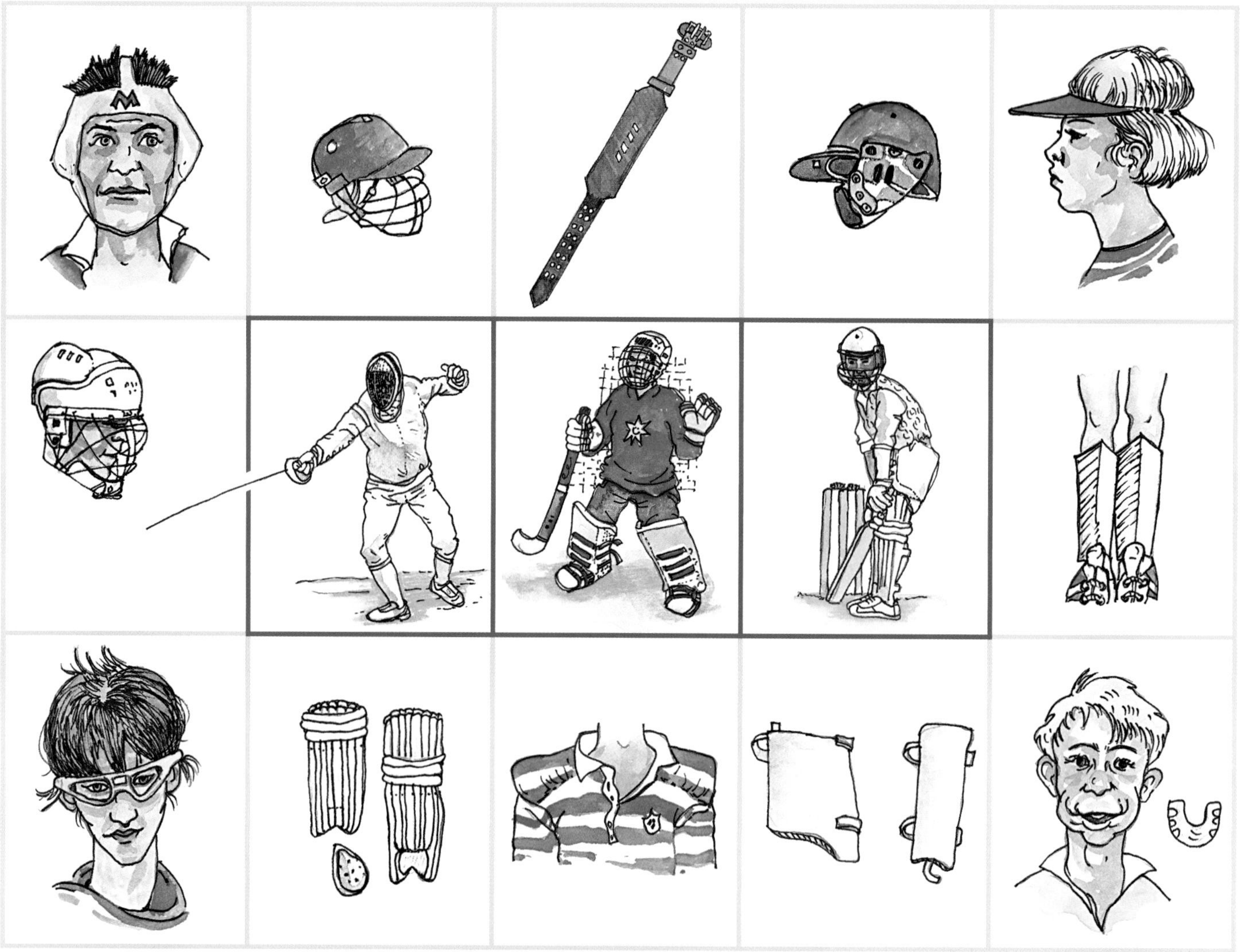

Task 2

What to do:

1. Choose a type of sportsperson and list the items they would need to dress for safety.

Use the pictures above to help with this task.

Active Challenge

With a partner, discuss and decide on as many items of protection in as many sports as possible. Now link each item of protection with an incident that could happen in a game.

Work down from head to toe, thinking of the protection a player may need.

Jewellery

Before a team game begins, players are checked for any jewellery they may be wearing. This may seem petty, but each type of jewellery has its own hazards. Sometimes players put a plaster over earrings so they are not as dangerous. In games where physical contact regularly occurs, it is essential that there is no jewellery to mark the wearer or the opposition.

- Rings – if fingers are jarred or a ball knocks the end of the finger (called 'stumped finger') the finger swells; a ring could be stuck on the finger and cut into the flesh. Also rings could get caught and cut the performer or an opponent.
- Necklaces – if caught and pulled could cause a scar around the neck.
- Earrings – if caught could injure the wearer or an opponent.

Personal presentation

Fingernails need to be clipped to prevent catching and scarring, especially in games like netball and basketball in which reaching for the ball around head height is common.

Hair should be tidy and not in the performer's eyes so players can see where they are going and it does not flick into another player's eyes.

If glasses are worn they should be made of plastic so if they break they do not shatter and injure someone.

Clothing worn for sport should be kept in good order. Ripped or frayed clothing can catch and be a danger.

Having tidy hair and short fingernails reduces the risk of injury. Here, the USA national football team display their impeccable personal presentation.

5 Attitude and Etiquette

Etiquette is the unwritten code of behaviour a player stands by when competing. Each sport has its own code of behaviour. A general example of this is shaking hands before and after a game. In tennis, new balls are used after the first seven games and every nine games after that; it is not a rule, but it is good etiquette for the player about to serve to show the ball to the opposition by raising it in the air.

Taking part is more important than winning!

A player may throw or kick the ball away in anger after a decision by the referee. This demonstration of bad sportsmanship can be punished by the referee in an attempt to discourage such behaviour from other players.

Play to win!

Judo players bow before a contest.

Tennis players shake hands after a match.

Task 3

What to do:

1. Read the two columns of part sentences below.
2. Link the beginnings of sentences with the endings.
3. When the sentences are complete, write them in your book.

Beginning of a sentence

1. Players are checked for
2. If a ball jars a finger,
3. Long fingernails can catch and scar,
4. Keeping a sports kit washed
5. Having sweaty and dirty feet
6. Keeping feet clean and dry between the toes
7. Verrucas are viral warts,
8. Verrucas can be treated quickly by being removed,
9. Etiquette is an unwritten code of behaviour
10. Shaking hands at the beginning and end of a match

Ending of a sentence

a. which spread in moist areas like swimming baths.
b. so the rules of netball state they should be short.
c. a player, wearing a ring, could cut their flesh.
d. is good etiquette.
e. can stop athlete's foot.
f. jewellery before a game.
g. players keep to for the good of the sport.
h. stops the spread of bacteria.
i. or over time with cream.
j. causes athlete's foot.

Key Terms:

Balanced competition ► grouping based on size, age or experience for an even match

Dehydration ► extreme lack of water in the body

Etiquette ► unwritten and unofficial codes of practice followed in an activity

Technique ► way in which a skill is performed

6 How the Rules and Officials Help

Each game has its own set of rules or laws. These rules are connected to the type of equipment and competition involved. They are designed to make the event safer and fairer. Its set of rules helps to give the game its own individual style.

The governing bodies of the sports make the rules. The players play to the rules. The referee, umpire or judge makes sure the rules are kept. Within the rules are a series of stages of discipline; often the player is given one warning to stop any bad play. If the foul play continues, a player will be asked to leave the game.

Yellow card; first warning in football for foul play. Thomas Gravesen is shown the yellow card.

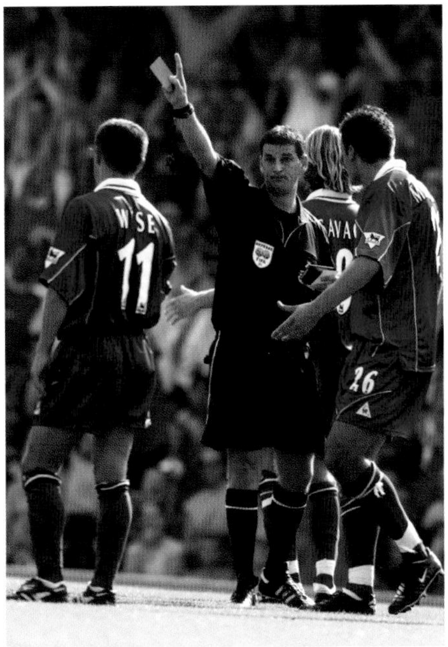

A second yellow (or violent act) earns a red card. Dennis Wise is ordered off.

In rugby and ice hockey, players are sent by the referee to 'cool down' in the sin bin.

In football, red card offences lead to disciplinary hearings where further action may be taken by the Football Association. It is in the player's best interests to obey the rules. Players may lose their competitive edge if the thought of another yellow card, and therefore a sending-off, is a possibility.

Officials make sure that there is safe and fair play. When the whistle blows, the game should stop immediately to prevent any further **infringements** and dangerous play. The referee is impartial and makes decisions according to the rules.

Referees make decisions on the spur of the moment and from where they are standing. In professional games, these verdicts are made under the extreme pressure of hundreds of fans who have their own viewpoints on the referee's decisions!

Players have a responsibility to follow the instructions of the officials and to carry on with the game as soon as possible. The flow of the game needs to be maintained and by getting on with the game quickly a surprise attack can begin. This can be especially successful if the other team is still concentrating on the incident.

Rules support referees in their jobs. In rugby, for instance, the 10-yard rule stops players arguing and using foul language.

Umpires use hand signals so that everyone can see clearly the decision made.

Task 4

What to do:

1. Write down four different responsibilities of a referee.
2. Choose four games or activities. For each one write down a rule that attempts to prevent injury.

Think of how the referee deals with rules, players and safety.

7 Reducing the Risk in Specific Activities

Venues

There are certain safety requirements a club must fulfil. These are to do with the safety of the sports area and safety for the spectators. People watching the event should be managed properly and be able to watch the match without intimidation from other supporters. The St John Ambulance Brigade attend large venues to deal with any first aid requirements necessary.

There are strict guidelines to do with venue exits, making sure the spectators are able to leave the venue safely. The players should also be able to play their game without fear of the crowd invading the pitch. In top-class events, stewards and police play a part in ensuring the players' safety.

The club is also responsible for the state of the playing surface. The ground should be level, have no litter or sharp objects on the ground, have correct netting and corner flags, a safe surface – not slippery, free from protruding objects and so on. The playing surface condition may change due to the weather, so guidelines are pre-stated so officials are able to make the most appropriate decision.

What to do:

1. Study the picture on the previous page. There are 12 hazards shown.
2. Record the hazards and the injury each one could cause.

It will help to think about personal presentation.

Specialised equipment

Using the correct equipment for the type of user is important for safety. Having equipment that is too big or too heavy could lead to injury and risk. The equipment should suit the size, age and experience of the user.

Invasion, striking and racket games

The size of the equipment should relate to the age and experience of the performer. Using full-size footballs for under elevens, for example, will not match the strength and skill of the players.

There are many **modified games**, which resemble the full game but have been adopted for a younger age group. These games have lighter equipment, smaller playing areas, smaller team numbers and simple rules.

Adapting the rules of the full game makes participation possible for all ages.

Gymnastics

Whether training or competing, the landing areas should be safe and stable. Competition landing areas are 120–200mm thick and have safety mats around them to a depth of 22mm–60mm. The landing, after a vault, for instance, needs to be technically correct for a good overall mark and also for the safety of the performer. A two-footed landing on the toes, cushioning the force of landing, reduces the risk of a jarring injury to the back. The safety requirements for landing areas are set out by the governing body.

A hall set out for a gymnastic competition.

The supports for the **asymmetric bars** and their fixings into the floor are specialised and fitted by professionals. This ensures they can withstand the forces put on them by gymnasts during practice and competition.

Equipment in school should be checked by a teacher before work starts. The correct technique should be taught for lifting and lowering vaulting boxes so back injuries are avoided.

Each piece of equipment must be set out so that it does not interfere with any other piece.

When using a trampoline, the setting out and putting away of this equipment should follow strict guidelines and always be supervised. The weight, size and tension of the trampoline are potentially dangerous.

Dance

The surface the dance is performed on should always be safe and non-slippery. It should be smooth with no splinters. Costumes reflecting the dance and adding drama to the performance should be fitted to each performer securely and allow free movement during the event.

Athletics

All surfaces to run on, throw from and jump off should be flat and free from obstacles and protruding objects.

Throwing events, such as the discus and hammer, require netting or a cage around the throwing area. These should be maintained regularly to prevent equipment escaping through gaps in the fencing. The throwing area should be clearly marked and marshalled. As the competition begins, warnings should be sounded to alert other judges, marshals and competitors that the throw is about to commence.

In jumping events, guidelines for the size, depth and composition of the landing areas are regulated by the governing body. Mats should have a continuous covering over them to keep them together. Throughout the high jump and pole vault competition a check should be kept on the correct placement of the landing area in relation to the bar.

Some equipment is dangerous, the javelin being an obvious example. There are special carry cages and trolleys for transporting awkward equipment. In schools, the training and drilling of moving such equipment, especially javelins and shot, should be reinforced in every lesson.

The throwing cage protects people at the event from a miss-throw. Dean Macey prepares to throw.

Equipment, such as javelins, needs to be stored correctly for safety reasons. Steve Backley selects a javelin.

Swimming

All safety information and equipment should be clearly on display at the pool side. Any change of depth in the pool should be clearly marked on the pool edge and visible on the wall too.

The surface around the pool should be non-slip and clean to prevent injury and infection.

Although it may be seen as unglamorous, the swimming cap is a safety aid in a variety of ways. It keeps hair out of the eyes, giving a clear view of the direction for the swimmer and it keeps hair out of the swimmer's mouth, allowing clear, unhindered breathing. Keeping the hair in a cap also helps prevent loose hair entering and blocking the filters.

Although a verruca can be painful, a person can still swim: they must take care when changing so they do not infect the floor and should wear a verruca sock when swimming to prevent it spreading.

Wearing goggles allows the swimmer to see underwater when their face is submerged. This allows turns to be made safely. Goggles also protect the eyes from the chemicals in the water.

Outdoor and adventurous activities

Personal equipment

The clothing taken on any adventurous activity should suit every kind of weather possibility. The clothing mountaineers take on an expedition should be appropriate for any extreme conditions that they might face. These clothes range from undergarments to the outer layers. Boots should be comfortable and sturdy, with a good grip. An activity may begin in warm and sunny weather but, as the day goes on, the weather may change. The temperature drops as the altitude rises on hills and mountains. Experienced mountaineers will be well equipped for this.

In addition to a compass and map a mountaineer may carry the following:

Personal safety kit:

- extra warm clothing
- extra gloves
- food and water
- bivvy bag (waterproof bag large enough for two people to shelter from the elements)
- whistle – for a distress call (a mobile phone would help but there are some areas where a signal cannot be picked up)
- torch.

Personal first aid kit:

- 2 crepe bandages: 1 ankle, 1 knee-size tubular bandage for sprains
- army knife with scissors
- sterile wipes for dirty wounds
- various-sized plasters
- 12-pack of swabs for compression
- 1 roll of tape for holding the swabs in place
- safety pin.

Safety equipment

The ability to use a map and compass properly needs specialist training and much practice. If walking over a long distance and in hostile terrain then it is important to be able to navigate. A route plan should be worked out before the party sets off. The plan should include escape points at certain parts of the route so if there is an accident or the weather deteriorates then they can be used. When visibility is zero, owing to the mist coming down, it is possible, as long as you know your position, to navigate with map and compass alone.

The safety equipment should suit all possible conditions of the day. This equipment may be bulky to carry, but it can be shared between members of the group. Often it will not be used but it is there should it be needed. If walking in the winter, specialised equipment is essential for safety, like crampons and ice-axes. Training and experience are necessary so that they can be used properly.

Regular checks on the condition of the equipment should be made. Ropes do not last for ever; they have a life determined by the number of hours used. After this time they cannot be relied on to do their job and so should not be used for climbing again.

Wearing the correct gear and carrying appropriate safety apparatus protects the performer from extreme elements and hazardous situations.

External forces

Before setting out on any expedition a detailed weather report should be studied. The Met Office can supply this for the British Isles. The weather at sea or in the mountains can change rapidly, so preparations should be made accordingly. By obtaining the weather report, predictions can be made as to whether it is viable to go out in the first place or what possible weather changes may occur during the day. If the elements are too much to handle, then it is sensible to turn back or take a safety route home. In mountainous areas the weather can bring wind, mist, rain, snow, heat, sun and storms all in the same day. The key is to prepare for the worst.

Experience of the leader and the crew

Major factors in the safety of the party are the experience, knowledge and ability of the leaders. They should plan the route taking into account the ability of each member of the group. They should have expertise in the use of a map and compass, carry safety equipment and know the safety procedures.

Leaders should be able to assess the group, encourage the weaker members and be able to adapt the pace to suit the whole party. Their ability to make correct decisions under pressure to suit a situation can help ensure the safety of the party. For long expeditions, leaders should have the personal ability to keep the morale of the group high, even in difficult and demanding conditions.

FACTORS AFFECTING THE SAFETY OF AN OUTDOOR ACTIVITY

Environmental conditions

- Does the sailor or canoeist know the tides and currents?
- Wind may blow the party off course. Rain may dampen morale. Is the group equipped for snow?
- In mist, would they still know where they were going?
- In a storm, would they know what to do?
- Are they prepared for the heat?

Planning the activity

- Is the plan accurate?
- Are there any escape routes?
- Does the route include rests?
- Is it suitable for all members of the group?
- Will it stretch the abilities of the group too far?

Experience of the leaders

- Do they know the area?
- Have they planned the route?
- Are they experienced in safety procedures?
- Can they use the safety equipment they have?
- Can they motivate the group?
- Will they set the pace to that of the slowest member?

Degree of difficulty of the activity

- Is the group able to complete the route?
- Has the group got the correct equipment for the route?
- Will safety be compromised due to the difficulty?
- Is the route too difficult for the conditions?
- Are group members strong enough to canoe the distance?
- Has everyone got enough and the right kind of protection for the climb?

Condition of the equipment

- Is that rope too old?
- Is there a record of the equipment's use?
- Is that compass still reliable?
- Is someone taking the correct map?
- Has that torch got good batteries?
- Is the equipment in good order?

Experience of the party

- Are they fit enough? Have they got the correct equipment?
- Have they enough experience for the degree of difficulty they may face?
- Have they the skills to finish the expedition?
- Do they know what is expected of them?

What to do:

1. Compile a list of outdoor and adventurous activities.
2. Name two specialised pieces of equipment required for each activity.
3. Write two sentences about the job of the safety equipment.

Use the photographs in this section to help you.

Use reference books or the Internet to help you.

Key Terms:

- **Asymmetric bars** ► a piece of gymnastic equipment used by females with bars at different heights
- **Cool down** ► exercises after the main activity gradually bringing the body systems back to a near resting state
- **Infringement** ► action in a game that breaks the rules
- **Main activity** ► period of training, competition or performance when all-out effort is applied
- **Modified game** ► a game with adapted rules, equipment and playing area based on a full game
- **Throwing cage** ► a secured enclosure around a throwing area
- **Warm-up** ► exercises putting greater stresses on the body systems so they are prepared for the main activity

Summary

With most activities there are risks involved and these increase if the competition is not equally matched. Through training and coaching players are made aware of the risks of the activity. Experience helps performers to predict and avoid hazardous situations.

Each sport or activity has its own physical demands. Training for the event prepares the body and its systems for the requirements of the activity. After training, the performer should have the right levels of strength, skill and stamina to compete more safely in the activity. By being able to use the correct technique when playing shots, landing, tackling and dodging, for instance, the player is less likely to suffer injury.

The rules are designed to allow the game to continue in a fair and safe way. Umpires, referees and judges make sure the rules are kept during the competition. They also ensure the conditions are safe, the equipment is set up correctly and whether the venue is suitable for the event when conditions change.

For most activities there is specially designed equipment. Some is designed to carry out the game and some for the safety of the performers. Both types should be kept in good condition as their effectiveness may be reduced if they are damaged in any way. For instance, if helmets are cracked they lose their protective quality. Whatever safety equipment is used, it should be worn correctly and strapped on properly.

Italian volleyball player Luca Cantagalli wears knee pads for protection.

Factors Affecting Individual Performance and Participation

What you will learn about in this section

1. School and Participation in Physical Activity
2. Social Groupings – People Who Influence Participation in Sport
3. Factors Beyond Our Control
4. Reasons for the Increase of the Leisure Industry
5. Changing Attitudes
6. Facilities Available

There are many factors affecting a person taking part in sport. What we see on the TV, or read in newspapers or magazines, may sway us in our thinking. The more we are in contact with an influence may result in it having more effect on us. School, consequently, can have an important part to play in the encouragement of exercise.

Sports day brings the whole school together through physical activity.

1 School and Participation in Physical Activity

Promotion Schools actively encourage participation in sport. Not only is it a legal requirement for all pupils to take part, but pupils can gain many personal benefits from sport at school. A school's physical education programme can encourage participation on several levels.

Demonstrates fitness levels Schools provide up to two hours of PE lessons a week for all pupils; statistically this is insufficient to improve a person's fitness. However, PE lessons can educate young people about safe levels and the amount of exercise that can be undertaken to have a positive effect on fitness.

Encourage a healthy lifestyle Some PE lessons involve general instruction on a balance of exercise, diet and the need to avoid harmful substances for a healthy life. A good health education can help young people make sound life choices which continue throughout adulthood.

Offer a range of activities By offering a wide range of activities, schools provide a variety of experiences for pupils where progress and achievement can be made. The mix of sports gives more chance of finding an area of interest and success for as many pupils as possible and, hopefully the confidence to continue taking part in physical activity after they have left school.

Extend skills learnt in class Many schools offer pupils the chance to join a school club or team. This provides an opportunity to improve and extend skills learnt in lessons through competition. Sometimes participation is purely for fun. Some clubs may be set up for a completely new activity not on the PE timetable to further extend pupils' interest.

Leisure pursuits By providing a wide variety of activities on the timetable and extra sessions after school, pupils may be sufficiently interested in exercise to continue participation after they have left school. The experience of visiting a local gym or sports centre whilst at school may provide the knowledge and confidence to go to these centres independently.

Experience different ways to enjoy sport Schools recognise the importance of giving pupils a chance not only to play the games but to take part in different ways too. Members of a class may regularly experience how to judge, coach, observe, officiate, captain, lead, organise or choreograph. These different experiences may appeal to children and lead to an interest in sport beyond actually playing the game.

Games

Outdoor and adventurous activities

The National Curriculum provides a chance for a variety of activities.

Teacher

By relating their enthusiasm for the subject, a PE teacher shows all of the good reasons for taking part in exercise. Although some pupils are not enthusiastic about physical education, a positive approach by staff can encourage most of the class to join in. By using different ways to deliver the information and encouraging more than just the acquisition of skill, the teacher can plan their lessons to inspire enthusiasm in their class.

Task 1

What to do:

1. Use the headings from the section 'School and Participation in Physical Activity' to form a spidergram. This will help you remember the main points.
2. Below each heading, write out a sentence, using your own words, expanding the idea.

The lesson

If traditional ways of teaching are used, for instance every lesson asks the pupils to tackle one problem, the same way and to one standard, which highlights the best and the worst in the class, then some pupils can be put off physical activity. If the teacher makes the tasks achievable, personal and varied, there is a possibility of more children having a good experience of PE and so, including exercise as part of their lifestyle in adulthood.

Pupils can referee to experience a different aspect of sport.

In class

The classroom can be a place where information is given and can also give the pupils the chance for the following:

planning – gymnastics and dance routines or strategy in a game
working out – finding answers to problems, such as how to beat the opposition
observing – learning the correct technique and looking for it in performances
communication – discussing useful instructions or coaching points
leadership – of a small group in class, as a captain or an organiser
choreography – in dance, children have the chance to make up their own routines
external examination – to increase the understanding of PE and aid the career of pupils
achieve awards – results in class may contribute to a recognised award scheme
links with the community – local sport centres and clubs may be used
cross-curricular links – made with other subjects to enhance the teaching
school facilities – the chance to use all available facilities
outside visits – links to see sports events, clubs and providers.

ICT – gives the opportunity to use the latest technology and link it with sport. Practice in finding information and results of performances on the Internet and recording their own results on computer gives pupils key skills in technology. Searching the Internet gives access to the heroes of the time and creates interest.

Social education issues – through sport, people can learn, in a controlled situation, how to act and react to different situations. The ability to play fairly and keep to the rules whilst playing in a team or as an individual are worthwhile qualities to develop. When assessing own and others' performances in sport, the ability to offer helpful and appropriate coaching points helps to develop co-operation and thoughtfulness.

Health awareness – learning what healthy living and safe practice is through sport can promote a healthy lifestyle for later life. A knowledge of a healthy and balanced diet, how to achieve and maintain a minimum level of fitness and where and how to access local facilities can be provided through a good PE programme.

Active Challenge

1. Think of a lesson where you have a role or job to do.
2. Put a name to the job using the previous section.
3. Briefly tell a partner what you did and what skills you developed as a result.
4. Try to think of three examples.

Extra-curricular activities

As an extension to PE lessons many schools provide extra sessions after school; these are called 'extra-curricular activities'. These provide even more benefits to the pupils, because they:

- become a member of a team
- have a chance to be a captain or leader of a team
- visit other schools and venues for matches
- may join organised trips to see top-class sport
- become a member of a club or society taking part for the fun of the event and not competition
- develop links with clubs and providers; for example, local coaches come into school to help coaching and local clubs offer their facilities to the school
- increase their sports performance by joining after school clubs to increase skill and in some cases reach a standard for awards and proficiency tests.

Many companies or products sponsor particular events and sports awards. Swimming benefits from the Kellogg's Frosties Awards.

Task 2

What to do:

1. List the ways your school promotes PE.
2. Find out about other companies or products that put their name to sports awards.

Think about the following: staff, clubs, teams and visits.

Key Terms:

Choreography	creating a series of steps and teaching others to follow
Coaching points	instructions given to improve technique
Extra-curricular activities	activities outside the regular school timetable
Healthy lifestyle	conducting life adhering to care on mental and physical well-being
National Curriculum	government instructions on what is to be taught in schools

2 Social Groupings – People Who Influence Participation in Sport

As well as school, there are other factors influencing participation in sport. These social influences can have a positive (and sometimes a negative) influence on participation in a sport or activity.

Parents

What parents think about sport, their experiences and the attitudes they have developed can have an effect on their children. If the experiences were good, then their enthusiasm may be passed on; if not, a negative attitude may make the child uninterested in exercise.

If a parent has ability, they sometimes actively encourage and spend time coaching their child to develop skills in that area, promoting the tradition of the children 'following in father's or mother's footsteps'. Many parents support their children in their interests by financing their hobbies. They provide the equipment, transport and subscription money so that their child can pursue their interests.

Parents often devote their time to encourage their children. Laila Ali, daughter of Muhammad Ali, celebrated her first world title win on 17 August 2002, with her father watching at ringside.

Peers

Peers are people of a similar age. They can be in the same class, same year group or at a different school. Peers can have a great influence on their friends; this is called 'peer pressure'. If a peer group takes part in a physical activity or sport, they could influence others to join in too.

What to do:

1. Put yourself in the position of these people:
   - parent
   - teacher
   - friend.
2. Write down three different comments, for each person, showing what they might say to a young person to encourage them to participate in sport.

3 Factors Beyond Our Control

Age

The age of a person may influence their chances of participating in certain activities. There may be age limits for participation or joining of some clubs, such as for golf, netball or rugby. Depending on the size of the club, each age group usually has its own section with separate competition and coaching. Guidelines may be set by the sports governing body to help organisation.

As the trend for a healthier lifestyle continues, older people see the need to keep exercising. Although they may be carrying an injury or a condition, if they are properly educated about the problem and are sensible about how much they take on, they will continue to benefit from exercising.

Older people have the chance to learn new skills as many public and private centres now cater for older age groups. More people are planning for their retirement but money may still be a problem for the older generation. In some cases, concessions are made for older participants and off-peak times are set aside for them.

As the age of the population increases there are more older people that want to keep fit. More opportunity and publicity of activities for this age group is necessary. There has been a slow increase in the television coverage of the seniors' golf tournaments and the occasional veterans' tennis matches. More coverage, promoting older people and top-class sport, is necessary if there is to be an increase of older, active sportspeople.

Gender

Both males and females are encouraged to participate in most sports. Ideally everyone who has an interest should be able to participate and compete in their chosen activity. However, there are constraints: some clubs may only offer single sex teams due to a lack of facilities and qualified coaches.

Although most sports are available to both sexes, generally each sex competes separately. This is for safety, due to the physical differences of size and strength, and fair play. Some sports have their own governing bodies for each sex; for example, tennis and golf. Two of the few major sporting events to have male and female competitors in the same event are show jumping and mixed-doubles matches in tennis.

Women in sport

Women's opportunities in sport are steadily increasing and becoming more financially rewarding. There is greater representation for women in the national authorities. The Sports Council supports women's participation in sport and has in place ways to raise levels of achievement. More governing bodies are recognising women's place in their sport. In 1972 the Women's Football Association (WFA) was formed.

The Women's Sports Foundation (WSF) also pioneers the female cause, working hard to increase media coverage, raising the awareness of top class women's sporting success. Events such as the Women's Rugby World Cup showed the highest level of women's sport, helping it to become more popular. There are increasingly more opportunities for women to have careers linked with sport in the media. This may be a first career or an occupation taken up after competitive life is over. On a local level, many sports centres make time during the day for women's activities. They provide crèche facilities to help as many women as possible take part.

Tradition and culture

An area may have a sport as part of its cultural heritage – for years, the Welsh valleys produced many world class rugby union players and had a successful national side. The success of a rugby, gymnastics or hockey club, for example, may be an attraction for new players or competitors and coaches, and so help maintain the traditional high standards of the club.

Family traditions may encourage children in a particular sport, even to the detriment of other sports. By focusing on one activity, there is a chance that talents for other sports are missed or overlooked.

Tradition, interest and facilities lead to a gold medal for the women's British curling team.

When success in new sports does emerge, the local authority may allocate more money for it in their budget or private sponsors may finance efforts to raise the profile, standards and participation levels.

In the Salt Lake City Winter Olympics, the British curling teams were solely made up of people from Scotland. This was due to the long tradition of curling in Scotland, where there are many curling rinks and the interest is high.

Access

Where facilities for certain activities are good, there may be more chance that more people will participate. The greater the involvement, the better the possibility of a higher standard which then attracts more players and coaches. In small communities, there may be an interest but not enough people to make it viable. Unless transport is available to towns with established clubs, the opportunity to play is lost.

What to do:

1. Read the three comments below made by keen and talented sportspeople.
2. Study their problems.
3. Think of possible ways they could overcome them and play the sport of their choice.

Key Terms:

Gender	male or female
Peers	people of a similar age
Tradition and culture	opinion or practice that is handed down to next generations or an established way of life

What is leisure?

Leisure time is the portion of the day a person has when they are free from the everyday duties of life. In this recreational time, a person voluntarily participates in sport for pleasure and enjoyment. Although every one is different, the day can be split up approximately in the following way:

- sleeping/eating/bodily functions
- working/school work
- domestic duties
- free time.

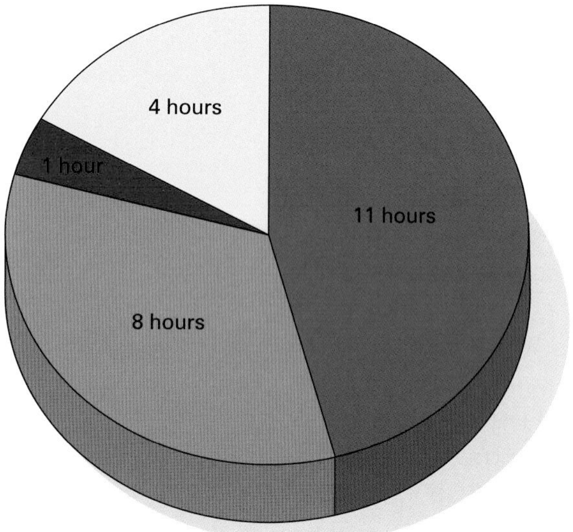

Approximate guide to how a person's day is filled.

Why is there more leisure time?

The overall time spent in the workplace is less than it was a decade ago. There are several reasons for this. An increasing number of people are taking advantage of working from home and so are rearranging their day so that time in the office is reduced. They can still be as efficient due to computer technology and excellent communication systems. By rearranging their working environment in this way it provides more flexibility to pursue and take advantage of leisure activities.

Since technology has taken a larger role in our lives there has gradually become an increase in leisure time. Machines have been built to do the jobs manual workers did years ago in the workplace. New technology does the job more efficiently and in less time than manual production, reducing the hours available to employees so they have a shorter working week. This increases the time available to take part in leisure pursuits.

Improved technology has provided people with labour-saving devices around the home, so freeing up time needed to complete housework and giving greater opportunity for leisure pursuits.

With the increase of more part-time work a chance to pursue more leisure activities may occur due to the greater time available.

Employers provide their work force with paid holidays per year. People therefore have the time and money to spend in the leisure industry.

People today are encouraged to plan for their retirement more carefully and many take early retirement. Although the retirement age is 60 for women and 65 for men, most people aim to be

A change in working hours allows more time to pursue leisure activities.

financially secure at a much earlier age. By subscribing to pension plans from an early age, people can stop working sooner, giving more time to pursue their leisure interests.

Retiring earlier and leading a healthier lifestyle allows people to enjoy their leisure time.

The overall population in the country is increasing due to the fact that generally people are living longer. One-fifth of the population in the UK is now over 60 years of age. By the year 2030 it is predicted that this figure will rise to one-third.

The rise in the number of unemployed has created a new group of people needing leisure provision. In order to include this group in the community, concessions are made and reduced fees are available for them so they can still be involved in leisure pursuits.

All these reasons for increasing the leisure industry create greater demands for more public and private facilities. The types of activities catered for range from the less active pursuits to providing fully equipped sports centres. Local authorities take on board the task of making available the public amenities for a wide range of user groups. They aim to target these user groups and provide them with a window in the week where they have the opportunity to take advantage of the facility. A mother and child, for instance, may have a slot during the day when a sports centre is quiet, with nursery facilities and at a concessionary rate.

What to do:

1. Write two sentences for each of the headings below, giving reasons for an increase in the leisure industry.
   - Working from home
   - Increased part-time work
   - Shorter working week
   - Early retirement
   - Improvement in technology
   - Provision for the unemployed

5 Changing Attitudes

The changing expectations of people and the way they live their lives has a bearing on the attitudes of a society. Over the years there have been many changes in attitudes to do with sport influencing participation levels.

Role models

There are many role models in sport; their following can be due to a combination of their play, personality and lifestyle. As there is more coverage of their play and everyday life in the media, these people become trendsetters in their sport and can shape the attitudes and behaviour of their fans – whether good or bad. Top-class sportspeople not only encourage people to participate in a sport and possibly play in a certain way but can also influence fashion choices on and off the field of play.

Top-class sportspeople have a great influence on society. Many fans of David Beckham emulate him by having the same hairstyle.

Active Challenge

Choose two sporting people in the public eye. Make a list of the positive and negative influences they each could have on you.

Women

In the early history of sport, women were not encouraged to participate as their place was seen as being in the home. It is only recently, now more women have followed careers giving them financial independence, that women have more choice to participate in sport. The women who played competitive sport were those from wealthy backgrounds that played sports such as golf and tennis. It was not until 1951 that the Ladies Professional Golf Association was formed in America. Although there is less prize money and fewer events for women generally, today there is an increasing opportunity for women to pursue sporting interests and ultimately earn a living from sport.

Coverage in the media of top sportswomen increases the amount of girls encouraged to participate. Other job opportunities in sport are open to women; there are more female umpires, officials, organisers and TV presenters making their name at the top of their career.

A major breakthrough came in April 2000 when Fulham Football Club announced its plans to become the first British and European club to have its own fully professional women's football team.

Increased TV coverage is a way of advertising women's sport.

Activities in and out of fashion

The popularity of an activity can change quickly as **trends** in sport fall in and out of fashion. In the short term, during Wimbledon week more people can be seen using local tennis facilities inspired by what they are seeing on the TV. A more long-term effect can come about by a national side doing well in a major tournament, which causes an increase in popularity in that sport, which may encourage local authorities to fund new facilities.

If a **minority sport** begins to receive greater coverage on the television this will lead to an increase in its popularity. In recent years snooker has gained in popularity, perhaps due to the coverage of the top personalities within the sport inspiring and attracting youngsters to the game. A sport could also decline in popularity with less people taking part; squash in recent years has taken a such a downturn. Courts in local sports centres, rather than remaining unused, are being adapted for trendier activities such as aerobics and yoga.

Key Terms:

- **Minority sports** ► sports where currently there are few participants
- **Role model** ► a person looked to by other people as an example to follow and whose behaviour and attitudes may be copied by others
- **Trend** ► a fad or fashion of the moment

6 Facilities Available

The provision of indoor and outdoor facilities depends on many factors. All areas of the country would like excellent local facilities but providing these would not be financially or practically workable. There are many issues taken into consideration when deciding on new facilities:

Location – certain sites naturally lend themselves to various activities. Outdoor pursuit centres are situated where there are hills, rivers, lakes and forests suited to the particular activities involved.

Funding – money to increase or improve the facilities can come from different sources: the government may set aside money in their annual budget; the lottery may meet part of the cost; an individual may personally finance a team.

Access – poor road and rail links to facilities may have a direct bearing on the amount of people that use a sports centre.

Expected use and demand – whether it is private or publicly funded, the aim is to have as many people use the facility for as much of the time as possible. When deciding on a site for a new facility enough people should be available in the area to make full use of it.

Summary

School can have a big impact on a young person. By providing an opportunity to exercise in a positive environment and have experience of the different roles in sport, interests can grow in ways other than the obvious one of playing the game. People who lack the skills or the inclination to participate or compete themselves may still have a positive role to play in sport as an administrator or officiator.

There are many factors that affect participation in physical activity. Usually it is the people or group a person is most in contact with that has the greatest influence. Parents may encourage involvement in an activity the family has a history in or peers may promote the newest craze.

The change in lifestyle over recent years has brought about a rise in leisure pursuits. People now have more control over their time than ever before. Many people set aside time in their day or week for exercise this has led to a greater demand for sports facilities. This has resulted in the public and private sectors increasing the amount of leisure amenities available as the industry continues to grow rapidly.

Individual sportspeople who are regularly in the public eye are often copied by admiring fans. More women are now becoming role models as their sport is increasing in popularity and so earns further coverage on the television.

The popularity of certain sports can vary from area to area and time to time. Seasonal sports have key times of the year attracting more participants. Some sports enjoy a short term of favour and then go out of fashion, making way for a new trend to take its place.

Sponsorship

What you will learn about in this section

1. Advantages of Sponsorship
2. Disadvantages of Sponsorship
3. Acceptable and Unacceptable Types of Sponsorship

Companies can choose to sponsor sport in different ways. Some prefer to put their name to leagues, events or sports facilities. Others choose to sponsor particular individual or team sports. Within a team, players may also have personal deals with their own sponsor and be used to endorse a particular brand or company. **The Institute of Sports Sponsorship (ISS)** predicts that the worldwide market for sports sponsorship will rise to $50 billion by 2010. This increase will be due to more attractive spectator and corporate facilities but mostly from televised coverage and sponsorship deals.

Year	Value (£m)	% change	No. of sponsors	% change
1991	238	–	759	–
1992	238	+ 0.4	659	– 13.2
1993	250	+ 4.6	745	+ 13.1
1994	265	+ 6	818	+ 9.8
1995	285	+ 7	939	+ 14.8
1996	302	+ 6	977	+ 4
1997	322	+ 6.6	995	+ 1.8
1998	357	+ 9.6	969	– 2.6
1999	377	+ 6.8	1172	+ 20.9
2000	400	+ 6.1	1200	+ 2.4

Trends in professional sports sponsorship expenditure.

1 Advantages of Sponsorship

Although football and motor sport dominate the market for sports **sponsorship** in the UK other sports like rugby, cricket, athletics, golf, tennis, equestrian, swimming and snooker enjoy significant support from sponsors.

Advantages for the sponsor

There are several reasons why companies sponsor sport. The most important is for financial gain. Before a sponsor puts their name to a sport, individual or team they work out the financial benefit of making the link to their product. This is usually in the form of increased sales of their product. In competition, which can range from local events to worldwide exposure with television coverage, the sponsor's logo is clearly seen. **Advertising** the brand name in this way saves companies money in comparison with the expense of using adverts in various forms of media.

Here, major and minor sponsors supporting rugby are advertised around the grounds.

By linking the brand name with a certain sport, it can develop a healthy image, making it more popular in the public's eyes. Sports can also benefit from being linked to a company with a good image, as they can be regarded as being successful in the same way.

To promote a caring image the sponsors can help promote minority sports. In schools, a company may provide sports equipment or put their name to an award scheme to help the interest and participation in a particular activity. This can be seen as a gesture of **goodwill** to help get people involved in the sport, whilst at the same time advertising their product.

The money sponsors make available to the sport can improve its standards by helping to provide better coaches, facilities, training and administration. Companies can become more popular and well respected because of their positive and loyal involvement with sport. Many companies finance a showcase event, like a league or major competition. This can increase the size and standard of the competition, attracting the best performers in the world. The sponsors not only finance the organisation, but the prizes or prize money too.

In 2001 Norwich Union became a major sponsor of UK athletics.

A company may gain financially through tax relief if they sponsor a sport. The amount they sponsor can be claimed against the tax that they pay and so save them money over the year.

In certain cases a sports equipment manufacturer may be researching and developing a new product. They will back a performer in return for them using the new product and giving feedback on its effectiveness. In this way improvements are made in the sport and the performer is supported in their training and competition.

In some cases, a company may sponsor a person or sport with no thought of financial return. Goodwill gestures such as these are a sign of a company's passion for the sport and its commitment to maintaining its standards and further progress. A company who sponsors an event can usually take advantage of corporate hospitality for their employees. They will be allotted good seats and sometimes meals at the events.

What to do:

1. Create a spidergram of the ways sponsors gain from advertising in sport.

Advantages for the performer

Taking part and competing at the highest level of sport is expensive. To reach the necessary standard an individual performer needs sponsorship so that they do not have financial worries, leaving the performer to concentrate on training and competing. The obvious way sponsorship helps is by supplying the equipment, clothing and training for the event.

There are other ways sponsors can help the sportsperson. Linked with training, the cost of special diets, to help the athlete's performance, can be expensive. Funds can be made available or local businesses can provide appropriate food direct to the athlete. The expense of travelling to an event may be paid for, whether by road or air. Car firms or garages may even supply a car for the exclusive use of the athlete. When Michael Owen, the Liverpool footballer, became successful and popular, Jaguar provided him with a car for his own use. The cost of the expenses and the entry fee necessary for a sportsperson to be involved in an event can be substantial, so the sponsors will take care of these financial outgoings. In some cases, an amount of money is given to the athlete, to distribute at their own discretion. Once all of the outgoings are paid, any excess money left acts as an extra income for the sportsperson.

Sponsorship is still vital for many new, young competitors in sport in order that they can reach levels of performance with those best in the world. With well-established performers, a sponsorship deal involves much more money. There can be extra money left over after all the sporting expenses are settled, so this goes to pay for a better lifestyle for the performer.

The top-class performers are sponsored for completely different reasons. Their faces are popular and companies want their name linked with them in order to sell more of their product. The individual will still receive clothing for their sport, but will also be provided with leisure clothing like baseball caps, trainers, sweatshirts and so on. These accessories, not directly linked with the sport, are given to the athlete so that they can further advertise the product. Many cricketers and athletes now wear designer sunglasses, tennis players receive watches to wear as they are playing and many sportspeople, in their leisure time, wear baseball caps with the sponsor's logo clearly shown.

Task 2

What to do:

1. Write five sentences on how a young, promising sportsperson may benefit from sponsorship.

Advantages for the teams

A team may solely receive sponsorship from one company or may have several sponsors helping with different aspects of the sport. A football team may have all their equipment provided by one company. This will include the team strip, training strip, footballs and other necessary equipment.

The UEFA Champions League logo and sponsors.

Bolton Wanderers' football ground is called the Reebok Stadium and the Surrey County cricket ground is now called the AMP Oval, both named after their sponsors. A motor sports team may advertise the names of the suppliers contributing to the working of the team. In the year 2001 there were over 230 sponsors for Formula One (F1), ranging from engineering and oil companies to food and fashion businesses.

The bigger the club, the bigger the sponsorship deal. As a result, smaller clubs unable to land support from national or international businesses seek sponsorship from local businesses. The expenditure of a smaller club is moderate and so the business can make a suitable and affordable contribution, still linking its name with sport and having its name advertised in the locality.

Flora sponsors the London Marathon. In 2002, Paula Radcliffe was the fastest ever Briton to complete the 26.2-mile distance.

Advantages for sport and the events

Some sports are seen to be so popular and an excellent advertising medium, both nationally and internationally, that larger companies will sponsor the whole sport. This gives the sport/event financial security for the future in that improvements can be made to its facilities and administration. The increase of money attracts the best performers, which in turn improves the standard and appeal of the sport/event. In return for the company having exclusive rights on advertising, the organisers, clubs and players benefit from the financial input.

Active Challenge

Look in your PE department for the names of companies helping sport. Look at award schemes, adverts for sports events, books and any local sponsors linked to school.

2 Disadvantages of Sponsorship

Disadvantages for the sponsor

Sponsorship does not automatically guarantee success; the sponsor takes a risk if backing new talent. The sponsor speculates on the performer reaching the top of their chosen field. One of the risks with sportspeople is injury, which may stall, shorten or even finish a career. The sponsor takes on this risk knowing that there may be limited return for their investment if an athlete is out of action.

Disadvantages for the performer

A sponsorship deal, while it lasts, can be a great benefit, but many are only short-term contracts, making the financial situation insecure. The power of the sponsor can sometimes be too great. They can expect the performer to wear a certain brand of clothing whether playing or not, resulting in the athlete feeling demotivated and used by the sponsor. A contract may also include a number of duties that the player is committed to outside sport. In the 1998 World Cup there was controversy with the Brazilian team and their sponsors Nike. Despite their major player, Ronaldo, being ill, the sponsors allegedly demanded that he take part in the final.

Disadvantages for the sports and events

If the sponsors get too much control over the sport then they begin to take charge of events and not the specialised sports bodies themselves. To make a game more marketable the rules of the sport can change due to the sponsor's demands. Cricket is a prime example of this. Rather than follow the traditional rules of the game and wear whites as their kit, each county team wear a different coloured kit for one-day games. In some cricket competitions the number of overs in the game has changed in order to make it more appealing to the television audience.

Sponsors can also control the timing of the events. Traditionally football matches used to start at 3:00 on Saturday afternoons. After BSkyB made an exclusive deal to broadcast live Premiership football, it influenced a change so that matches are played on Sundays, have various starting times and later kick-offs for midweek matches. The sponsors have demanded the changes in order to capture the primetime viewing slots for the television coverage. For international matches similar changes to starting times have been made to suit viewing audiences. Although the changes are good for the audiences they are not always in the best interests of the performers.

In extreme cases, the sports become reliant on the sponsors for a major part of their financial existence. When ITV Digital bought the rights to broadcast Nationwide League football games and then the company collapsed, this caused financial concerns for clubs with some, such as Bradford City, being forced into administration.

Sponsors are attracted to the major sports and the most successful performers as they want their product to be linked with success. This creates an imbalance not only in sports coverage in the media but also in competition, where the best-financed performers have more resources to compete and win at the highest level. For the less popular sports, it is difficult to get sponsorship despite the sports being worthy in their own right.

In an attempt to promote minority sports the government has set up the 'Sportsmatch Scheme', targeting under-funded, amateur and minority sports. Any money given by a company to sponsor such a sport will be matched pound for pound by the government. The minimum grant is £1000 and the maximum is £50 000. In England the ISS is responsible for the scheme, but in Scotland, Wales and Northern Ireland it is administered by their own Sports Councils.

Many sponsors will only put money into a high profile sport, as this is the easiest way of getting the best return. Ten years ago, many athletes found it difficult to get sufficient sponsorship to compete at the highest level. It is only recently, now that the image of athletics has risen, due to the personalities in the sport and increased television coverage creating an international appeal, that sponsors are more willing to direct money towards sport. For some involved in sport, the importance of making money for the sponsor spoils the enjoyment of the sport.

3 Acceptable and Unacceptable Types of Sponsorship

Generally when sports seek sponsorship they do so from companies that have an appropriately healthy, positive and wholesome image. However, some products traditionally linked with sports in today's society are losing their credibility. Two prime examples are alcohol and tobacco.

These products, although continuing to have a link with sport, have restrictions on them so that they can only have a link with adult events. Tobacco companies are a major sponsor of F1 racing and have been so for many years. The link to cigarettes is now so controversial, as smoking is increasingly associated with poor health conditions, that the sponsorship is scheduled to stop in 2006.

Michael Schumacher's suit advertises cigarette companies. Tobacco is clearly linked with poor health, so Formula 1 will end all tobacco sponsorship in 2006.

What to do:

1. Make a list of the advantages and disadvantages of sponsorship. Answer from both the performer's and sponsor's viewpoints.
2. From what you have read in this section write your opinions on why some sponsorship is seen to be unacceptable and others acceptable.

Key Terms:

Advertising	►	displaying a product, name or logo in public
Goodwill	►	supporting a performer or sport financially without any monetary return
Institute of Sports Sponsorship (ISS)	►	promotes best practice in sponsorship, working closely with sports bodies, government and the media
Sponsorship	►	backing performers financially in return for advertising a product

Summary

In most sponsorship deals, both the company and the performer gain from the partnership. For the performer, having financial backing relieves the stress of how a training and competitive programme is funded. This gives the performer freedom to choose the best methods in order to challenge the top sportspeople in the world. For the company, they are seen to support a particular sport, putting them in a favourable light with the public whilst advertising their product nationally or internationally.

The sponsor may feel that the more money they provide, the greater their influence in the running of the sport. This, at times, has a detrimental effect on the performers and can change the traditions of the sport itself. Some sponsors who care about the sport they are involved with can ensure the standards of the sport are maintained and developed in the future.

What you will learn about in this section

1. Types of Media
2. Types of Television Broadcast
3. Satellite Television and Sport
4. How the Media Helps the Understanding of Sport
5. Radio, Press, IT and Sport
6. Positive and Negative Effects of Media Coverage

1 Types of Media

Sport uses all the different forms of media to bring itself to the widest audience. In each newspaper there are the sports columns; there are programmes and whole channels on TV and radio devoted to sport; and information technology (IT) provides access to many websites devoted to a particular sport.

The different forms of the media include TV, radio, press (magazines/specialist publications) and information technology.

Task 1

What to do:

1. Copy the spidergram shown above.
2. Add to each category names of TV channels, newspapers, magazines and websites that have connections with sport.

2 Types of Television Broadcast

Terrestrial television includes BBC1, BBC2, ITV, Channel 4 and Channel 5. All televisions can receive these channels providing they have an aerial to pick up the signal. The BBC programmes are financed by revenue from TV licence sales, whilst the independent channels pay their way by advertisements between and at the end of programmes shown. Certain programmes may even be sponsored by particular products, which are seen at the beginning, end and intervals of the programme.

The competition between terrestrial and **satellite television** companies is such that the Independent Television Commission (ITC) has to organise the allocation of sporting broadcasts between them as they feel that some sporting events are of major importance and should be available to everybody. This prevents the wealthier satellite companies buying up all the best sporting events. As a result, there are some sporting events which are protected by the ITC so that terrestrial TV can broadcast them. These sporting events make up two groups, A and B. Events on the class A list are legally bound to have the rights of their live coverage on the free TV channels. The B list can be shown on satellite or digital TV as long as there is provision made for highlights and delayed coverage for terrestrial TV. There are strict guidelines for B-list events concerning regulations on the length of the highlight coverage and how long after the live event it should be transmitted. Protecting the events in this way guarantees the traditional channels, which the majority of the population still only have access to, broadcasting rights to some top quality sport.

The revised list of sports events protected under Part IV of the Broadcasting Act 1996

Group A
(full live coverage protected)

The Olympic Games

The FIFA World Cup Finals Tournament

The European Football Championship Finals Tournament

The FA Cup Final

The Scottish FA Cup Final (in Scotland)

The Grand National

The Derby

The Wimbledon Tennis Finals

The Rugby League Challenge Cup Final

The Rugby World Cup Final (Rugby Union)

Group B
(secondary coverage protected)

Cricket Test Matches played in England

Non-finals played in the Wimbledon Tournament

All other matches in the Rugby World Cup Tournament

Six Nations Rugby Tournament matches involving Home Countries

The Commonwealth Games

The World Athletics Championships

The Cricket World Cup – the Final, Semi-final and matches involving Home Nations' Teams

The Ryder Cup

The Open Golf Championship

Active Challenge

With a partner decide on changes to the A and B list you would make so sports of your choice could be seen on terrestrial television.

3 Satellite Television and Sport

Subscription television was first transmitted into homes by BSkyB in 1989 and has completely changed the way broadcasting operates. The main companies for this type of transmission are BSkyB (British Sky Broadcasting Group PLC), Cable TV and Freeview.

For companies to gain the right to broadcast particular events, not on the A list, each have to make a bid for the rights to do so. The successful bid, which is largely based on the amount of money offered, earns exclusive rights to that sporting event. The more popular the sport the more expensive it is to buy the rights. Although winning the bid costs multi-millions of pounds, by selling the coverage the companies make their money back.

There are several specialist sports channels provided by BSkyB, broadcasting a wide variety of sports for all tastes. Eurosport is a sports channel showing a variety of events taking place in Europe. The coverage is of a wide variety of activities, including those that have yet to make their mark in Britain. This broadens the number of sports shown and so giving people the chance to see a sport for the first time and possibly be interested enough to participate in it.

Viewers can watch sports events interactively. This facility allows viewers a variety of choices when watching sport, which include different matches to watch, a choice of commentary, access to player profiles and the ability to view the match using a different camera angle. The new options provide greater freedom and give detailed information to the viewers, which can increase their interest and knowledge in the sport.

Pay per view

If a person subscribes to BSkyB they are eligible to watch sporting events that are broadcast on neither terrestrial nor BSkyB channels. These are **pay per view** events – the customer pays a certain amount of money to receive the event. Boxing is one of the main sports that are broadcast in this way. Here the companies feel that there will be such a demand to see the event that they can make money by showing it in this way.

Task 2

What to do:

1. Write a paragraph on how 'free to air' and subscription television differs.

4 How the Media Helps the Understanding of Sport

The various methods of the media help improve people's understanding of sport and current affairs, popularise personalities and provide sports' entertainment. Each form of media employs a series of experts (past players, pundits, presenters and journalists) to give their judgements, opinions and views on the sport in question.

Types of coverage

There are several different types of sporting broadcast, each with a different way of presenting the subject. For each event the director has an influence on how the information comes across: what and how it is said and particular points to be discussed. Therefore, the public see and hear what the director decides. Presenters may put their own slant on what they say during a broadcast as long as it is within stated boundaries, or a script may be used and read off an autocue.

Television programmes can be classified as informative, educational, instructive and entertaining. This reflects the general content and aims of the programme. Many programmes contain different elements.

Informative programmes

News, news bulletins and sport update programmes, together with Ceefax and Teletext services, are all in the informative programme group. They are based on facts, intending to give the viewer more information about a sport, event, club or performer. They are designed to give the public updates on results, future events and current issues regarding a sport or activity.

Educational programmes

Educational, schools and skills programmes are productions dealing with coaching and helping people learn about the skills, tactics and strategies of a game or activity. Sometimes, school programmes will suggest ways for further development and give information of where to take up an activity in the area. Some broadcasts are documentary-based and so are concerned with the facts about an event or activity, like the history of a sport for example. For some people, knowing more about a sport is interesting, increases their understanding of the game and can increase its popularity.

On the spot interviews after a match capture the emotion of the moment, making them entertaining.

Instructive programmes

This type of coverage is closely linked with educational programmes, but is mainly interested in teaching the viewer about a specific sport. They appeal to a specialist market interested in a particular activity. Some programmes mix the type of coverage shown. The broadcasting of the cricket test matches, largely under the heading of entertainment, have in the lunch break a 'master/super class' section, where experts and coaches relay coaching points, instructing young players on how to improve their technique. This part of the programme would fall under the informative title.

Entertaining programmes

These programmes are designed for enjoyment. They can include coverage of live matches and special events, highlight programmes and celebrity quiz shows. The drama of a game, for some, can be entertainment enough, but the addition of the commentary gives greater information and insight and can enhance the appeal even more. To add to the entertainment, a series of presenters, pundits and experts are employed to give their opinion on the event. Expert commentators, who have often competed at the highest level themselves, give in-depth views that are accurate and factual. Those currently involved in the sport can give up-to-date information on the issues relevant at the time. Live coverage matches are cheap to produce and attract large audiences even when broadcast in off-peak viewing time.

A Question of Sport is a popular TV quiz show

Highlight programmes, showing the events of the day, pick out the best of the action in the time they have available. Here the audience see exactly what the director wants them to see. This is usually the best of the action and any contentious moments too (particularly in football). These isolated incidents can be over-sensationalised by the panel of experts, becoming more talked about than the play itself.

Sports quiz shows have high ratings on television. This is due to the popular personalities on the show attracting the audiences. The quiz seems secondary to the antics of the personalities. The appeal to the public may be that they see respected sportspeople having fun and making people laugh. Guest appearances of current, popular sportspeople can attract a bigger audience, as people want to know more about and have greater access to their sporting role models.

Manchester United have such a following that they produce their own programmes broadcast on their own channel. This gives fans up-to-date information on players, club and fixtures.

What to do:

1. Write two sentences on each of the four types of television broadcast.

Task 3

Radio

Radio broadcasts regularly produce specialist sports programmes. These include coverage of live matches, discussion programmes and informative programmes. There is little rivalry between radio and television, as television regards itself as far more popular. Radio is therefore allowed to broadcast all sporting events live. There are several channels devoted solely to sport and news including Five Live, Talksport and BBC Radio Four's coverage of the cricket test matches. Cricket enthusiasts take their radios to the matches so that they can hear a commentary whilst they are watching the match live. Some people watch an event on television with the sound down, whilst listening to the radio commentary.

Press

The back pages of most newspapers are devoted to current sporting news. Each newspaper employs journalists and photographers to gather up-to-the-minute information about the matches and events for publication in the morning press. With this form of media the reader sees the match through the eyes of the journalists who are able to put their opinions forward and influence the reader.

Sports magazines devoted to the specialised reader are a large expanding market, the most popular subjects being football and golf. These publications contain entertaining, instructive and informative articles.

Title	Sport	Average issue readership	Total average net circulation per issue
Golf Monthly	golf	73 589	661 000
442	football	82 539	554 000
Golf World	golf	70 019	449 000
Rugby World	rugby	36 926	405 000
Angling Times	fishing	60 487	370 000
Match	football	70 398	300 000
Shoot!	football	30 222	219 000
Total Football	football	24 954	188 000
Yachting Monthly	yachting	37 516	175 000

Circulation of leading sports magazines.

IT

This is the newest and quickest-developing form of media. IT provides a way to access up-to-date information about sports, events and personalities in sport for those with access to an on-line computer. (It is worth remembering that some websites remain unchanged for a long time, so they may not be that current, but generally there is a note at the end of the website saying when it was last updated.) Many sports governing bodies, major clubs and smaller teams provide a website for those interested to learn more about them. The Internet also provides an advertising vehicle for retailers. Goods can be bought and sold quickly and easily using this service.

6 Positive and Negative Effects of Media Coverage

Positive Effects of Media Coverage

- Keeps people informed of current trends and players.
- The more information given to the spectator, the better they can appreciate the event.
- Seeing the sport on TV may encourage more participation.
- The more coverage a sport has in the media, the more supporters it may attract.
- The more coverage there is, the easier it is to attract sponsors and so more money is available to the sport.
- People become familiar with the players who become sports personalities and, hopefully, become positive role models in sport.
- Coverage of minority sports can popularise them.
- Money from broadcast bids goes direct to the sport.

Negative Effects of Media Coverage

- Major sports have most of the coverage to the detriment of the minority sports.
- Effect on attendance – as people watch in the comfort of their own homes.
- The demand to see the personalities in the media gives them little privacy.
- Small incidents can be exaggerated and often sensationalised.
- Newspaper columnists put their slant on how they see a game or personality.
- The directors of the programmes dictate exactly what is seen and so viewing is through their eyes.
- Traditional daytime sports may be influenced by the media to change to night matches, so that there are more viewers for instance cricket night matches, changes to the playing season.
- Subtle rule changes may be made to the sport so that it has greater appeal for the TV spectators, such as the tie-break in tennis.
- The timing of the events may have to change due to the timing slot of the TV broadcast, causing delays for the audience.
- Replaying incidents in the game may undermine the official's decisions through the pundits' comments and analysis. This can disregard the fact that the referee only has a split second to assess and apply the ruling.
- Sports not broadcast may, as a result, become less popular.

What to do:

1. Simplify the lists on the previous page by making two spidergrams – one for the positive, one for the negative effects of media coverage.
2. Work out the main idea (shown in bold in the example) and then write your own phrase.

   Examples:

   Keeps people **informed** of **current** trends and players = provides current information.

   Effects on **attendance** as people watch in the comfort of their own home = live coverage affects attendance.

What to do:

1. Write two facts about each of radio, press and information technology.

Include:
- any rivalries that may exist
- who uses them
- what services they provide
- how the media are developing.

BSkyB television brings money into football and boxing, but the fans can only watch live matches and fights if they pay.

Key Terms:

Pay per view ► extra sporting events, bought individually by the viewer and available only to subscription viewers

Satellite TV ► extra programmes available to those who purchase a receiver and pay a subscription

Terrestrial ► programmes available to everyone with a television and an aerial

Summary

Sport is such a popular and marketable commodity that all forms of media devote time, space and money to it. There are several successful television channels specifically devoted to sport. The influence of the director of the programme or columnist of the paper is massive on the viewer or reader, enough to persuade them to think in a certain way. Although there are many advantages of the media's involvement in sport, there are also disadvantages as well; for the benefit of sport getting the right balance is important.

What you will learn about in this section

1. Conduct of Players and Officials
2. Social and Antisocial Behaviour of Fans
3. Strategies Employed to Combat Hooliganism
4. Comparison of Behaviour in Different Sports
5. Political and Financial Issues
6. Amateur and Professional Sportspeople

1 Conduct of Players and Officials

Both players and officials have responsibility to the game, themselves and the fans. The referee implements the rules according to the play and the players attempt to outplay the opposition within the confines of the rules. With each sport there is an unwritten set of rules that is obeyed for the good of the sport and forms the etiquette of that sport. (This is looked at in more detail in 'Safety and Risk Assessment' page 145.)

2 Social and Antisocial Behaviour of Fans

The role of spectators is to show their support and favour to their team. This can play a major part in the success of their team. The encouragement of home support can have a great effect on both the home and away players. For the home team it can be an advantage. They will be subject to greater encouragement, appreciation of good play and a positive atmosphere. If the team play well, then the crowd give positive signals. The away team may be influenced by the hostile attitude of the fans and this may affect their performance. However, if the home team plays poorly then there may be the opposite effect. The crowd become restless, dissatisfied and aggressive.

Tim Henman recognises that crowd support can lift a player's game.

If the game is a local derby (a match between two teams from the same area) then there is added tension to the game. There may be stronger tackles and generally a more physical game. This can transfer to the crowd who can respond adversely to what they are seeing on the field of play. The crowd's reaction can influence the performance of the players and this can be transferred to the play. Tim Henman was helped by the Wimbledon crowd to raise his game and reach four consecutive semi-finals at the championships.

Active Challenge

Discuss with a partner the ways a crowd of fans can influence the play.

3 Strategies Employed to Combat Hooliganism

In 1989, 96 lives were lost in a crush of people at an FA Cup semi-final football match taking place at the Hillsborough Stadium, Sheffield. As a result of the Hillsborough disaster, there was a special inquiry by Lord Justice Taylor. The Taylor report was completed in 1990 and contained over 70 recommendations designed to improve spectator safety at football matches in Britain. The main changes were: the improvement of the stadiums, stopping ticket touting, new laws against racist comments and missile-throwing and dealing with older offenders.

With the introduction of all-seater stadiums and the improvement of football stadiums in general, there has been a decrease in hooliganism. Each fan buys a ticket for a particular seat. This keeps home and away fans segregated and reduces the chance of any violence between the two groups. Stewards and marshals are employed by the clubs to help the spectators. They help supporters to their seat and are a reassurance to fans that should there be any trouble they can quickly deal with the situation. They also check that supporters bring nothing dangerous into the stadium and are not under the influence of alcohol.

To further help with the movement of crowds the police are at hand, employed and paid for by the clubs, to keep any possible disturbances to a minimum.

What to do:

1. In your own words, say how changes have encouraged spectators to behave. Include six–ten changes.

4 Comparison of Behaviour in Different Sports

Each sport attracts its own fan base. Each group behaves in response to the nature of the game, the action that they see, the importance of the game and what is seen to be acceptable in the game. A supporter of tennis and rugby will act differently at each event.

The golf and snooker crowds know to be quiet when a shot is being played. The individual players performing the isolated skill can be easily distracted; the crowd appreciate this and in order to see the best quality play they act accordingly. Generally, invasion games can be played with a great amount of crowd noise. A rugby crowd, for instance, will shout encouragement throughout the game and at times it can have a positive effect on the play.

Team players get encouragement from their supporters, which can have a positive effect on their play.

Rules

If the rules are obeyed and the official has charge of the situation then the atmosphere may be more controlled. The crowd can become agitated and hostile when it is evident that there is a lack of control. The rules clearly define what is right and wrong. It is vital when strong, motivated and competitive players are engaged in competition that they know and keep to the rules.

Rugby uses interim rules for foul play. The 10-yard rule moves the play forward if there is any argument with the referee and the sin bin extracts players for a period of time from the game. The spectators see that there is a degree of punishment and a series of impositions in force for different infringements. Sports learn from each other; football has adopted the 10-yard rule into the game in an attempt to bring about better behaviour from the players. Hockey now uses the sin bin system to penalise players' foul play.

Task 2

What to do:

1. Spectators watching different sports change the way they behave. What makes fans act in a different way depending on the event? In your own words, write a paragraph on this subject.

5 Political and Financial Issues

The government sees sport as an important part of life in this country. In Parliament there is a minister for sport who travels the world attending meetings and conferences promoting British involvement in sport. This minister provides a link between sport governing bodies and the government and advises them on new initiatives and procedures. The government helps to finance sport through taxes and the Lotto. Parliament legislates (makes the rules and regulations) for safety in sport and the improvement of sport in general.

Many countries abroad, especially the former USSR, made sport their priority. They picked out the potential champions and trained them in government-run centres, improving standards and levels of performance. This gave talented sportspeople the chance to shine, but as the government made decisions for everyone, the individuals had no say in anything. It was seen as their duty to their country. This way of training for sport positively raised the standard of other countries' performances in their attempt to keep up with the communist countries.

At times, there are worldwide politically difficult issues which overlap with sport. The feelings are such that individuals, teams or even national sides boycott major competitions, showing their views publicly. In the UK, when there is a politically difficult situation involving our sportspeople the government leaves the decision to the individual or governing body concerned.

Different countries have historically used sport as an advert for their opinions. Major events are seen worldwide and so political activists use this coverage to demonstrate their beliefs. The Olympic Games is the largest showcase sporting event in the world. It is a typical example of how sport is used as a political tool.

Many incidents have been linked with athletics. Many of the Olympic Games have been associated with political issues.

- Berlin 1936 – Games used for propaganda by Hitler.
- 1940 & 1944 – Games cancelled due to war.

- London 1948 – Germany, Japan and the former Soviet Union are non-participants.
- Helsinki 1952 – Germany excluded. The East–West rivalry begins (Communism v Democracy).
- Melbourne 1956 – There are many disruptions:
  - Egypt and Lebanon withdraw because of the Suez crisis
  - Spain, Holland and Switzerland withdraw because of their disapproval of the former Soviet Union invading Hungary
  - China withdraw because Taiwan, previously part of China, entered their own team
  - Germany are re-admitted.
- Rome 1960 – South Africa enter an all-white team. China forced to compete under the title Taiwan: they do so under protest.
- Tokyo 1964 – South Africa banned because of apartheid.
- Mexico 1968 – American black athletes raise black-gloved fists protesting about treatment of black people in the USA.
- Munich 1972 – Palestinian terrorists kill 11 Israeli Olympic athletes.
- Montreal 1976 – many African nations withdraw due to New Zealand rugby tour to South Africa.
- Moscow 1980 – Over 60 nations refuse to attend because of the Soviet Union invasion of Afghanistan.
- Los Angeles 1984 – Soviet Union boycott the Games, their reason being that there were poor security arrangements.
- Seoul 1988 – IOC refuses to allow events to take place in North Korea, so they boycott.
- Barcelona 1992 – South Africa compete in the Games after an absence of 30 years.
- Atlanta 1996 – Bomb explodes near to stadium.
- Sydney 2000 – Australian authorities make attempts to bridge the gap between themselves and the Aborigine people.

Major sports events, such as the Sydney Olympics 2000, can have a positive political impact. Midnight Oil underscored lyrics about returning Australian land to the Aborigine people by wearing black T-shirts and track pants with the word 'sorry' emblazoned in bold white letters. Aussie chart toppers Savage Garden's singer wore a T-shirt displaying the Aborigine flag.

A variety of other sports have had their share of political interference too. Here are just three examples:

- rugby 1949 – New Zealand rugby team not allowed to play in South Africa as it had a Maori player. At the time, in South Africa, no black player could play on the same team as a white one.
- cricket 1970 – South African tour of England cancelled by the government.
- football 2000 – Ivory Coast national football team held prisoners for losing at football. Many played domestic football in Europe, so there was a question as to whether they should have to play for their country again in the future.

Task 3

What to do:

1. Describe how different countries organise training for sportspeople.
2. Why have major sporting events been used as a political weapon?
3. What political issues have been linked with sport in the past?

Financing major events

The hosting of major international events can improve the profile of a country. The reasons for choosing a particular country to host a major sports event may be made on political grounds, historic sporting traditions, recent sporting success or the need to promote the sport in that region.

If a bid is to be successful then several matters have to be addressed:

- Do the facilities meet the required standard?
- Is the provision for competitor accommodation good enough?
- Are the spectators able to gain access to the competitions?
- How will the event be financed?
- Is there adequate security for the event?

Hosting a major event promotes sport in that country and brings increased revenue from the event. The World Cup 2002 was held in both Japan and South Korea.

To fulfil all the requirements of the governing body, enormous financial investment is required. Sports stadiums and villages are a major cost, as they need to be built or updated. To meet the costs, sponsors contribute money in order that their product is linked with the event and television rights are sold worldwide. Further income is generated from nationwide appeals and merchandising.

The cost of hosting a major event like the Olympics takes a great deal of organising. Many of the past Games have proved to be very expensive to the host countries. The Montreal Games began with the stadium unfinished and the country ended up in debt after the games. Los Angeles was the first Games to make a substantial profit. The Sydney Olympics 2000 attracted many sponsors: there were ten contributing 50 million Australian dollars for the right to have their company's product associated with the games. The estimated running cost of the event has been worked out at 2.4 billion Australian dollars.

The differences between amateurs and professionals

Mick Hill, professional athlete, during the Aqua-Pura Commonwealth Trials.

Phill Sharpe, amateur athlete, javelin winner at the English Schools Championships.

Professionals

- To the professional player, sport is their job.
- They receive financial reward for participating and this is how they make their living.
- In top-class sport, the rewards can be enormous, providing a luxurious lifestyle to the sportsperson. The greater the success, the bigger the financial rewards.
- Professionals train on a full-time basis and are usually controlled by the club, such as in the case of footballers.
- Each player signs a contract not only to play for the club, but to be engaged in other events to do with the club.

Amateurs

- Amateurs use sport as a leisure activity, which takes place in their own time and is totally separate from their work.
- There is no payment for their participation; in fact with annual subscription and match fees, it costs the amateur to participate.
- As their livelihood does not depend on playing sport it is their choice to take part.
- Sport provides an enjoyable interest outside of the workplace, relieving stress, keeping the body healthy and is a means to socialise.
- Many amateurs will train to improve their skill, but not to the same extent as a professional.
- In any competition, they will have to keep to a set of rules laid down by the governing body just like professional players.

How amateurs make a living

Some amateur sportspeople gain money indirectly for participating. Although payment to amateurs is illegal, loopholes are found so they can still receive 'payments' for their services.

Expenses – under the label of travel and personal expenses, these can exceed the actual cost of the travel and food needed and so would be a payment for playing.

Gifts – presented to the performer for taking part or winning an event. Some gifts could be cashed in and so indirectly act as a payment for performing.

Scholarships – the athlete is accepted, free of charge, into a university and receives expert training as part of the course at no expense.

Trust funds – money is deposited in a fund for use by the athlete when they retire.

Occupation – a token job is given to the athlete for which they are paid. This allows them to be financially secure so they are able to take part in their chosen sport. Often, in foreign countries a job in the armed forces covers this kind of payment to a talented sportsperson.

Sponsorship – a company supplies the team with money or equipment in return for their logos on the clothing.

Illegal payments – some performers receive illegal payments for their inclusion in an event. This was common in amateur football, where money was placed in the boots of the player on completion of the game, so it became known as 'boot money'.

Athletics was traditionally viewed as an amateur sport. The International Amateur Athletic Federation (IAAF) was founded in 1912. In recent years the International Olympic Committee (IOC) relaxed their rules about payment to performers in order to keep the standard high. This means that athletes are able to train and compete on a full-time basis. This move towards a more professional sport was particularly recognised in 2001, when the IAAF Congress voted unanimously for the organisation's name to be changed to the International Association of Athletics Federations.

How professionals earn their money

Wages – many performers have agents who negotiate contracts for the players before they sign to a club or sponsor. Their job is to get the best wage deal for the player.

Bonuses – these are negotiated at the contract-signing stage and rely on the success of the player or the team.

Appearance money – the best sportspeople are a great attraction at an event; they will increase the number of people coming to watch. These people are paid to participate whether they do well in the competition or not. Golfers and athletes are often paid in this way.

The rewards today are so enormous that, for financially secure tennis player Pete Sampras, his motivation now is to beat the record of grand slam wins held by Rod Laver and not necessarily to win more money.

Transfer fees – when players are bought by other clubs they can receive a percentage of the fee.

Media work – TV appearances, radio work and magazine articles generally have a fee attached negotiated by the agent.

Sponsorship – a player receives a financial reward from a company to help with training. This is usually for advertising a product on sports clothing or using their equipment.

Endorsements – the well-known performers are paid to promote a product.

What to do:

1. Make a list of the differences between professional and amateur sport.

Open competitions

'Open' events invite all performers to compete whether they are amateur or professional. This brings together sportspeople from all backgrounds and previous experience. In golf, the British Open is a good example. The prize money to the winner is enormous. If an amateur were to win, then they would receive a medal as best amateur, but no financial reward for their efforts. In this sport, there is a clear distinction between the two levels of player.

Improved sports facilities and an increase in leisure time mean that amateurs can commit themselves to their sport. They will have time to increase their fitness and skill levels. As the golfing example shows, a dedicated amateur can compete on an equal footing with the professional.

As an amateur Justin Rose came third in the British Open competition. He received the amateur medal for his success.

Some amateur competitors may see these 'open' events as a way of gaining money and ignore the recommendations of the governing bodies of the sport. In some cases turning professional is more appealing than remaining an amateur. If the player had been a member of their national amateur squad, then this will weaken the country's amateur team. As players make progress in their sport, small clubs may be unable to make it financially viable for them to remain there.

For some amateur performers, as they become more successful, their desire to win at all costs grows too. As they progress, they form an elite of amateur performers, making amateur competitions predictable and less appealing. Open competitions can undermine the amateur ideal of playing for the love of the game.

Advantages of being a professional sportsperson

Making the grade as a professional player is difficult and making it right to the top of a chosen sport is harder still. There are many young people who go for trials for football teams and suffer the disappointment of not making the grade.

Those who do achieve top-class status enjoy a luxurious lifestyle. High earnings can give financial security to a sportsperson for the rest of their lives. The top competitions take place all over the world so for the best sportspeople, they have the opportunity to travel and visit new countries as part of their job.

Players are often in the public eye and can earn great popularity with their supporters. A high-profile player, with a good reputation, can attract a variety of employment opportunities during and after their sporting days are over, giving them job security.

The rewards are high for footballers, if they make the grade.

Key Terms:

Amateur	► performer who competes for pleasure without monetary reward
Antisocial behaviour	► behaviour against other people
Boycott	► refuse to have anything to do with a person or event
Endorsement	► promoting a product for money
Gentlemen cricketers	► wealthy men, who played cricket in the nineteenth century
Professional	► performer playing and training full-time for financial reward
Taylor Report	► 1990 report attempting to outline possible improvements to football spectator safety in Britain

Gary Lineker, previously a top-class footballer, is now a TV presenter.

TV personality Sue Barker, here interviewing Lleyton Hewitt at the 2002 Wimbledon finals, was at one time ranked number 3 in the world for tennis.

Disadvantages of being a professional sportsperson

Although the lifestyle is good, a professional player's career is very short in comparison with the working life of the average person. They face the problem of finding a new career midway through their life. Every time a sportsperson trains or competes, there is the risk of injury shortening their career even further. Also, it must be remembered that not all sports at professional level pay equally well.

There are many pressures for the top class performer:

- Once they have reached the top there is the stress of staying there.
- There is strain to keep motivated in training in order to maintain and increase performance.
- In a team game, there is much competition for the few first team places, so there is constant pressure to be at the top of the game.
- All sportspeople have to keep motivated to train and keep winning too. Some performers feel a need to win at all costs and so succumb to cheating in order to keep winning.
- Any mistakes made are seen by all and can lead to negative press and unpopularity.
- The player and their family are constantly in the public eye and often suffer from their privacy being invaded.
- Performers are increasingly required for interview after a competition, even if they are uncomfortable in front of a camera. This is becoming such a major part of sport that there are courses for sportspeople, teaching them how to handle the media positively.

Active Challenge

Discuss with a partner the advantages and disadvantages of being famous and how you would handle the pressures involved.

History of change

Initially all sport was amateur; people played because they loved the game and there was no need for financial reimbursement as they were usually the wealthy middle and upper classes.

In first-class cricket, the changes began to be made in the mid-nineteenth century. The sport began to use the skills of working class players who could not afford to self-finance their play. As a result there became a distinction between the 'players' (professionals who were paid to play) and the 'gentlemen' (amateur) cricketers.

Most sports today have a professional section, but the history of how willing each were to take on the professional code is varied, as the timeline below shows.

How the role of the player has changed

1846	Football Association formed by undergraduates at Cambridge encouraging a common code.
1860	All cricket players were wealthy amateurs. There were no money rewards for success, but prizes were given to the winners. Play was more for fun by the 'gentlemen amateurs' of the upper and middle classes who earned their living by their non-sporting professions.
1860	Golf becomes professional with the first British Open Golf Championship held in Scotland's Prestwick Club.
1877	First Wimbledon competition for all amateurs, a gold prize for the winner and a silver one for the runner-up.
1880	More working class players in cricket that played top class cricket but needed their full-time jobs to support their families. The rules on professionalism had to change as the numbers of working class players increased. The governing bodies controlled the changes so that fair practices, fair competition and the values of the sport were kept intact.
1880	Amateur Athletics Association (AAA) formed.
1885	Professional football legalised.
1888	Lawn Tennis Association (LTA) formed.
1893	Rugby League formed: players are paid for playing.
1894	International Olympic Committee (IOC) formed by Pierre de Coubertin. Its philosophy was to 'enhance human development ...' and 'blend sport with culture and education ...'
1900	Women compete for the first time in the Paris Olympics.
1904	FIFA founded to promote football and safeguard the sport.
1920	Professional tennis players started to make money from tennis. Although there was an increase in professional sports players some governing bodies kept their game amateur: rugby union and athletics are prime examples. The Olympics governing body, the IOC, saw their event as amateur. They tried to keep participation pure with no payment and competing for enjoyment alone. The standards were rising and each country wanted to improve their athletes' performances.
1927	First professional snooker championships.

1930	First football World Cup.
1954	UEFA formed: responsible for football in Europe.
1963	First professional boxing convention and the World Boxing Council formed.
1967	LTA abolished the distinction between professionals and amateurs.
1968	International Tennis Federation (ITF) approve open professionalism. Rod Laver wins the men's singles at Wimbledon and a prize of £2000, whilst Billie-Jean King wins the women's and receives £750.
1973	British Amateur Rugby League Association (BARLA) formed to give amateurs a say in Rugby League decisions.
1979	Trevor Francis transfers to Nottingham Forest and becomes Britain's first £1 million player.
1988	European Ladies Professional Golf Association formed (USA formed theirs in 1951).
1995	Rugby Union made professional.
2001	Fulham Ladies FC become the first British and European professional ladies club.
2002	David Beckham first British footballer to receive £100 000 a week.

What to do:

1. Using the timeline above, create individual timelines for the following sports:
   - football
   - tennis
   - athletics.

Effect of professional sport

Professional sport raises the standard of competition, since it enables athletes to train on a full-time basis and earn a living from it. As the performers become better at their chosen activity, the competition is more attractive to watch. Companies wishing to advertise themselves see sport as a way of showing off their product in the market place and will invest money in sport to do so.

This additional money has several effects on the sport. The governing bodies of the sport can increase their resources for administration and so develop and improve events and competitions into 'showcase' events. This in turn will attract better performers and more spectators. New stadiums with improved facilities can be built, making venues more attractive to spectators. This increases the numbers watching the events.

Nike and the mobile phone company, O_2, sponsor Arsenal. The deal with O_2, which began as a shirt sponsorship, has since evolved into the first fully interactive partnership between a football club and sponsor designed to generate revenue for the club (see photo).

Professionals travel widely to play and earn high salaries. Here, French, English and Dutch internationals play together in London for Arsenal.

Task 6

What to do:

There are many jobs related to sport – not just as a player or performer.

1. Make a list of these jobs.
2. Write some skills that school could teach to help with experience.

Summary

The players and referee influence how a game turns out. The players are responsible for keeping to the rules and being competitive. The conduct within the game seems to influence the mood of the fans and they react accordingly. As a result of the Hillsborough disaster, the Taylor Report took steps to improve football in Britain. It brought in rules to make stadiums safer, deter racism and aggressive behaviour, stop illegal ticket touting and generally improve the image of sport.

Each sport engenders different behaviour from their fans. The same people may watch several different live sports events and at each react differently according to the accepted behaviour of that sport.

The way sport is organised varies in each country and reflects how important it is to the government. Sport can be used as a way of showing off the strength of a country on the world stage. Sometimes major events, broadcast all over the world, are used as a means to advertise political issues.

Many sports have professional and amateur status. Performers fall into amateur and professional categories. Pure amateurs receive no money and play for pleasure in their leisure time. People competing at a high level, in what is seen to be an amateur sport, can receive money indirectly for their efforts. Professionals train on a full-time basis and play sport as their job.

Influences of Local and National Providers

What you will learn about in this section

1. Public Funding for Sport in the UK
2. Private Provision for Sport
3. Sports Clubs and Their Members
4. Ways of Financing Sports Clubs
5. The Role of the Different Sports Organisations

The amount of facilities available in an area has a direct effect on the participation levels. A community with local access to good facilities will be more inclined to take part in sport. Better facilities may also attract a higher standard of coach and so increase the skills of those taking part.

1 Public Funding for Sport in the UK

Local government may operate on a parish (village and rural communities), town, city or district council level. The facilities can be run by the councils themselves or a private company can be contracted by the council, with the aim of running the centre at a profit within stated guidelines. If a centre cannot finance itself then the local council can help by meeting any shortfall. Such subsidies help to keep the centre open.

In the UK, the government filters money for local sport through to the local councils. In turn, local government has elected councillors who have the responsibility of making provision for leisure in their locality.

The Department of Culture, Media and Sport, created in 1992, influences sport in Britain. Since 1994, it has been responsible for the distribution of the national lottery (Lotto) fund, including that allocated for use in sport. The DCMS provides grants to central bodies, like Sport England.

Collectively, the sports councils have over £1billion per year allocated to them by the government for sport. The government also provides guidelines to the councils affecting the building of facilities and the amount of land available for sport use at a local level. With UK trends moving away from participating in team games and more toward individual gym and general health pursuits, policies drawn up by the politicians change accordingly.

Each county council has a designated officer for sport. They create a link between local, regional and national sports bodies. Their local knowledge and interest recognise where there is most a need for improvement. The general aim is to encourage and enable sporting prospects for all.

Local authorities provide 1600 public leisure centres in the UK. These offer a wide range of sports and activities with sports halls, swimming pools and outside facilities. These facilities make sport available to all members of the community at a reasonable cost. There are subsidies made for particular users and time slots reserved for certain groups, to attract as many types of people as possible.

Task 1

What to do:

1. State the connection between local and national government provision for sport in the community.

2 Private Provision for Sport

Sport centres come under three categories – commercial sports centres, private clubs and employee sports centres. The demand is so great for gyms and health clubs that private provision has had to increase in this area in order to meet the demand. In 2002, there were over 3500 private health clubs in the UK, with the number still growing. There are many small business providers for this type of leisure pursuit, but there are seven main companies sharing a million members.

Company	Main club boards	No. of members in UK	No. of UK sites
Whitbread	Marriott	300 000	110
Fitness First	Fitness First	210 000	90
Esporta	Esporta	167 000	37
Cannons	Cannons Courtney's	160 000	57
Holmes Place	Holmes Place	132 000	42
Hilton Group	Living Well	115 000	88
De Vere	Village & De Vere Greens	98 000	41

Leisure companies in the UK

Source: Leisure and hospitality business, fitness focus supplement, August 2001.

Commercial sports centres charge membership fees and sometimes a joining fee. They may also charge extra for particular activities or for the use of health and beauty treatments.

Private clubs usually offer one major sport, but can sometimes specialise in two areas successfully. Wimbledon is such a club offering two sports, its full name being Wimbledon Lawn Tennis and Croquet Club. Private clubs are self-financing through club membership and, in the case of Wimbledon, earn money from holding a showcase event annually.

An employer can also set up sporting provision for their employees by providing a sports centre. In some cases, a subsidised membership fee may be charged, or some companies provide the facility free of charge. By offering such facilities the company has a healthier work force, the extra provision may make employees more loyal to the company and for certain jobs fitness may be necessary to do the job well, so the company can increase effectiveness of their workforce.

3 Sports Clubs and Their Members

In order to play many sports there is often a need to join a formal club. (Some activities, like swimming and rambling, are an exception.) These clubs are classed as voluntary organisations and many exist all over the country. Many of them offer the opportunity to compete not only with those in the club, but other teams too. There are millions of people who join clubs to improve their skills, compete against others and meet other people with similar interests.

Number of UK sports clubs and their members for selected sports.

Sport	No. of clubs	No. of members	Average no. of members per club
football	42000	1500 000	36
snooker	5300	1500 000	283
golf	2877	1126 000	391
tennis	2450	750 000	306
bowls	8600	500 000	58
sailing/yachting	1620	450 000	278
motor sports	750	420 000	560
rugby union	2026	284 000	140
martial arts	1000	175 000	175
athletics	1750	135 000	77
hockey	2000	90 000	45

Source:
Sports associations/NTC Marketing pocket book/keynote.

The purpose of joining a club is to play a sport or participate in an activity. For this to happen there is much work and organising to do behind the scenes. Members often take on the various jobs involved in the running of a club voluntarily. These people form a committee, who meet regularly to discuss issues involved in club matters and its development.

A committee is usually formed from the playing members of the club, but skilled people who do not play can also be involved. This can be especially true in a large club where there is a large annual turnover of money: the treasurer may be a trained accountant who does not play the sport.

A chairperson conducts the meeting making sure everyone has their chance to put their views forward. The secretary records what is said in the meeting in a written form called 'minutes'. Part of the secretary's job is to store the minutes of past meetings and in most clubs display those of recent meetings for all to see.

Money is needed to run the club: this is generated from subscriptions, match fees, grants from particular agencies and fund-raising events held throughout the year. The treasurer keeps a check on club finances and regular reports are produced to check the club stays in credit.

The fixtures for a club can be organised by the league or by a designated member of the club. If matches have to be cancelled, then postponed matches are rearranged by the fixtures secretary. The results of the matches are sent to the league and displayed in the club for all to see. In many cases there is a results secretary who is responsible for displaying scores on the club notice board.

On the committee is the captain of the club who represents the players. A vice-captain is elected so that they can deputise in the absence of the captain. A social secretary helps with events, bringing members together and raising money for the club.

Some committees have a representative liaising with the governing bodies of the sport or the local council. This keeps the club up to date with regulations and policy that might affect the club. Their job may also involve linking with the community so that schools can make use of their facilities too. Making the facilities available in this way may encourage young people to join the club in the future. Using the expertise in the club will help skill development and improve performance as well as give the opportunity to pupils of using the best facilities.

People often forget what goes on behind the scenes of a sport and how events get organised. Many people, not just the athletes, are needed to ensure a club is run successfully.

Active Challenge

With a partner, discuss ways schools could use local sports clubs for their pupils.

All members are eligible to have their say in club matters. However, having a meeting of every member would be difficult to hold, so the committee members make the decisions representing the whole membership. Important people in the club, but not necessarily on the committee, are the ground staff and the designated umpires or referees of the club. Any issues they have can be raised at a meeting through any of the committee representatives.

What to do:

1. In your own words, state the importance of having a committee in a club.
2. For each committee member, write a description of their job to go in the recruitment section of a newspaper.

4 Ways of Financing Sports Clubs

Sports clubs are run as a business and aim to break even or make a profit. They have to generate their funding themselves, as they receive no support for the general running of the club by the government. They employ several ways to do this:

- Membership fees – those wanting to join the club pay a membership fee. This can be as a player or as a social member. As the membership grows, so too does the amount of money brought into the club.
- Fund-raising – raffles, open days, events. Large sports clubs benefit from a supporters club, which helps with fund-raising and can provide donations.
- Sponsorship – attracting companies to give financial support to the club, which can go towards buying the kit, equipment and improvements to the ground.
- TV rights – major sports attract a large viewing audience and the clubs receive a share of money from TV companies.
- Gate receipts – for clubs with a large following, gate receipts are a major contributor to club funds.
- Merchandising – many large clubs produce an assortment of merchandise for supporters to buy.
- Grants from agencies – the national sports councils distribute lottery money to various clubs and the Sports Aid Foundation gives money to the governing bodies of sport to dispense.
- Some clubs operate on private land provided by an individual. Usually this person has an interest in promoting that particular sport.
- Profits made by providing catering or social events at a club contribute to club funds. This occurs at many golf clubs, for instance.

What to do:

1. Give examples of how different clubs use the various ways of funding.

Example: Professional clubs, like Bath Rugby Club, charge the public to watch their matches, which contributes to financing the club.

5 The Role of the Different Sports Organisations

There are many national authorities and organisations working to promote sport in the UK. Each group target specific sections of the community and work towards helping their involvement in physical activity. At a government level, there are the sports councils, helping sport in general. There are also national organisations, which partly fund themselves and receive additional funds from the regional sports councils. Some national authorities run on a purely voluntary basis.

The Department of Culture, Media and Sport

The DCMS, created in 1992, influences sport in Britain. Since 1994, it has been responsible for the distribution of the lottery fund, including that allocated for use in sport.

The DCMS provide grants to central bodies like Sport England to subsidise various sports. The DCMS published the government's plan for sport in the publication *A Sporting Future For All* in 2001. In this document, it emphasises the importance of sport and the community:

> Sport is an important dimension of life for the community ... . Sport and the cultural services should therefore be at the heart of an authority's community planning.

The DCMS have specific goals for sport, some of which include:

- encouraging excellence at every level
- more participation in sport ... particularly among young people, women, ethnic minority groups and people with disabilities
- modernising and reform of sports governing bodies
- enabling athletes to participate equally in drugs-free sport
- ensuring role of sport in education in schools and lifelong learning is enhanced
- better training and education in sports coaching and for officials
- bringing more major international sporting events to the UK.

National sports organisation in the UK 2002

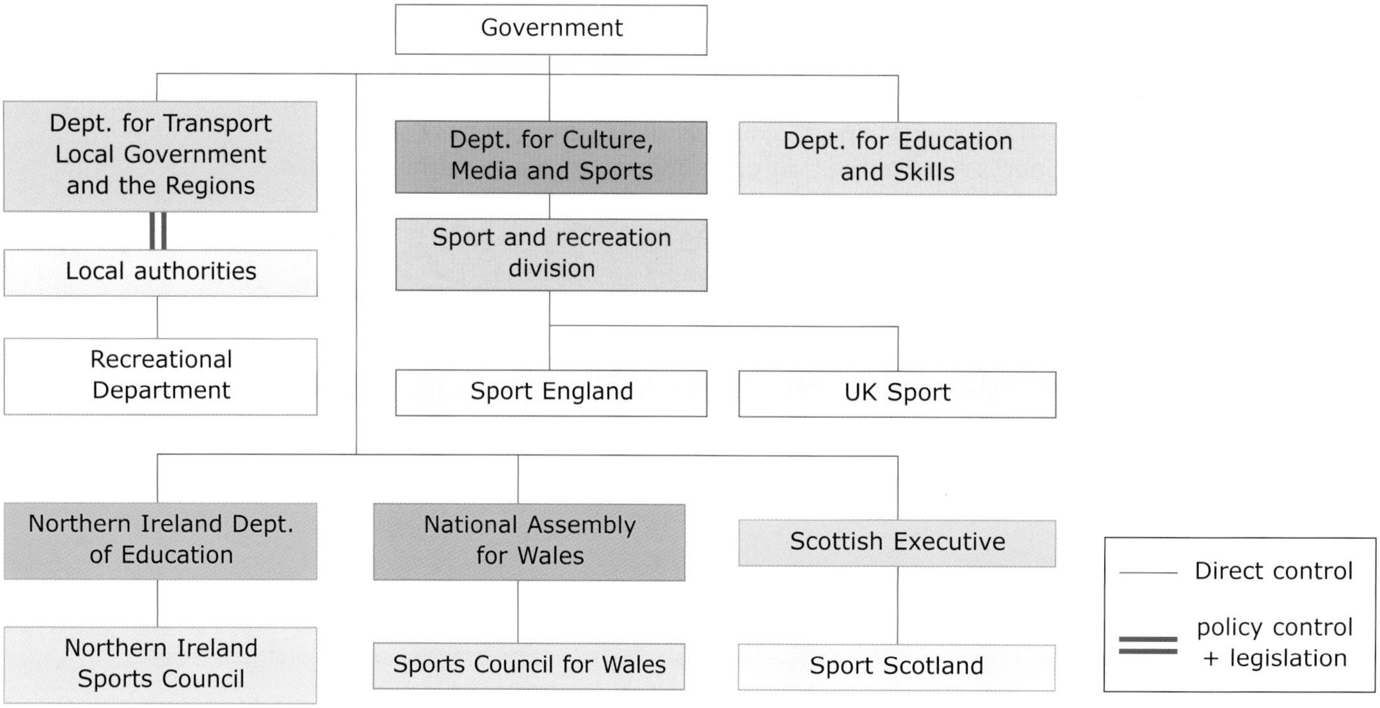

Sports Council

The UK Sports Council is divided into five distributing bodies. One is UK Sport – a national body and the other four are regional bodies: Sport England, Sport Scotland, Sports Council for Wales and Sports Council for Northern Ireland.

The job of the Sports Councils is to distribute the money raised for sports by the national lottery to the five independent bodies. The money that comes in does not have to be spent in that financial year, as in the case of local councils' funds, so large sums of money can build up for major facilities and projects. They aim to work on existing ideas and proposals but have a view to develop new ideas too.

National Sports Council – UK Sport

This council concerns itself with high performance in sport at the national level and a drug-free involvement of the athletes. It helps top-class performers to compete on the world stage. It does this by making sure the system for the structure and development of sport is capable of producing world class performers. The World Class Performance Programme aims to support and fund the athletes in many ways:

- providing world class coaches
- sports science and medicine back-up
- warm-weather and acclimatisation training
- international competition programmes (including travel and accommodation)
- athlete development programmes
- training facilities
- performance directors to bring it all together.

UK Sport also uses the lottery money to promote the UK as a suitable venue to host major sporting events. By doing this, it allows the athletes and the public to benefit from home events.

Regional Sports Councils

Each regional sports council receives money to promote sport in their area. This money comes from the lottery and is in addition to money provided by the government through taxes. Each body can choose the way it uses the money according to the needs of the region.

National – UK Sport
Focuses directly on high performance sport at the UK level, with the aim of achieving sporting excellence on the world stage.

Regional – Sport England
Sees a responsibility to
– young people
– the community
– those striving to raise their standard of performance.

Regional – Sport Scotland
Promotes sporting opportunities for all Scots at all levels, whatever their interest and ability.

SPORTS COUNCIL
money raised from National Lottery goes to – 1 National and 4 Regional councils

Regional – Sports Council for Wales
Its vision is to increase participation and performance in sport and plan for a bright sporting future.

Regional – Sports Council for Northern Ireland
Its aims are to increase and sustain committed participation, especially among young people and to raise the standards of sporting excellence.

The Sports Councils and their stated aims

National – UK Sport

Focuses directly on high performance sport at the UK level, with the aim of achieving sporting excellence on the world stage.

Sports Council

Money raised from the lottery goes to one national and four regional councils.

Regional – Sport England

Sees a responsibility to: young people, the community and those striving to raise their standard of performance.

Regional – Sports Council for Wales

Its vision is to increase participation and performance in sport and plan for a bright sporting future.

Regional – Sport Scotland

Promotes sporting opportunities for all Scots at all levels, whatever their interest and ability.

Regional – Sports Council for Northern Ireland

Its aims are to increase and sustain committed participation, especially among young people and to raise the standard of sporting excellence.

Sport England

Also known as the English Sports Council, aims to increase participation in sport, provide more sporting venues and be a support to those who are committed to excellence in their sport. Sport England concentrates work on the following three programmes:

- **More people** involved in sport
- **More places** to play sport
- **More medals** through higher standards of performance.

It receives its funding from the exchequer and the lottery and is accountable for its actions to parliament through the Secretary of State for Culture, Media and Sport (DCMS) and the Public

uk sport

SPORT ENGLAND

THE SPORTS COUNCIL FOR WALES
CYNGOR CHWARAEON CYMRU

sportscotland
widening opportunities • developing potential • achieving excellence

SPORTS
COUNCIL NORTHERN IRELAND

Accounts Committee. The funding from the government goes towards maintaining the general running of sport in the country. The lottery money, set aside for sport in England, goes to bids made by groups or individuals for sports development.

The head office of Sport England is in London, but its staff keep close links with nine main regional offices around the country. The network of contacts include those in the public and private sector such as local authorities, sports governing bodies, national and regional organisations dealing with sport, recreation, education and the environment.

Part of the role of Sport England is to create links with other groups. Regional officers organise events and competitions in their area and open them to children in the locality. Representatives of Sport England are keen to involve school children and so create links with local schools. They discuss future events with teachers, encouraging them to enter teams and take advantage of the competitions. Further links are made by inviting the organisers of public facilities, local clubs and schools to host these events.

Sports governing bodies

Every sport has a governing body, to which the local club will affiliate. In the UK, there are about 400 national governing bodies. Their job is to maintain the standards of the sport whilst promoting the sport's image to the rest of the world. The sports councils support the governing bodies by providing them with grants. The extra finance goes to help administer, promote and develop each of the activities.

Generally, the same body controls the sport whether it is at amateur or professional level, drawing up its rules, standards and codes of conduct. Each body supports participation at all levels from the local club to the national performer. They organise competitions, education programmes and awards and certificates promoting their particular sport.

Most governing bodies have associations or links, but they may also operate as federations (which are groupings of different associations). The Amateur Swimming Association is a good example of having links with other sports as it organises events and development for diving, water polo and synchronised swimming.

The following are some of the largest governing bodies. They are placed in order of their membership size.

The Football Association – the governing body of the game in England and seeks to develop football at all levels. The Football League is an association of the largest professional clubs in all divisions.

Royal and Ancient Golf Club of St Andrew's – this governs golf in the UK and sets the rules worldwide. The sport has a number of associations separating amateur and professional and male and female golfers, such as the Ladies Golfing Union and the Professional Golfer's Association.

Marylebone Cricket Club (MCC) – the club is based at Lord's Cricket Ground in London and administers the rules of the game.

Lawn Tennis Association – this body represents tennis on a national level. The main event in the UK – The Championship, held at Wimbledon, is organised by the All-England Lawn Tennis Club.

National Federation of Anglers – this is made up of different fishing associations and organisations for the different types of fishing.

Amateur Swimming Association – this is made up of the federation of over 1600 swimming clubs in England.

Keep Fit Association – this is an English group organising participants in aerobic exercise, dance exercise and eurythmics.

Task 4

All sports governing bodies are affiliated to the international organisation for that sport. For example, the Football Association is affiliated to UEFA – Union des Associations Europeennes de Football and worldwide to FIFA – Federation Internationale de Football Association.

What to do:

1. Compare the following different sports organisations:
   - Sports Council
   - national sports council
   - regional sports councils
   - sports governing bodies
2. Make a written account of their areas of responsibility.

School and sports development

Sport England is committed to giving young people the best start in physical education and sport. It has set up the Active Schools programme in order to support its intention. Active Schools is a crucial part of the More People programme.

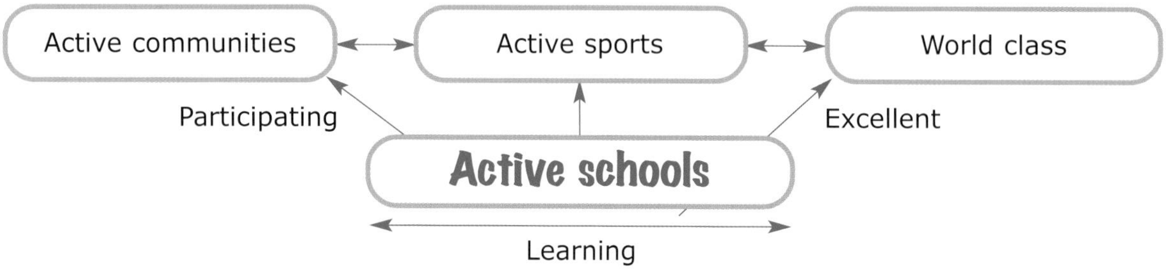

There are several schemes in place to encourage schools to raise their standards of sport. Each scheme encourages skills development in staff, more participation by the pupils and opportunities in a wide range of activities.

TOP programmes

TOP Play and TOP Sport are jointly organised by the Youth Sports Trust and Sport England. They are designed to support the National Curriculum and help children improve their skill and involvement levels in sport. They cover a variety of games and activities such as athletics, gymnastics, outdoor activities and swimming. TOP Play is for 4–9-year-olds and TOP Sport is for 7–11-year-olds. All primary schools are eligible for the scheme. Accompanying the scheme are resource cards, equipment bags and training for teachers.

Sportsmark

The Sportsmark award scheme is directed at secondary schools. Qualifying schools are rewarded by government accreditation for their standards of sports provision and broad and balanced curriculum. For a school to achieve a Sportsmark distinction it must have in place the standards set out in the guidelines of the scheme.

The schools should offer two hours of physical education per week on the timetable. Outside of lesson times, at least four hours of extra-curricular activities should be offered. These extra sessions can take place before and after school, during lunch times and at weekends. These sessions can be for recreation or as team practices.

All pupils should have the chance to compete against other schools. Children should also have the opportunity to take part in award schemes set up by the governing bodies of the sport. Links should be made with local clubs so that pupils can take part in activities independent of the school.

Systems should be in place so more teachers are encouraged to gain qualifications in order to be able to lead sports teams and improve their coaching skills.

What to do:

1. Write why sports campaigns and programmes are important for sport.

Key Terms:

Department of Culture, Media and Sport (DCMS)	► responsible for distributing lottery money
Private facilities	► available only to those who are members
Public facilities	► available to all members of the community
Regional Councils	► councils for each country – England, Northern Ireland, Scotland and Wales
Sport England	► alternative name for the Sports Council of England
Sports Council	► organisation responsible for overseeing sport in the UK
Sports governing body	► organisation looking after the interest of a particular sport and its members
UK Sport	► national council for sports performance and promotion in the UK

Summary

Sport in the UK is financed by the government through taxation and by the DCMS who allocate money from proceeds from the lottery. This financing covers public facilities and the promotion of top-class performers. Private sport clubs are self-financing and the number of private health clubs is continually on the increase.

UK Sport supports performers, nationally, at the highest level. The regional sports councils develop sport in their area according to their specific needs. They promote sport from grass roots level, attempting to increase participation and the number of available sports facilities.

Each sport has a governing body overseeing the rules and standards of the sport. Each governing body usually controls both the amateur and professional levels of the sport, maintaining its values whilst, at the same time, promoting its image worldwide.

Analysis of Performance

What you will learn about in this section:

1. Personal Training Programme
2. Necessary Skills to Analyse and Improve Performance
3. How to Determine Strengths and Weaknesses
4. Improving Quality and Effectiveness
5. Showing Development of Leadership Skills
6. The Final Examination

The *Analysis of Performance* part of the course requires you, the candidate, to recognise the strengths and weaknesses of a performance and to understand and demonstrate ways to improve it. To do this you will experience a variety of roles and responsibilities linked with physical activity. As your personal performance continually develops, so should your abilities in the five areas making up the analysis and performance section.

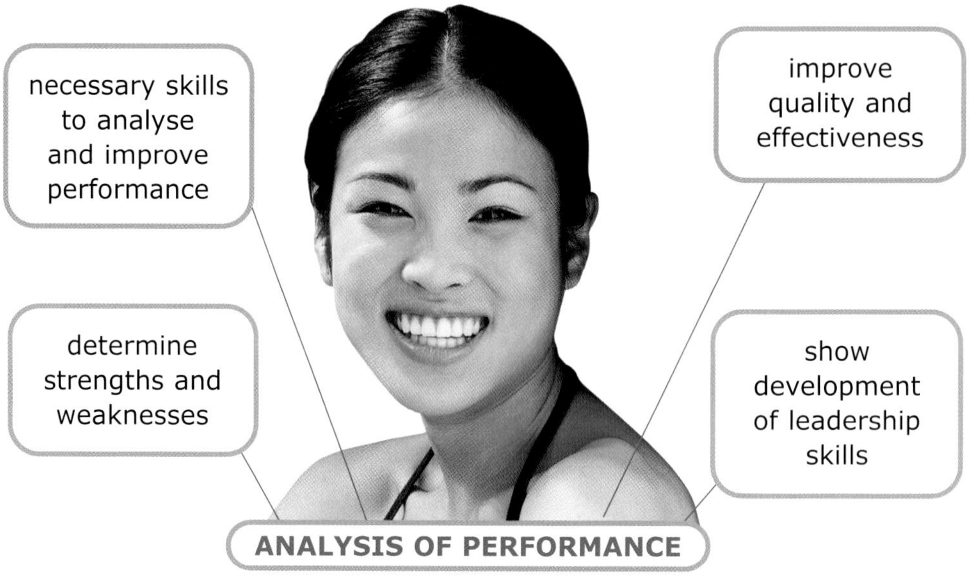

This section of work will develop your skills as an official, coach and leader in your chosen sport. It will link together the application of skills with factors affecting participation and performance parts of the specification. Your overall success in this part of the course relies on reaching a good standard in each component. A weak area will affect your overall analysis of performance mark.

The following coaching model is useful when breaking down the parts that are important for analysis.

Performance
Actions made by player/participant.

→ **Observation**
Action watched carefully by another.

→ **Analysis**
Parts of the performance studied in detail.

↓ **Evaluation**
Performance compared with the 'perfect model' and past performances.

← **Planning**
Working out what training will be best for future improvement based on the strengths and weaknesses of the performance.

← **Feedback**
Information given to the performer responding to the results of competition and training.

↑ (back to Performance)

1 Personal Training Programme

A personal training programme (PTP) is a series of exercises or practices put together for a particular person. The exercise sessions follow all the guidelines of the principles of training to make them safe and suitable for the performer. To be effective, the PTP should be performed regularly and over a period of weeks. There will come a time when the programme is physically too easy to have an effect on the performer. This can happen about week 5 or 6 of the programme. At this stage, reviewing the programme is necessary. By applying the principles of training, the programme may be made more demanding.

Link the PTP with the effects of exercise

The diagram shows how the PTP develops. It always starts with the individual and their needs and capabilities, moving on to the planning, performing and then to the reviewing. The review of the programme is most important if progress is to continue to be made. Re-testing the individual will show how their body has adapted to the programme. Increasing the FID principle according to the results will ensure further progress.

Devising a PTP

Look at the individual and consider:

- test results
- cardio results (resting heart rate)
- respiratory results (VO_2 max.)
- body composition (how much of the body is fat, muscle and bone?)
- which exercises they prefer
- whether they like training on their own or in a group.

What is the purpose of the PTP?

- general health
- sport specific
- rehabilitation
- strength improvement
- flexibility
- muscular endurance.

Plan the programme, choosing from a variety of training methods:

- circuit
- weights
- continuous
- interval
- fartlek
- altitude
- aerobic and anaerobic.

Review programme by applying the FID principles of training:

- increase how many times individual trains – frequency
- increase the intensity
- increase time exercising
- vary the type of exercise.

What to do:

1. Using the ideas from 'Devising a PTP', write your own action plan of how a PTP should be organised.

Preparation for testing and measuring

To plan and prepare a programme of exercise for an individual, the clearest picture of their fitness level should be made. This is called a 'fitness profile'. This can be a general understanding of the heart rate and lung capacity or it can be made more detailed by testing aspects of skill. It is useful when assessing games players as they will need many different skills to play their game properly and the test can be designed to include these skills.

TESTING

Why test?

- to have an idea of the next performance results
- to show weaknesses
- to show improvements
- to show how successful a training programme has been
- to motivate the performer.

How to evaluate

- choose the fitness component to measure
- choose a way of measuring it
- record the results
- work out what the results imply
- decide on the best exercises to do based on the results
- put the exercises into a training programme.

How to test

- each test should concentrate on one fitness component only
- the test should be easy to complete
- the performer should completely understand the test
- the test should be carried out the same way every time.

2 Necessary Skills to Analyse and Improve Performance

Many people can look at a sporting activity, but only the trained eye can see what the performer is really attempting to do. The observation and analysis part of the course requires you to train these skills and make a judgement on quality, success and ways of improving a performance.

Skills needed

The skills you will develop are similar to those needed by coaches in order to get the best out of their players.

Applying rules – show knowledge and application of them; practice and experience in this area can be gained from officiating or judging a sport. Choose sports in which you feel confident, interested and have some experience of.

Using specialised terminology – each sport has its own language for describing skills, tactics and strategies. An ability to use this language shows an understanding of the sport.

Analysing – be able to break down the action of the performer.

Recording – making a record of the performance gives information, which can be analysed and acted upon; sometimes a training session is changed according to the results.

Evaluating – is the ability to watch a performer in action and work out how close their performance is to what is known as the 'perfect model'.

Identifying the perfect model – when analysing the performance, knowledge and understanding of what the best performance looks like is very important. Any performance can then be compared to this 'perfect model'.

Seeing strengths and weaknesses – each performance has positive and negative aspects and both must be recognised by the observer.

Communicating – being able to communicate an analysis of the action to the performer so improvement can be made. Even in weak performances it is important to comment on a good aspect in order to keep the performer motivated.

Planning – by working out the successes and failures of the performance, planned changes can be made to training, tactics and strategies so improvements can be made.

Applying knowledge – of training methods and principles is essential when linking with weaknesses and strengths of the performer. The principles and methods will determine what goes in the training programme.

Understanding leadership – good leadership is the ability to get the best out of the performer. Give examples of successful captains, coaches and managers. Examples of this include: leading through example, motivating, setting up achievable targets and rewarding progress.

What to do:

1. For each of the 11 skill areas make a list of the experiences you have already.
2. Re-list the skills with the areas you most need to work on at the top, moving down to the ones you are most confident in at the bottom.

Observation

Observation needs to be planned. In order to observe a performance meaningfully, then an understanding of the perfect model is necessary. Where to observe the action from is important too. Standing at different positions in relation to the action will give different views and so more than one viewpoint may be necessary for a full picture of an activity.

Equipment

Whatever method of analysis you use it will be useful to have a record of the performance you see. This will act as evidence and can then be used to analyse the results of the performance with other data at a later date. Plan your observations well. Record sheets, pencils and something to lean on are all basic and obvious requirements to do the job. Knowing that you have prepared the equipment you need in advance will allow you to concentrate on the process of observation. You may prefer to photograph or video the performance, in which case, greater planning is necessary in booking the equipment before the date.

The view

Where to watch from may vary according to the sport. A team game has lots of action so being near to the performer's positional area is good. A raised viewpoint is often useful. For smaller playing areas like volleyball, badminton and tennis, court side is effective and if possible a raised position may give a better view.

The spidergram indicates possible places to view a large team game from.

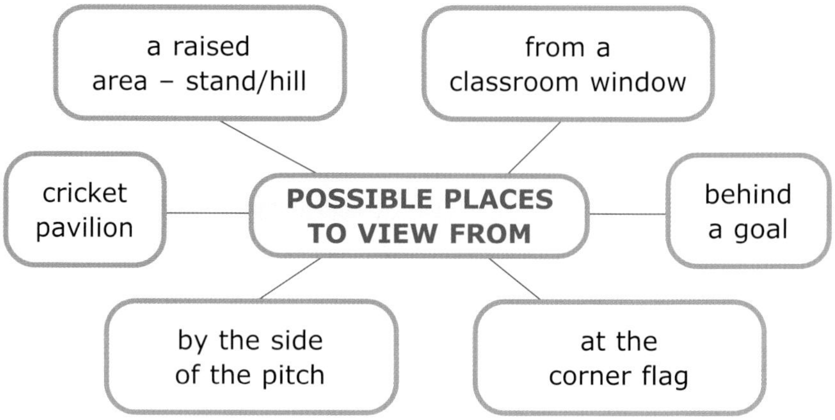

Task 3

What to do:

1. For three sports, decide on the best viewing position for each. You can use diagrams in your answer if you wish.
2. Say why you think some sports are best viewed at different positions, such as judo viewed at ground level, but team games from a high position.

Gaining observational experience

There are different ways you can build up your observational skills. Using as many methods as you can will give you the broadest information base from which to work.

By watching an activity and then discussing the performance with others, you develop your knowledge, language and understanding of what you see.

Listen to the coaching points given by a teacher in class and then compare them with how a person performs the activity. This gives experience of linking the description of the correct action with a beginner's attempt.

There are many coaching manuals and books available for sporting activities. Reading them will give you the knowledge of what the perfect model should look like. These books break down the skill and illustrate or describe the parts of the action to concentrate on. This knowledge of the components of the correct skill can be watched for and compared with that of the observed performance. You can than decide on the strengths and weaknesses of the action you see.

Once you understand the skill you will appreciate how it can be broken down. For instance in gymnastics, a judge will look for the following when marking a vault: flight on, flight off, elevation, shape of the body, distance carried, body alignment and controlled landing. It is these areas that the observer must be aware of in order to understand the action. As the vault only takes a short time to complete, videoing the action will help you concentrate on one part of the action at a time. You can then build up your observation and appreciation of the whole action after several replays.

Your knowledge and experience of a game helps you know what to look for. Knowing the game well allows the observer to anticipate the action, prepare a mental picture of the best performance and compare it with what they see. This expectation of the action also allows the effectiveness of the build-up play to be observed too.

Ways to observe

There are various ways of watching top-class performers, each with positive and negative points for the observer. Some of these methods are readily available through watching television and reading newspapers and magazines, whereas some need seeking out through libraries and the Internet.

Knowledge of skill-related fitness

What you have learnt about skill-related fitness and its application to different sports will help with your observations. You will know which components to look out for in your chosen activity.

SKILL-RELATED FITNESS COMPONENTS

- **Balance** – the ability to keep the body stable whether still, moving or in a different shape by keeping the centre of gravity over the base.
- **Agility** – the ability to change direction quickly and still keep control of the whole body.
- **Speed** – the fastest rate at which a person can complete a task or cover a distance.
- **Reaction time** – the time it takes to respond to a stimulus.
- **Power** – the ability to apply a combination of strength and speed in an action.
- **Co-ordination** – the ability to use two parts of the body at the same time.

Active Challenge

Using a sport of your choice state a basic, an intermediate and an advanced skill. Discuss your examples with a partner.

Ways to analyse

Comments made on a performance can be based on subjective or objective evidence: each can comment about the same action but in a different way.

Subjective

Subjective analysis is related to how the observer thinks the player is performing in comparison with the other players. Two people may have different opinions about a particular performance. The list below includes subjective statements:

'She is crossing the ball better.'

'That's the best goal I've seen him score.'

'He is moving more quickly to the ball.'

'There seem to be fewer double faults than in previous sets.'

'I thought that shot had more pace.'

'She looks to be serving better.'

'He has more energy than the others.'

Objective

Objective analysis is based on fact, not personal opinions. The aim is to have results and statistics to back up the observations. This is very helpful to the coach and performer as it identifies explicitly the strengths and weaknesses of the performer. Objective analysis provides:

- statistical record of aspects of the performance
- records of heights jumped, distances thrown and speeds run
- comparisons made between performer and the decided criteria (perfect model).

What to do:

1. For a sport of your choice complete the following:
   a. Give three examples of subjective comments.
   b. State why objective comments are more accurate.
   c. Give examples of how an individual can be seen to be successful in the sport.

Analysis

There are a variety of areas that can be analysed when looking at performance. Some are more complex than others. The most straightforward range from individual, closed and basic skills to the complexities of the open complex, advanced skills.

There are different skills required by different players on the pitch so the observer must be mindful of this in the analysis. An attacker may not need information on the number of tackles they make, but for a defender it would be an important part of the analysis. A strong team may be often on the attack, so their defence is only rarely involved. As a result, a defender may only make a few passes in the game, so for them, the percentage rather than the actual number of successful passes made may say more about his or her personal play.

The skills required for good play are different for a defender and attacker.

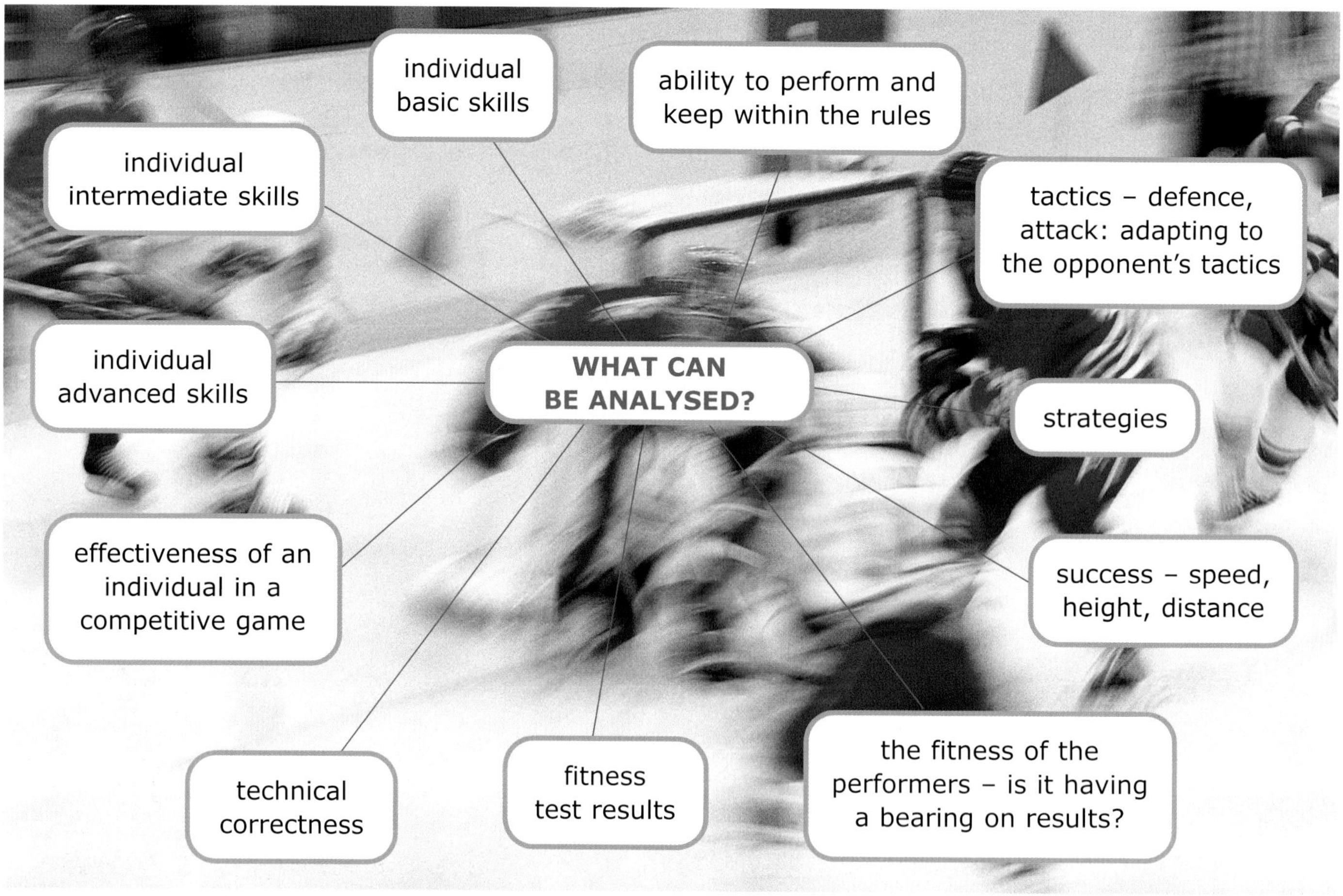

Different ways to record and analyse

Keeping a record of a person's performance can be used in several ways. Records taken at different times in the season are useful as they can show individual progress, the effectiveness of training and strengths and weaknesses of performance.

The methods used to record performance vary and can include:

Making notes on the performance – detailed notes are made by the observer based on the action of the performer.

Check list for performance – this lists the parts of the action the person needs to perform to complete the action and represents the perfect model. The observed performance can be compared to the components on the list and a simple 'tick off' system can be used.

Individual's performance in the game – this records the actions of an individual in the game situation. The success or failure of the performer is recorded each time they are an active part of the game and can be indicated by a plus or minus response to stated criteria. In tennis, for example, there are many parts to the game important to record; such as the number of points won on first or second serve, or number of double-faults recorded.

Team performance – this records the effectiveness of the team performance. It reflects the success of the chosen tactics and can include:

- where successful shots come from
- where on the pitch/court the attacks start
- where the opposition attacks come from
- how much possession the team has
- how many corners the team earn.

Active Challenge

With a partner, choose a basic skill you are confident in performing. Break down the skill listing, in order, the different actions needed to complete the action.

What to do:

1. For a sport of your choice:
   a make a list of the parts of the game that can be recorded to give useful feedback to the coach
   b make a record sheet of your list that could be used when observing the game

3 How to Determine Strengths and Weaknesses

Perfect model

In order to realise whether a sporting action is good or not an understanding of how the action should look in its perfect state should be appreciated. This is the 'perfect model' you will mark any performance against. There are several ways you can observe the perfect model:

- world class sports coverage (TV or video)
- training videos
- coaching manuals
- action photos from magazines and books of world class players

When developing an understanding of the perfect model it is useful to use video recordings of the best performers. This allows replays and pauses in the action to be made, giving time for you to appreciate the performance in question.

When looking at a performance the shape of the body in action will indicate how close it is to the perfect model. Some areas to look for are the head position, where the centre of gravity is, a balanced body position and how the weight is distributed.

Task 6

What to do:

1. Look at the two photos above and compare the differences in the following:
   - head position
   - balance of the body
   - centre of gravity
   - weight distribution.

Expectations of the observer

Many factors can influence the way a skill is performed. These are sometimes in the control of the performer and sometimes not. The observer should distinguish between the two and adapt the comments given in feedback accordingly. For instance, a player may well have shown success in a skill in the past, but changes in the weather (it may be a windy day) may cause the skill to break down.

ALWAYS HAVE IN MIND THE PERFECT MODEL

FACTORS AFFECTING PERFORMANCE	REACTIONS AND COMMENTS
rules	comment on good aspects of performance
fitness	comment on main area to improve
experience	have a knowledge of how bad play can be improved
weather	suggest ways to improve
standards of game	make allowances for difficult circumstances
degree of difficulty of the skill	
open skill	
closed skill	

Factors influencing the expectation and reaction of the observer.

4 Improving Quality and Effectiveness

Evaluating a performance by comparing it with the perfect model is the process after analysis when the observer works out the success or failure of an activity. Evaluation tells us where strengths and weaknesses are and how training should be adapted to the findings in order to make progress.

Knowledge of the perfect model may come from a photograph, video or coaching manual. Understanding the perfect model will make it easier to evaluate what is seen and suggest improvements to be made.

The evaluation process may look like this:

1. Perfect model – know what you are looking for.
2. Make observations of the performance.
3. Compare the performance with the perfect model.
4. Decide on and state the main positive point to express.
5. Decide and state the main fault and express it.
6. Communicate how the performance can be improved in the next attempt (short-term).
7. Communicate how training will need to be adapted and a new plan made (long-term).

Feedback

To work on and develop skill every performer needs feedback. An athlete may have technical feedback after their event, but a team may need a combination of skill and tactical feedback. Whatever the content of the feedback, if it is not acted upon then it is of no use. The observer may include comments on motivation, tactics, commitment, skill, determination and effort.

There are factors that you should be aware of when giving feedback and they should influence what you say and how you say it. For instance if someone has only just started participating in the activity there may be many mistakes and negative comments would be inappropriate. Detailed comments on their faults may well demoralise the performer.

It is the coach or manager's role to supply feedback to the performers. They choose the most appropriate way to deliver the information, which may be given individually, to the whole team, or to groups within the team – like the defence and attack.

Feedback can benefit the performer by keeping them motivated, working towards achievable goals, allowing them to see development in fitness and in fitness tests results. The coach can plan the training programme around the feedback, use it as a motivating tool and change tactics to hide weaknesses and show strengths.

What to do:

1. This work involves practice in analysing results and feeding back information. Study the analysis sheet of a game of tennis. Interpret the results by including comments on:

   Where is the most successful play coming from?

   Where is the least successful play coming from?

   How should the tactics change?

   What training should be included in the programme as a result?

Tennis analysis sheet

Tennis	Set 1	Set 2	Set 3
aces	1	3	2
1st serve percentage	52%	70%	72%
2nd serve percentage	60%	74%	70%
speed of serve	120mph	122mph	123mph
double faults	2	1	0
forehand winners	8	6	7
backhand winners	5	7	5
volley winners	11	18	19
unforced errors	8	6	6

How to gain experience of what to say

Saying the right things is important. Too many negative comments and the performer will lose confidence and the skill will remain poor. Too much praise and they may stop trying or become complacent.

There are several ways to gain experience of what to say to a performer. Listening and watching different types of TV sports programmes, radio commentary, coaching points given by a teacher and interviews with sportspeople and their coaches will help you to build up the correct language. Each method has its own style and content – a certain style may suit you better than others. Language used will include technical terms, comments on skill, opinions on performance and factual comments on analysis.

Educational, instructive and coaching videos will all use technical language. They will put the language in context giving you a greater understanding of the activity. The Internet, specialised CD-ROMs and award schemes run for a particular sport will also provide technical terms and language in your chosen area.

Active Challenge

Think about what technical terms you know for your chosen sport and how these will help you when giving feedback.

How to communicate what you see

It is important to make comments to the performer as clear, positive and to the point as possible.

- Pick out the skills to comment on.
- Look for good points – speed, aim, body position, movement, direction of performer.
- Start with praise – how the performer was successful.

- Identify the most ineffective part of skill and say how it can be improved, for example, 'more height in the rebound by using your arms, swinging them in the air above your head'.
- Suggest how this skill can be worked on – for example, improvement of leg strength, more vigorous arm action, better co-ordination and be more determined to get the ball.

What to do:

1. Decide on a skill to analyse or refer to the photograph of Kath Johnson below. Use the indicated points to make comments about the performer.

Factors building up to the perfect model.

Plan

Having made an account of the action and put it all together, you now need to use it to improve performance. Your findings will determine change to the practices and training sessions in the future. When looking at the information you need to know whether the player is a defender or attacker. Some skills or parts of play may look poor but these skills may not be vital for that player's success. Gary Lineker was a successful footballer for club and country, scoring many goals. Statistically, however, his tackling ratio was poor, due to the fact that he was a striker and concentrated on attacking rather than defending. It is important to know the main skills needed for the player and concentrate on them.

How to read the results

Reading and interpreting results is essential to planning. A coach (or analyst) may look at an individual performance, compare two players, the team performance or how the two teams' statistics compared.

- Count the actions to identify strengths.
- Count the actions to identify weaknesses.
- Compare success and failure of each action.
- Compare with past performance records.
- Compare two players' or teams' performances.

Considerations for the coach

The coach will also take into consideration questions like:

- When did the faults occur – if late in the game is fitness the problem?
- In what situation was the error – did the fault(s) happen in pressured situations?
- Is the fault in skill – will identifying the component of skill-related fitness and training that area help?
- Is the skill new – was the player playing out of position?
- What were the opposition like – was it the hardest match of the season?
- Was the error tactical – would working on using judgement and understanding of the tactics improve performance?
- Has the performer reached a plateau of improvement? (Seemingly no progress is made for a time, skills must be broken down and worked on separately, this is frustrating for the performer and coach – patience will have to be shown to give time to go beyond this.)

Decisions to be made

After deciding on which areas need improvement, the practices and training plans are adapted. The coach may show the performer examples of the perfect model or the new targets to work towards, so a clear picture of what is necessary is identified.

Changes

- New training programme put in place with increased emphasis on weak areas.
- Make sure that skill practices are relevant and help the performer to improve.
- In practice sessions performer should perform the skill slowly and then build up the pace.
- Set new achievable targets – number of repetitions, weights to lift.
- Use static opponents to build up the skill and confidence in the performer and gradually progress to realistic opposition.
- Fitness training with an emphasis on aerobic work will provide stamina so a player can maintain a performance throughout the match.

A coach needs to take note of the player's performance, identify areas that need to improve and put them into the training programme. A good coach will discuss reasons for changes to training sessions with the performer based on past results.

Task 9

What to do:

1. Using your chosen sport as the example, write three sentences on each of the following as though you are the coach:
   - stamina
   - strength
   - co-ordination
   - speed
   - passive and aggressive opposition
   - tactical awareness
   - identifying the perfect model

Example:
'You narrowly missed out and came second in your last race. More work on a quicker sprint finish will give you a better chance. We will start by doing speed work at the end of the next training session.' (Speed)

The importance of rules

It is important that you gain as much information as you can of the rules of your chosen sport. You will have gained knowledge already through your experience of taking part in sport activities and this foundation of knowledge can be built on. Ways to increase your knowledge and understanding:

- watch sports events on TV and listen to the commentary of the experts
- play the game to as high a standard as you can
- read coaching manuals
- discuss rules with your teacher
- practise refereeing or umpiring, preferably at school within PE lessons to ensure safe practise
- read the rules of your sport, perhaps use the Internet to find information on rules.

Active Challenge

For your chosen sport find five books you can use to help with your knowledge of the rules. Use your school and local libraries and the Internet to help find the titles of these publications.

Leadership and your sport

People who can motivate and get the best performance out of others, even in difficult circumstances, have leadership qualities. There are many personalities in sport who are successful leaders. Managers, coaches and captains all play their part in motivating their team. As football is so widely televised many of their leaders are well known.

How leadership enhances performance

- Style of leadership influences the performer.
- Leader sets achievable goals.
- Leader keeps players informed on their progress.
- Leader is respected for their knowledge, experience and history in the sport.

Role of the captain

- To influence their team and individual players on and off the pitch.
- Lead by example as a role model.
- Talk to players throughout a game to encourage, praise, change play and so on.
- Encourage or lead others through their fear.
- Give instructions on tactics.
- Keep the team playing together and working hard.
- Act as the link between thc players and the officials.

Role of the coach

- Take training sessions.
- Identify and recognise strengths and weaknesses.
- Give individual help to performers.
- Treat performers as individuals as far as possible.
- Know the players and set achievable goals that suit their personality.
- Reward good work.
- Organise players' diets.
- Motivate training sessions.
- Make training interesting and fun.

Role of the manager

- Organise team.
- Put the right blend of characters together – they may not be the most skilful but they work hard for each other.
- Support and discipline players.
- Praise and criticise play.
- Represent the team in the media.

Active Challenge

Choose a coach, captain or manager who has really impressed you. Prepare a short account, to say to the rest of the class, on why they have done so. (Try to use an example other than football if you can.)

To gain experience of what it is like to be a coach take a session based on your performer fitness testing and analysis of performance. This is a good way to put into operation your understanding of the work. It may not be right first time, so listen to help given by the teacher and improve on your next effort.

Leading a Warm-up

At any time during the course, a warm-up session can be organised. You can choose your own activity or sport, so make your decision on your experience, knowledge and expertise.

Remember the three phases of a warm-up:

- aerobic phase
- stretch and flexibility phase
- skills and intensive exercise phase.

You will be marked on the following areas:

1. Suitability of exercises

Make sure the exercises warm up the body gradually and concentrate on the muscles to be used in the game.

2. Appropriateness of the exercises to the sport

Think of the skills of the activity and include them at a basic level in the warm-up. Basic catching and throwing challenges are suitable for netball, basketball and rugby, for instance.

3. Ability to organise and lead the group

If you are not used to taking a group it is important to work out easy ways to organise the group: use a whistle to get the groups attention; if certain numbered groups are needed, assemble them quickly, so the class's attention is kept; be enthusiastic about what you do; praise good work to keep the group motivated.

4. Verbal communication skills

Keep your instructions clear, talk slowly and use the appropriate terminology.

5. Use of non-verbal communication skills

Make sure your demonstrations are accurate. Try to be competent demonstrating for left as well as right-handers.

6 The Final Examination

For the analysis and performance part of the course you will be assessed on your ability to show the following:

- determining the strength and weaknesses of a performance
- improving its quality and effectiveness.

This will include assessing your own performance as well as that of others. To do this you will need to develop all of the following areas for the best results:

- rules and their application in sport
- observation and analysis
- evaluate by comparing with the perfect model
- planning to improve performance
- leadership and your sport.

Your chosen sport

Throughout the course you will be asked to assess your own and others' performances. Gain as much experience as you can by analysing performance in practical sports lessons. For the examination, you will have to name the sport you are analysing, so make yourself as familiar with that sport as possible. Factors affecting your choice may be:

- it is your favourite sport or your best performance sport
- it is the sport you know most about
- it is the sport with lots of readily available information available
- it is the sport with simple tactics and basic skills, easy to understand and analyse.

Preparation

Use this list to check that you have done as much as you can to earn the best mark:

- know your sport
- know the perfect model
- be able to use the terminology
- know tactics – basic, intermediate, advanced
- gained experience watching and reading about your chosen sport
- joined in class discussions to increase your confidence in verbally expressing your thoughts
- have umpired/refereed or judged your sport so you are confident with the rules, regulations and procedures
- have completed, recorded and saved for reference several examples of your analysing of the activity
- have records of past analysis to hand to revise from
- practise recording performance so it can be done quickly, allowing concentration on the action.

On the day

- If possible, organise your favoured position for observing the action.
- Have all the equipment you need to record the action.
- Have in mind the 'perfect model' performance.
- Be confident that you have revised well enough to succeed.

You will be asked questions about a performance in your chosen sport. What to do:

- listen to the instructions
- listen to the questions
- think it through in your head before you speak
- keep calm and give a full, informative, clear answer, as brief as necessary without being vague
- if appropriate, give examples from your knowledge of the 'perfect model'.

You are bound to be a little nervous but you can draw confidence from the fact that, if you have completed all the necessary preparations, tasks and analysis as coursework, you are being examined from a position of strength.

Glossary

A

Abduction moving a limb or bone away from the body

Adduction moving a limb or bone towards the body

Aerobic 'with oxygen'; when exercise is moderate and steady, the heart can supply all the oxygen the working muscles need

Aesthetic quality how good an action looks

Agility the ability to change the position of the body quickly and to control the movement of the whole body easily

Altitude training training at a place situated high above sea level

Alveoli tiny air sacs of the lungs where gaseous exchange takes place

Anaerobic 'without oxygen'; when exercising in short, fast bursts, the heart cannot supply blood and oxygen to the muscles as fast as the cells can use them, so energy is released without oxygen present

Antagonist a muscle whose action counteracts that of another muscle and so allowing movement

Aorta the main artery of the body, blood vessel transporting oxygenated blood to the body tissues

Arterioles blood vessels that are sub-divisions of arteries, leading into capillaries

Asymmetric bars a piece of Olympic gymnastic equipment used by females with bars at different heights

Atrophy decline in effectiveness; when muscles atrophy they weaken and lose their strength and size

B

Balance the ability to retain the centre of mass (gravity) of the body above the base of support with reference to static (stationary) or dynamic (changing) conditions of movement, shape and orientation

Balanced competition grouping based on size, age or experience for an even match

Balanced diet daily intake of food containing right amounts and types of nutrients

Basal metabolic rate the level at which energy is used without exercise

Blood doping method of increasing the oxygen carrying capacity of the blood, by increasing haemoglobin levels and red blood cell count

Body composition the proportion of body weight that is fat, muscle and bone, normally measured as a percentage

C

Calcify harden by conversion into calcium carbonate

Calcium an essential element for strong healthy bones; dairy products provide a good source of calcium

Cancelluos bone name for spongy bone; has air pockets so it looks like a sponge

Capillaries blood vessels of hair-like thinness that connect the arteries with the veins

Carbohydrate loading eating large amounts of carbohydrate-rich foods to build up glycogen levels in the body to use in endurance events

Cardiac muscle only found in the heart, never tires

Cardiac output the amount of blood pumped by the heart in one minute

Cardiovascular relating to the heart and blood vessels

Cardiovascular fitness the ability to exercise the entire body for long periods of time; this is dependent on the fitness of the heart, blood and blood vessels

Cartilage whitish, tough, flexible tissue found at the end of bones; more widespread in infants, as during growth it is replaced by bone

Cervical vertebrae bones of the vertebrae forming the neck

Circuit training a series of exercises completed in order and for a certain time limit

Circulatory system transports blood, using the heart, through all parts of the body

Classification a way of sorting or organising groups

Coccyx small fused triangular bone at the base of the vertebral column

Compact bone strong, hard bone

Compound/open fracture break of the bone that pierces the skin, causing a risk of infection

Concussion injury to the brain, caused by blow to the head, may cause a person temporarily to lose consciousness

Continuous training aerobic exercising, at a moderate to high level, with no rests lasting for a sustained period of time

Convalescence period of time when body is rested to aid recovery

Cool down exercises after the main activity gradually bringing the body systems back to near resting state

Co-ordination the ability to perform complex moves using two or more body parts together

D

Dehydration extreme lack of water in the body, usually as a result of exercising in hot conditions or heavy sweating

Diaphragm a dome-shaped muscle that divides the chest cavity from the abdominal cavity

Diaphysis shaft or central part of a long bone

Dilate open up or become wider

Dislocate disturb the usual arrangement of bones so that they move out of their usual joint arrangement

DRABC **D**anger (to casualty or first aider?) **R**esponse (different levels of casualty response – alert/unresponsive; presence or absence of voice/pain?) **A**irway (is there a blockage of the airway?) **B**reathing (is casualty breathing?) **C**irculation (is the blood circulating?)

Drugs substances (other than food) that, when taken into the body, cause a change; socially unacceptable drugs are drugs that are illegal to possess

E

Ectomorph body type with little fat or muscle and a narrow shape

Element a part that contributes to the whole

Emergency procedures series of actions to be followed in a crisis

Endomorph body type that is apple or pear shaped, with a large amount of fat

Endothelium internal space of the blood vessels

Endurance the ability to keep working over a period of time without tiring or losing skill

Energy drinks fluids containing carbohydrates

Epiphysis end of a long bone

Etiquette a code of polite behaviour

Exercise a form of physical activity done primarily to improve one's health and physical fitness

Expiration breathing out, exhalation

Extension increasing the angle at a joint

F

Fartlek training 'speed play': changing speed, distances and times of exercise, with rests in the same session

Fast twitch muscle fibres used in events requiring quick reactions and power; muscles contract rapidly providing strength and so tire quickly

Fatigue extreme tiredness and physical exhaustion

Fibrinogen a protein found in blood plasma that helps clotting

Fitness ability to meet the demands of the environment

FITT frequency, intensity, time and type

Flat bone also called plate bone, mainly linked with protection

Flexibility joints' ability to move to their full range

Flexion decreasing the angle at a joint

Forced breathing breathing during exercise

Friction action of two surfaces rubbing together creating heat

Fused two or more bones knitted together so no movement occurs

G

Glycogen the form in which carbohydrates are stored in the muscle and liver

Governing body a group responsible for rules, procedures and fixtures of a particular game or event

H

Haemoglobin found in red blood cells; transports oxygen to body tissue

Health a state of complete social, mental and physical well-being

Heart rate the number of times the heart beats per minute

Heat exhaustion fatigue brought on by the body temperature rising

Hypertrophy when muscle increases in size due to regular exercise

Hypothermia condition of the body when its core temperature falls below 35°C

I

Individual needs personal requirements for training

Inflamed reddened and swollen

Infringement action in a game that breaks the rules

Insertion the point where a tendon attaches a muscle to bone where there is movement

Inspiration the drawing in of breath, inhalation

Interval training mixing periods of hard exercise with rest periods

Involuntary muscles muscles that work automatically, controlled by the involuntary nervous system

Irregular bones bones that have no uniform shape

Isometric muscular contraction muscle contraction with no movement; there is increased tension but the length of the muscles does not alter, e.g. when pressing against a stationary object

Isotonic muscular contraction muscle contraction that results in limb movement

J

Joint the point where two or more bones meet

L

Lactic acid produced in the muscle tissues during strenuous exercise, as a result of insufficient oxygen availability

Leverage the use of force or effort (muscle power) to overcome resistance

Ligament tough, rounded, elastic fibre attaching bone to bone

Long bones those bones that are the longest in the body which make up the arms and legs

Lumbar vertebrae bones of the vertebrae in the lower back region

M

Main activity period of training, competition or performance when all-out effort is applied

Masking agent a legal substance for a sport, hiding the presence of an illegal one

Maximum heart rate calculated as 220 minus age

Mesomorph body that is characterised by being muscular

Metabolic rate the speed at which energy is used up

Minimum level of fitness (for health) the resulting fitness level when over a period of weeks three to five exercise sessions of 20 minutes, raising the heart rate to 60–80% of its maximum, are completed

Moderation balancing training and not over-training

Modified game a game with adapted rules, equipment and playing area based on a full game

Movement in motion, could be an action like running or swinging a racket at a ball

Muscle definition muscle shape

Muscle tone muscles in a state of very slight tension, ready and waiting to be used

Muscular endurance the ability to use voluntary muscles, over long periods of time without getting tired

Muscular strength the amount of force a muscle can exert against a resistance in one attempt

N

Nausea feeling of sickness

Newton a unit of force

O

Obese a term used to describe people who are very overfat

Optimum weight ideal weight for a person, giving them the best chance of success in an activity

Origin the point where the tendon attaches the muscle to a fixed bone

Ossification the development from cartilage to bone

Osteoblasts bone-forming cells

Osteoclasts bone-eroding cells

Overfat a person having more body fat than is recommended for their gender and height

Overload following the principle that the body can only be improved through training more and harder than normal

Overuse injury this can be caused by using a part of the body too much or by too much repetitive training

Overweight having weight in excess of normal; not harmful unless accompanied by overfatness

Oxygen debt the amount of oxygen consumed during recovery above that which would have been consumed in the same time at rest (this results in a shortfall in the oxygen available)

P

Performance how well a task is completed

Performance-enhancing drugs substances that artificially improve personal characteristics and performance

Periosteal collar also known as periosteum, membrane surrounding the shaft of a bone

Personal exercise programme (PEP) training designed specifically for one individual

Posture the way the muscles hold the body when still or in motion

Power the ability to complete strength performances quickly; power = strength x speed

Prime mover contracting muscles that cause movement

Principles of training ideas behind effects of training

Progression starting slowly and gradually increasing the amount of exercise completed

Protect guard against threat

Pulmonary circuit system of blood vessels that transports deoxygenated blood from the heart to the lungs and re-oxygenated blood back again

R

Reaction time the time between the presentation of a stimulus and the onset of a movement

Recovery rate the time it takes for the heart and metabolism to return to resting after exercise

Regularity repeating exercise sessions in a week to bring about improved fitness

Rehabilitate recovery from injury

Residual volume the amount of air left in the lungs after a maximal breath out

Resting heart rate number of heart beats per minute when the body is at rest

Reversibility any adaptation that takes place as a consequence of training will be reversed when a person stops training

RICE rest, ice, compression, elevation; order of treatment for a minor injury

Rotation movement in a circular or part-circular fashion

S

Sacrum bones of the vertebrae, fused in adults, making part of the pelvic girdle

Septum wall of muscle dividing the right and left sides of the heart; septum can also mean a dividing wall between two cavities elsewhere in the body

Shaft long, thin part of a long bone

Shape form or outline

Short bone smaller bone found in the hands and feet

Simple/closed fracture break of the bone when the skin is not broken

Skeleton the arrangement of the 206 bones of the human body

Skill-related fitness physical motor abilities of the body adapted to specific sports

Skin-fold calliper equipment used to measure a fold of skin with its underlying layer of fat

Slow twitch muscle fibres muscle fibres required in endurance events

Somatotype particular body type and shape of an individual. There are three types: ectomorph, endomorph and mesomorph

Specificity concentrating on specific kinds of activity or exercise to build specific body parts

Speed the differential rate at which an individual is able to perform a movement or cover a distance in a period of time

Stress a state of mental or emotional strain leading to anxiety and nervous tension

Stress-related illnesses illnesses such as heart attack, ulcer, high blood pressure

Stroke volume the amount of blood pumped out of the heart by each ventricle during one contraction

Synovial capsule tough fibre surrounding the synovial joint

Synovial fluid fluid helping to lubricate a synovial joint

Synovial joints freely movable joints with ends covered in cartilage

Synovial membrane lining inside joint capsule where synovial fluid is produced

Systematic training planning a programme for an individual as a result of the effect of previous training

Systemic circuit part of the circulatory system concerned with transporting oxygenated blood from the heart to the body and deoxygenated blood back to the heart again

T

Target zone level of effort applied, often keeping within aerobic levels but depending on specified training intensity

Tendon strong, non-elastic tissue attaching bone to muscle

Thoracic vertebrae bones of the vertebrae in the chest area

Throwing cage a secured enclosure around a throwing area

Tidal volume amount of air breathed in or out at rest

Training a planned programme which uses scientific principles to improve performance, skill, game ability and motor and physical fitness

U

Unconsciousness state of unawareness, an unwakening sleep

V

Valves openings allowing blood flow in one direction, found in the heart and veins

Vena cava blood vessel transporting deoxygenated blood back to the heart

Vertebral column irregular bones (vertebrae) that run the length of the body from head to rear; the column protects the spinal cord

Vital capacity the maximum amount of air that can be forcibly exhaled after breathing in as much as possible

VO_2 max maximum amount of oxygen the body can take in

Voluntary muscles skeletal muscles, attached to the skeleton, work consciously by the brain

W

Warm-up exercises gradually putting stresses on the body systems in preparation for the main activity

Weight training progressively lifting heavier weights to improve strength or lifting weights more often to improve stamina

Y

Yellow bone marrow substance found in the shaft of a long bone

Index

C

D

E

F

G

H

I

J

K

L

M

N

O

P

Q

R

S

T

U

V

W

Y